WALKING IN THE VALAIS

1. Bettmeralp   4. Mattertal   7. Val d'Hérens   10. Val Ferret
2. Lötschental 5. Turmanntal   8. Val de Nendaz   11. Vallée du Trient
3. Saastal   6. Val d'Anniviers 9. Val de Bagnes

BERN

BASEL

ZÜRICH

BERN

BRIG

MARTIGNY

GENEVA

ZERMATT

THE VALAIS

Lac Léman

LEUKERBAD

SIERRE

RHÔNE VALLEY

SION

6 Val d'Anniviers

7

Val de Moiry

5

Dents du Midi

CHAMPERY

MARTIGNY

8

HAUTE NENDAZ

Val d'Hérens

Val de Nendaz

Val d'Hérémence

ZINA

Weisshorn

11

VERBIER

LES HAUDERES

CHAMPEX

Val de Bagnes

Dent Blanche

Ober Gabelhorn

Val d'Entremont

9

 AROLLA

FRANCE

Val Ferret

LA FOULY

BOURG ST-PIERRE

Mt Blanc de Cheilon

Mt Collon

Pigne d'Arolla

Matt

Tour Noir

Mt Dolent

10

Gd. Combin

ITALY

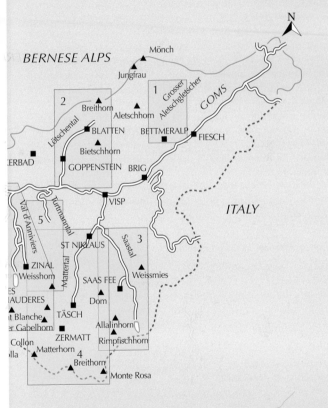

N

BERNESE ALPS

Mönch

Jungfrau

GOMS

2

Breithorn

Aletschhorn

1

Grosser Aletschgletscher

Lötschental

BLATTEN

BETTMERALP

FIESCH

Bietschhorn

ERBAD

GOPPENSTEIN

BRIG

VISP

ITALY

Turtmanntal

5

Val d'Anniviers

ST NIKLAUS

Saastal

3

ZINAL

Weisshorn

Mattertal

SAAS FEE

Weissmies

Dom

AUDERES

t Blanche

er Gabelhorn

TÄSCH

Allalinhorn

Collon

ZERMATT

Rimpfischhorn

olla

Matterhorn

4

Breithorn

Monte Rosa

0   10   20km

ABOUT THE AUTHOR

Kev Reynolds, author of this guide, is a freelance writer, photojournalist and lecturer whose first title for Cicerone Press (*Walks & Climbs in the Pyrenees*) appeared in 1978 and is still in print. He has published many books on the Alps, a series of trekkers' guides to Nepal and, nearer to home, several guides on walking in southern England. He also writes regular features for the outdoor press, produces brochures for tourist authorities, and leads walking and trekking holidays in various high-mountain regions. The first honorary member of the British Association of European Mountain Leaders (BAEML), and a member of the Alpine Club, Austrian Alpine Club and Outdoor Writers' Guild, Kev's enthusiasm for the countryside in general, and mountains in particular, remains undiminished after more than 40 years of activity. When not trekking or climbing in one of the world's great ranges, Kev lives among what he calls 'the Kentish Alps', and during the winter months regularly travels throughout Britain to share that enthusiasm through his lectures. Check him out on www.kevreynolds.co.uk

Cicerone guidebooks by the same author

100 Hut Walks in the Alps

Alpine Pass Route

Annapurna: a Trekker's Guide

Central Switzerland

Chamonix to Zermatt, Walker's Haute Route

Écrins National Park

Everest: a Trekker's Guide

Kangchenjunga: a Trekker's Guide

Langtang, Helambu & Gosainkund: a Trekker's Guide

Manaslu: a Trekker's Guide

The Bernese Alps

The Cotswold Way

The Jura (with R Brian Evans)

The North Downs Way

The South Downs Way

The Wealdway & Vanguard Way

Ticino – Switzerland

Tour of Mont Blanc

Tour of the Vanoise

Walking in Kent Vols I & II

Walking in Sussex

Walking in the Alp

Walks & Climbs in the Pyrenees

Walks in the Engadine – Switzerland

Alpine Points of View

Tour of the Jungfrau Region

WALKING IN THE VALAIS

by
Kev Reynolds

2 POLICE SQUARE, MILNTHORPE, CUMBRIA LA7 7PY
www.cicerone.co.uk

Third edition 2003
Reprinted with amendments 2007
ISBN-13: 978-1-85284-388-5
ISBN-10: 1-85284-388-8

First edition   1989
Second edition   1994

A catalogue record for this book is available from the British Library.

DEDICATION

To all who go to the mountains to find peace and spiritual
refreshment – may you be fulfilled.

Front cover: Hohbalmen, high above Zermatt, gives some of the finest views
of the district

CONTENTS

PREFACE TO THE THIRD EDITION

Having an opportunity to produce a third edition of this guide is welcome, not least because it has provided the perfect excuse to return to one of my favourite Alpine regions yet again, to walk some much-loved routes and to include several new walks discovered since the second edition was published nine years ago. In the intervening years it has been my pleasure to make a number of visits to the Valais, twice to trek across the mountains, at times to concentrate on the area for writing or photographic assignments, and sometimes to lead walking holidays and introduce others to scenes of visual drama and enchantment. That is what this book is all about - the discovery of landscape beauty and an enrichment of one's days.

I cannot claim to have rewalked every route included in this new edition, but am extremely grateful to a number of correspondents for update information, among them: M.I. Bromfield, Tim Ford, Bob Gibbons and Sîan Pritchard-Jones, Nigel Greenwood, the late Andrew Harper, Gordon Hatton (who provided some new routes for inclusion), Anthony Jones, and David and Jenny Norgrove. Their letters and post-cards brought the Valais to me in a positive way, and I thank them for their contributions to this book. At various times I've shared the trails with my old trekking and climbing partner Alan Payne, my good friend Roland Hiss, my ever-patient wife and daughters, and the many fit and eager folk who accompanied me on walking holidays and not only added to the pleasures of each day among the mountains, but also taught me to see the routes through the eyes of others and to reassess their finer points.

For this new edition, much of the text has been rewritten. In addition many more illustrations have been included, new maps have been prepared, and the layout redesigned by the Cicerone team, to whom I am deeply indebted not only for their skill and talent, but for their continued support and encouragement.

Finally, all information contained in this guide is given in good faith, and the routes described are offered in the hope that readers will gain as much enjoyment from walking in this magnificent region as I have during the many weeks of research. But I am fully aware that changes occur from time to time, not only to resort facilities, roads and huts, but to the landscape too – sometimes through natural causes, but also by the hand of man. It may be that you will discover paths that have been rerouted or landscape features altered to such an extent that some of the descriptions are no longer valid. Should this be the case, I first of all sincerely hope that such changes in no way spoil your holiday and, secondly, would appreciate a note giving details in order that I can check them out for future editions of this guide. A postcard sent to me c/o Cicerone Press Ltd, 2 Police Square, Milnthorpe, Cumbria LA7 7PY would be gratefully received.

Kev Reynolds, 2003

The Grosser Aletschgletscher is the longest icefield in the Alps (Routes 1–3)

MOUNTAIN SAFETY

Every mountain walk has its dangers, and those described in this guidebook are no exception. All who walk or climb in the mountains should recognise this and take responsibility for themselves and their companions along the way. The author and publisher have tried to make the information contained herein as accurate as possible before the guide went to press, but they cannot accept responsibility for any loss, injury or inconvenience sustained by persons using this book.

International Distress Signal
(To be used in emergency only)
Six blasts on a whistle (and flashes with a torch after dark) spaced evenly for one minute, followed by a minute's pause. Repeat until located by a rescuer. The response is three signals per minute followed by a minute's pause.

The following signals are used to communicate with a helicopter:

Help required:
raise both arms
above head to
form a 'V'

Help not required:
raise one arm above
head, extend other
arm downward

Note: mountain rescue can be very expensive – be adequately insured.

Emergency telephone number: ☎ 144
(Organisation cantonal valaisanne de secours)

Weather report: ☎ 162 (in French, German or Italian)

Map Key

～	ridge
～	river/watercourse
••••••	international boundary
■	village/habitation
～～	road
⬆	refuge
▲	summit
⋈	pass
‖‖‖‖‖‖‖	railway
├————————┤	cablecar
┄┄┄┄┄┄┄	tunnel
⬭	lake
⬭	glacier

INTRODUCTION

The valley of the Rhône is a long, deep furrow cut by a plough of ice. Ice-melt fills its rivers, and the mountains that rear majestically to both north and south are laden with permanent snows that give birth to literally hundreds of glaciers, among them the largest in the Alps.

And yet the Rhône is not a frosty, arctic region at all. On the contrary, it's a warm and sunny valley, its slopes terraced with vineyards and orchards of apple, peach, pear and apricot. Its climate is more akin to that of the Mediterranean than the high Alps, and the fertility of its broad, flat bed is there for all to see. But in marked contrast the tributary valleys which feed it are mostly narrow, tight-walled and rock-girt. Tiny villages hug abrupt hillsides. Above them ancient chalets and haybarns represent alp hamlets that command some of the loveliest views in all of Europe. These views are (forgive the cliché) simply breathtaking. They incorporate shapely peaks and long ridges bristling with spires. They dazzle with snowfields, hanging glaciers and the chaos of icefalls exposing several shades of blue in the eye-squinting light of summer. They include soft green pastures and the deeper forest green-that-is-almost-black, the shadowy-grey of ravines, the silver spray of cascades, the azure sparkle of a mountain lake. Wild flowers freckle the meadows in early summer with yellows and blues, pink and scarlet and mauve; a bewildering kaleidoscope of colour and fragrance is created, the air thrashed by butterflies' wings as they flit from one pollen-heavy flower-head to another.

Walling these valleys, or standing sentry-proud at their head, are mountains straight out of dreams: the Bietschhorn, Matterhorn, Monte Rosa, Dom, Weisshorn, Täschhorn, Zinalrothorn, Ober Gabelhorn, Dent Blanche, Dent d'Hérens, Mont Collon, Pigne d'Arolla, Mont Blanc de Cheilon, Grand Combin, Mont Dolent... the list goes on and on of peaks that formed the backdrop to the adventures of Alpine Club pioneers who were active among the Pennine Alps a century and more ago. Yet although the foundations of mountaineering were set upon these peaks, one need not be a mountaineer to fall under their spell. One need not feel compelled to climb them in order to enjoy their company, for by taking to the footpaths that weave among their shadows we can bask in their glory and become, for a few fleeting hours, days or weeks, figures in their landscape.

The footpaths of Switzerland's Alpine regions are highways to a wonderland. Along them the fit and

Near the head of the Lötschental, the Uisters Tal tributary glen provides outstanding views of the Gletscherstafel wall (Route 7)

healthy, young and old, can become absorbed by a world of infinite beauty that may only be imagined by those who remain road-bound. The 8000km network of paths in canton Valais (Wallis to German-speaking Swiss) leads, surely, to some of the very best that this extravagantly picturesque country can boast. So, whether your wandering is limited to valley-bed trails, along the mountainsides from alp to alp, or more energetically over passes that conveniently breach some of the high ridges, there will invariably be something of scenic drama to see and to experience, thereby adding a richness to your Alpine days.

The Valais region has its own distinctive character, be that of its mountains, its valleys, the native population or the architecture of its villages, some of which came late into the twentieth century. Even today a number of these villages retain an air of welcome simplicity that has long been lost in some of the area's bustling resorts, which bear a closer kinship with European capital cities than they do with the pastoral communities gathered nearby. The vernacular architecture of the Valais, best represented by the beautiful old villages and alp hamlets, is heavily dependent upon wood, and practically every valley is characterised by chalets of dark brown (almost black) timbers on a stone foundation standing side by side with traditional *mazots* (haybarns or granaries). These *mazots* are also constructed of dark brown timbers, usually lengths of horizontally laid pine logs fitted one upon another, and stand on staddle stones (*Mäusesteine* – 'mouse stones') to resist the attention of rodents. Chalets and haybarns close ranks alongside narrow cobbled alleyways, seemingly unaltered in appearance for hundreds of years. At their windows boxes of geraniums and petunias add welcome colour, while small square vegetable plots are kept trim with chard and lettuce growing in neat rows. The aroma of cut grass and cow dung hangs over many of the villages, and it's not unusual to see women tackling everyday chores dressed in traditional costumes of long black skirts, white blouses and black bodices embroidered with red and white threads, and with red scarves loosely tied. Some of the older folk wear traditional bonnets too – not for show, not for the benefit of tourists or for Sunday mass, but because it is simply their way.

Mostly, of course, tourism has had a major impact on village life and on the mountain scene, especially where downhill skiing dominates the locality's income. Above Zermatt and Saas Fee, for example, cableways whisk visitors to remote summits or viewpoints where restaurants and gift shops stand on rocks that once were known only to climbers and Alpine choughs. Engineers have even tunnelled into the mountains to create underground railways – remarkable feats of engineering, no doubt, but unwarranted acts of vandalism on a fragile mountain environment.

In several valleys enormous dams have been constructed, reservoirs created, and hundreds of kilometres of tunnels and aqueducts laid as part of the complex Grande Dixence hydro-electric scheme, a scheme that transformed large areas of the Pennine Alps of canton Valais in the latter half of the twentieth century, and which conservationists today are anxious to prevent from spreading further.

Fortunately such developments are not experienced everywhere in the region, and there are scores of enchanting areas where the mountain wanderer can tread in the footsteps of the pioneers with nothing of the twenty-first century to tarnish his vision of untamed wildness. For although the peaks and valleys of Switzerland have all been mapped, named, measured and photographed, although their exploration has been recorded in so many different languages that it seems there is nothing left to discover, the perceptive wanderer who takes to the steeply winding trail across the alps of the Valais with his eyes alert and senses tuned will find many a surprise waiting just around the corner or over the next hillside bluff.

This guide will lead you to some of those surprises...

THE VALAIS REGION

Canton Valais, third largest in the country, is that region of southwest Switzerland which surrounds the Rhône valley. It begins at the Rhônegletscher between the Grimsel and Furka passes, and then flows southwestward as the valley of Goms through Fiesch and down to Brig at the foot of the Simplon pass. Just beyond Brig the valley swings to the west, then curves southwest again at Sierre, which stands close by the language frontier. All to the east is German-speaking Wallis; to the west, French-speaking Valais.

The Rhône flows on towards the canton's capital, Sion. This historic town, extensively modernised and developed, has at its core a pair of rather incongruous castle-topped hills that catch the eye as one approaches. Beyond them, with vines on the northern slopes and orchards to the south, the river reaches Martigny, a busy town at the hub of major through-ways. To the southwest the Col de la Forclaz road winds up among more vineyards on its way to Chamonix; to the southeast runs an international highway to the tunnel and pass of the Grand St Bernard, the long-established route to Italy. But the Rhône swings at right angles away from Martigny, heading almost to the north now to pass the wall of the Dents du Midi before spending itself in the huge teardrop of Lac Léman – the Lake of Geneva.

Around 15% of the canton is covered by glaciers, for on either side of the Rhône stand the largest snow ranges of the Alps: the Bernese Alps

The Mattmark reservoir lies below the Monte Moro pass (Route 22)

to the north and Pennine Alps to the south. Both are great spawning grounds for glaciers, but the largest of all these icefields is the 22km-long Grosser Aletschgletscher which, fed by other glaciers, curves like a vast arctic highway from Oberland giants such as the Jungfrau, Mönch and Fiescherhorn before coming to a halt near the Aletschwald, some 1200m above Brig. At the Konkordiaplatz the ice is said to be around 800m deep and 1800m wide, but in common with other Alpine glaciers the Grosser Aletschgletscher is in retreat, and measurements show that the annual rate of shrinkage is about 20m, while its depth is also being dramatically reduced.

As for the mountains of this scenically spectacular region, the chain of the Pennine Alps which stretches between the Col du Grand St Bernard and the Simplon pass claims a greater number of 4000m peaks than any other Alpine region, and includes the highest mountain standing entirely in Switzerland (the Dom, 4545m), above Saas Fee; the largest massif in Western Europe (Monte Rosa); and the Alps' second highest summit after Mont Blanc (the Dufourspitze on Monte Rosa at 4634m), which is located a few metres west of the Italian border above Zermatt.

Perhaps the most attractive and challenging of Valaisian mountains on the north side of the Rhône is the 3934m Bietschhorn, which stands guard over the entrance to the Lötschental, dominates that valley

17

with its elegant cone shape, but is also clearly evident from many paths and valleys of the Pennine Alps to the south.

THE VALLEYS

It is the lateral valleys which cut into these mountain ranges that provide the Valais with its essential charm, its scenic qualities, character and magnetic appeal. These valleys include the Saastal, Mattertal and Turtmanntal, the Vals d'Anniviers, d'Hérens, Nendaz and Bagnes, Entremont and Ferret and the Vallée du Trient, and the splendid Lötschental that carves into the wall of the Bernese Alps above Gampel. Each one has its own particular contrast of peak, pasture and glacier to ensure that walks tackled among them will provide a host of memorable experiences to relive in the months ahead.

Bettmeralp

This is not a valley but a tiny car-free resort perched high above the Rhône on a slope of meadowland facing across the valley to the Pennine Alps. Behind the village runs a modest ridge spur which forms a bank to the lower end of the Grosser Aletschgletscher, and it is along this bank that some of the best walks are to be had overlooking the glacier and along its moraine-banded length into the icy heart of the Bernese Alps. Bettmeralp is accessed by cablecar from Betten-FO on the Grimsel/Furka road about 12km northeast of Brig.

Lötschental

Midway between Visp and Sierre a side-road cuts north, snaking above Gampel before plunging into a tunnel, from which it emerges alongside the important trans-Alpine railway. Road and railway soon part company at Goppenstein, entrance to the Lötschbergtunnel, which carries the motor-rail through the mountains to Kandersteg and northern Switzerland. Beyond the station the valley remains a narrow defile until at Ferden the Lötschental curves to the northeast and opens into a sunny trench full of charm. A string of small villages (Kippel, Wiler, Ried and Blatten) stands above the right bank of the river, and high above them another collection of alp hamlets is linked by a footpath which carries the Lötschentaler Höhenweg, one of the finest of all the walks in the Valais. The Lötschental is the longest and by far the loveliest of those valleys which drain from the Bernese Alps into the Rhône, a romantic, unspoilt backwater, full of simple beauty.

Saastal

About 7km due south of Visp, Stalden stands at the confluence of the two most important valleys of the Valais – in terms of tourist appeal, that is: the Mattertal, which leads to Zermatt; and the Saastal, with Saas Fee its major attraction. The southeastern stem is the Saastal (served by postbus from Visp), which pushes deep into the eastern end of the Pennine Alps,

At the foot of the Chessjen glacier below the Britannia Hut, the Weissmies is turned on its head in this small pool (Route 30)

climb to remote mountain huts. Cableways provide opportunities to access high routes without major effort, while more gentle riverside rambles go from village to village through flower-filled meadows. The Saastal also makes a good base for a climbing holiday. Hard routes are to be found on the steep walls of the Mischabel group; there are snow climbs on Allalinhorn, Alphubel and Rimpfischhorn, and easier rock climbs on peaks neighbouring the Weissmies on the eastern side of the valley directly above Saas Grund.

Mattertal

It's tempting to concentrate on Zermatt and its rim of 4000m mountains when describing the Mattertal, but the valley does have other places worth visiting – Grächen and Gasenried, for example, at the northern end of the valley above St Niklaus. The first is a sprawling resort with a sunny position and views across the Rhône, while Gasenried, much smaller, huddles below the Ried glacier, which hangs from the Nadelhorn and has its own undeniable magic. Across the valley the tiny hamlet of Jungen is indescribably lovely, a gathering of barns and chalets on a plunging hillside. Halfway between St Niklaus and Zermatt lies Randa, just far enough above the river and on the right side of the valley to have escaped obliteration by a massive rockfall in 1991 – the debris remains as a sober

with several attractive villages lining the bed of the valley, while car-free Saas Fee itself is located some 250m above the Saaser Vispa in a fabulous glacial cirque at the foot of the Mischabel wall, crowned by the Täschhorn, Dom, Lenzspitze and Nadelhorn. The valley extends further south beyond Saas Almagell, its highest village. The roadhead is at the Mattmark dam, but walkers can go on beyond that and climb to the Monte Moro pass on the Swiss/Italian border to gaze on the majestic East Face of Monte Rosa.

This is but one of countless very fine walking opportunities from and within the Saastal. There are extensive balcony paths that stretch almost the complete length of the valley, trails that edge the glaciers, and others that

The Grindjisee is one of the most attractive tarns above Zermatt (Route 44)

reminder of the fragile nature of the seemingly solid mountain walls. To all intents and purposes Täsch appears to be a car park for motor-free Zermatt, but move away from the railway and you'll find an attractive, traditional Valaisian village, while the narrow valley that cleaves the mountains behind it leads to peaceful Täschalp and some wonderful mountain views.

That brings us to Zermatt and the Matterhorn. Zermatt, one of the busiest resorts in all the Alps, lies at the foot of the most distinctive of mountains. Once seen, never forgotten. The town has been a focus of attention for mountaineers since the mid-19th century. Nowadays most of the climbs involve long routes on snow and ice, but there are, of course, difficult test-pieces such as the North Face of the

Matterhorn. Easier ascents exist for competent alpinists on the Monte Rosa massif, which boasts no less than ten 4000m summits, and on other peaks that wall the Swiss/Italian frontier: Liskamm, Castor, Pollux and Breithorn. All these mountains are on display to walkers tackling routes described in this guide without the need to set foot on ice or snow, and when viewed in their full spectacular spread above the Gorner glacier, the scale is almost Himalayan.

Turtmanntal

The Weisshorn is one of the most conspicuous peaks in the Mattertal, standing tall and proud west of Randa. It's a massive peak whose icy West Face plunges into the Val de Zinal (the upper reaches of Val d'Anniviers), and whose northern aspect overlooks the little Turtmanntal, one of the shortest of the Rhône's tributary valleys draining the Pennine Alps. It's an undeveloped valley with a summer-only village, Gruben-Meiden, nestling among the pastures between two walkers' passes used by trekkers on the classic Chamonix to Zermatt Walkers' Haute Route.

Val d'Anniviers and Val de Moiry

The road into Val d'Anniviers wriggles south of Sierre into the jaws of a gorge that obscures the valley's wonders, but once you emerge from that, one delight after another is announced. A few small villages and hamlets cling to the steep hillsides on both sides of the valley, and at Vissoie the road forks, with a secondary route branching off to Grimentz and the Val de Moiry. The

upper stem of the main valley takes its name from Zinal, the highest of its villages which serves as an important, though small, mountaineering and walking centre. Reached by postbus from Sierre, Zinal lies just short of the glacial amphitheatre that closes the valley in an arc of towering peaks: Weisshorn, Zinalrothorn, Ober Gabelhorn, Dent Blanche, Grand Cornier and Les Bouquetins. Thanks to the steepness of these walling mountains and the long ridges they push north, some of the trails in Val d'Anniviers are quite demanding, but the visual rewards they give more than compensate for the effort required to tackle them.

One of these routes crosses Col de Sorebois into the Val de Moiry. Much shorter than the main valley, the Moiry glen is known for the tightly

Col de Sorebois, boundary between the Vals de Zinal and Moiry (Route 75)

21

packed and flower-choked village of Grimentz, and for the impressive icefall on the Moiry glacier near its head. The Cabane de Moiry enjoys a privileged close view of this icefall, and is approached by an entertaining walk along the moraine crest. Below the glacier a dammed lake forms part of the Grande Dixence hydro complex, its eastern shore tight against abrupt rock walls, its west bank rising to pastures, a farm and a few smaller natural lakes that make an obvious focus for other walks.

Vals d'Hérens and Hérémence

These two valleys, which divide after a few kilometres, lie southeast of Sion and provide plenty of opportunities for walking holidays. Val d'Hérens is the more important of the two, with Evolène, Les Haudères and Arolla acting as low-key resorts, but there's some very fine wild country to explore at the head of Val d'Hérémence, too, where the Cabane des Dix is perched on a plug of rock in full view of Mont Blanc de Cheilon's North Face. East of the hut, across the Cheilon glacier, the ridge that divides the two valleys is breached by a pair of walkers' passes and a highly recommended route to Arolla. Huddled among meadows in the bed of Val d'Hérens, Evolène and Les Haudères are typical Valaisian villages, while Arolla stands in isolation at the roadhead with snow-crowned mountains as its backdrop. Arolla remains unfussed and little changed by the advance of tourism, and is one

of the best centres for aspirant alpinists in the Pennine Alps, as well as being a splendid walking centre with mountain huts, alp hamlets and tiny lakes to visit. Rising above the village some of the mountains are ringed with glacial moats, like Mont Collon, Pigne d'Arolla and Mont Blanc de Cheilon; the big wall of rock east of the village is jagged with spires and teeth, while to the west the Aiguilles Rouges have their own unique appeal.

Val de Nendaz

Immediately to the west of Val d'Hérémence, the little Val de Nendaz is often bypassed and ignored in summer, while the ski station of Super Nendaz (Siviez) is linked with the winter playground of Verbier by a series of lifts. At the southern end of the valley lies the dammed Lac de Cleuson, beyond which the landscape grows increasingly wild. Up there the rapidly shrinking Grand Désert glacier is draped down the face of the 3336m Rosablanche, while all around lies a chaos of rocks, boulders and old moraines. Walking in the lower valley is gentle among shrubs and flower meadows, while in its upper reaches the contrast is astonishing.

Val de Bagnes

Accessed by train from Martigny and Sembrancher, Val de Bagnes makes a long southeasterly sweep towards the gigantic Mauvoisin dam, with modest villages like Le Châble and Fionnay in the valley, and Verbier perched 700m above it on an open terrace facing west. Rising vast and high above the valley, the graceful Combin massif is, from choice viewpoints, a Mont Blanc look-alike with three summits over 4000m, a great dome of snow, and long fingers of ice carving from it. Some of the walks described in these pages are dominated by its dazzle of white, and it comes as no surprise to discover that the Grand Combin offers one of the classic ski ascents – first tackled in 1907. South of Lac de Mauvoisin the valley headwaters retain a sense of wild remoteness, with the Italian border traced along the walling ridge, and the Cabane de Chanrion perfectly placed to accommodate both walkers and climbers in the pastures below.

Val d'Entremont

Branching southeast of Orsières, this valley carries the road to the Col du Grand St Bernard and edges the western side of the Combin massif. Its villages, apart from Orsières at its entrance, are the modest settlements of Liddes and Bourg-St-Pierre, both fortunately bypassed by the road to Italy. Bourg has been used as a mountaineering base, and from it routes climb to a brace of mountain huts on the slopes of Mont Vélen and the Grand Combin, while the western side of the valley is largely snow-free and much lower than its neighbour. Here the Combe de l'A makes a long inroad into the mountains and offers a

way over a col at its head into the upper reaches of the Val Ferret.

Val Ferret

Traversed by walkers tackling the Tour of Mont Blanc (TMB), the Val Ferret is a distinctly pastoral valley that lies on the outer edge of the Mont Blanc massif. Several small villages and hamlets inhabit the valley, but these mostly disregard the needs of visitors. Only La Fouly, which gazes into a cirque topped by Mont Dolent and the Tour Noir, devotes itself to walkers and climbers, and it is well worth seeking out for there are some splendid walks and views to enjoy. Like the Vals d'Entremont and Bagnes, the valley is reached from Martigny via Sembrancher. The St Bernard Express (a very slow train despite its name) continues as far as Orsières, where the Vals Ferret and d'Entremont part company. Just out of Orsières a road breaks away to climb in numerous hairpins to Champex, a delightful, small but attractive resort also visited by trekkers on the TMB. With the unspoilt Val d'Arpette behind it, Champex is another worthwhile base for a few days of a walking holiday.

Vallée du Trient

This, the most westerly of the region's valleys, lies to the southwest of Martigny, by which it is reached across the Col de Forclaz. A very short, glacier-carved glen, Trient is its only village (discounting neighbouring Le Peuty, which is just a hamlet),

On the approach to the Grand Col Ferret, the Grandes Jorasses rises as a vast wall of rock (Route 103)

but being on the route of both the Tour of Mont Blanc and the Walkers' Haute Route it has a disproportionate amount of accommodation almost entirely aimed at the outdoor fraternity. The village looks up to glaciers that hang from abrupt rocky slopes, the view framed by dark pinewoods. It's an appealing sight, and the various walks on offer make the most of such views. One of the recommended routes climbs easily to the French border at Col de Balme, where an unforgettable scene reveals the Aiguilles Verte and Drus, and the massive snow dome of Mont Blanc shining in the distance. As Alpine connoisseur R.L.G. Irving once wrote: 'If that view does not thrill you, you are better away from the Alps.'

GETTING THERE

By air

Readers are warned that information about air travel is especially vulnerable to change. Even without mentioning a host of different fare structures, schedules are frequently rearranged, routes introduced and cancelled, airlines go out of business and others are formed year by year to increase competition. Information given below can, therefore, be offered only as a rough guide. The best advice is to either visit your local travel agent for current offers or browse the Internet. In any case, shop around.

Switzerland's main international airports are at Geneva and Zürich, both of which are just an escalator ride from a mainline railway station. Bern and Basel are also used, but by a smaller number of flights, and involve bus transfers to the nearest stations. Geneva is the most convenient airport for a visit to the Valais, with a direct rail link to all main Rhône valley stations.

Daily scheduled flights are operated by British Airways from London Heathrow and Gatwick to Geneva and Zürich. BA also fly direct from Manchester to Zürich and, six times a week, to Geneva. Less convenient for visitors to the Valais, BA also fly between Heathrow and Basel. For travellers from Ireland, BA has a service from Dublin to Geneva via Gatwick (www.britishairways.com).

SWISS (the national carrier formed after the collapse of Swissair) at present offers 42 daily scheduled departures from London Heathrow, London City, Birmingham, Manchester and the Channel Islands to Geneva, Zürich and Basel (☎ 0845 607 3000, website: www.swiss.com).

Swisswings Airlines (a Swiss regional carrier) operates a daily service between London City and Bern.

Currently by far the cheapest scheduled flights are by Easyjet, which operates between London Gatwick and Geneva and Zürich, Luton and Zürich, and also Liverpool to Geneva (www.easyjet.com).

Several airlines fly from North America to Geneva and/or Zürich, with departures from Boston, Chicago, Los Angeles, Miami, New York and Washington. Check with www.travelocity.com or www.expedia.com for the latest fares.

BAGGAGE TRANSFER

When flying you can take advantage of a unique 'Fly Rail Baggage' scheme which enables you to check in your baggage at the departure airport, and on arrival in Switzerland it will be transported directly to the railway station of your chosen resort. There's no waiting at the arrival airport's carousel or hustling your baggage from plane to train. The system is straightforward, safe and convenient, and also works on the homeward journey. But you pay for each item of luggage transferred. When booking your flight, ask for details.

Note: Only 'Nothing to Declare' baggage can be included in this scheme, which is not available on Go or EasyJet airlines, or for British Airways passengers with 'E' tickets.

By rail

By a combination of Eurostar (London Waterloo to Paris via the Channel Tunnel) and TGV (Paris to Geneva or Lausanne) high-speed rail travel offers an alternative to flying, although the overall cost may be no less than an air fare. Assuming connections are made, the journey time from London to Geneva or Lausanne can be as little as 8 hours, although you should allow for 12 hours or so to reach your final destination.

At least 14 Eurostar trains per day travel between Waterloo and the Gare du Nord in Paris, the journey time being around 3 hours. In Paris transfer to the Gare de Lyon for the TGV departure to either Geneva or Lausanne – there's a choice of several trains each day and the journey time is around 4–4½ hours (timings vary from season to season).

For up-to-date rail information contact: Rail Europe (☎ 08705 848 848, website: www.raileurope.com).

By road

If planning to drive to Switzerland, remember that French motorways are toll roads, and that a special sticker (Vignette) must be purchased for travel on the Swiss motorway system. This is available at border crossings, or in advance from the Switzerland Travel Centre, 10th Floor, 10 Wardour St., London W1D 6QF (☎ 00800 100 200 30, e-mail: stc@london.com, website: www.MySwitzerland.com). The minimum age to drive in Switzerland is 18, and both UK and North American drivers' licences are accepted.

TRANSPORT WITHIN THE VALAIS

Switzerland's extensive public transport system is second to none. It is truly integrated, famously efficient, clean, punctual and of great value to the walker. Schedules are dovetailed not only between different train operators but also to concide with bus services. In short, travel by public transport in Switzerland is a pleasure, not a frustration.

Pra Gra is one of the most attractive alps in the Valais, its chalets looking across the valley to Mont Collon (Routes 89, 90)

A main-line railway runs the length of the Rhône valley providing fast and frequent links with other parts of the country. From Visp a branch line (the BVZ) extends through the Mattertal to Zermatt; from Martigny the St Bernard Express serves Sembrancher, Le Châble (Val de Bagnes), Orsières, and the Val d'Entremont; while further north, in Val d'Illiez below the Dents du Midi, a branch line runs from Monthey to Champery.

For access to the Lötschental, a rail link is provided by the Brig–Kandersteg line via Goppenstein, from where a connecting postbus ferries Lötschental-bound passengers into the valley proper.

For timetable information visit www.rail.ch.

The yellow postbus travels practically everywhere there's a motorable road, and is as predictably punctual as the rail system. In village centres the main bus stop will be outside the Post Office (PTT). Elsewhere the postbus calls at railway stations and main points of habitation, but the PTT Haltestelle sign is also seen at strategic locations such as a junction of valleys or where there's access to a popular walk.

Various incentives are available to holiday makers to encourage use of either the railways or postbus services. These are outlined below, and can be purchased in the UK from the Switzerland Travel Centre in London (☎ 00800 100 200 30, e-mail: stc@london.com, website: www.MySwitzerland.com; further information is available on www.rail.ch/sts).

Swiss Pass: This entitles the holder to unlimited travel by postbus, rail and lake ferry for periods of 4, 8, 15 and 22 days, or a month. Discounts are also given on most forms of mountain transport.

Swiss Youth Pass: Advantages are the same as for the Swiss Pass, but young people under the age of 26 can obtain the Swiss Youth Pass at a discount of 25%.

Swiss Flexi Pass: Similar to the above, except that the Flexi Pass is valid for 3, 4, 5, 6 or 8 days within a month.

Swiss Half-Fare Card: Valid for one month, the card allows unlimited purchase of train, bus, boat and some cablecar tickets at half price.

Swiss Transfer Ticket: The STT is useful for visitors planning to stay in a single base. It is valid for a period of one month and gives one free round-trip to any destination in Switzerland. The trip can start at any Swiss airport or border, and each leg of the trip must be completed on the same day. Holders of the Swiss Transfer Ticket can also claim discounts on most mountain lift systems.

Swiss Card: An extended version of the Swiss Transfer Ticket, the Swiss

Card gives the holder a 50% discount on all further train, bus or boat travel.

Swiss Travel System Family Card: Children under 16 years of age travel free if accompanied by at least one parent in possession of a Swiss Card, Swiss Pass or Flexi Pass. Non-family members between 6 and 16 years old receive a 50% discount. The Family Card is available free of charge from the Switzerland Travel Centre in London.

Regionalpass Oberwallis: Within the Oberwallis region (the German-speaking part of the canton), this 7-day pass gives 3 days free travel – simply enter the days of your choice on the pass – and reductions of 50% and 25% on the other 4 days. The Regional Pass can be obtained from all public transport stations and tourist offices in the Oberwallis.

ACCOMMODATION

A wide range of accommodation is available within the area covered by this guidebook, from the most basic campsite to the ultimate in hotel luxury. Outline details are given within the main body of this guide, but for specific information you are advised to contact the local tourist offices, which can usually supply printed lists of facilities, addresses and prices (tourist office contact details are given in the introductory section of each valley covered in the guide). It is perhaps worth stressing that good accommodation may not be as expensive as imagined. Prices are often more modest than the official star-rating might suggest.

Official Campsites

Most of the region's valleys have official campsites. Some of these are rather basic, while the majority have first-class toilet and washing blocks, and some boast laundry facilities and drying rooms. Do not assume that the larger the resort, the better the campsite, for the converse is often true! Note that off-site camping in Switzerland is officially forbidden. Annual lists of camping and caravan sites are published by the Touring Club of Switzerland (www.tcs.ch) and the Swiss Camping Association (www.campingswiss.ch). Another website which lists campsites throughout the country is www.camp-ingnet.ch, while the Switzerland Travel Centre will send a camping guide to the Valais on request.

Youth Hostels

Swiss Youth Hostels (Auberge de Jeunesse Suisse or Schweizer Jugendherbergen) provide reasonably priced accommodation, are affiliated to Hostelling International, and are open to all young people holding a current membership card. Small dormitories and family rooms are generally available. For a current list visit www.youthhostel.ch or contact Schweizer Jugendherbergen, Schaffhauserstr. 14, Postfach, CH-8042 Zürich.

Gîtes d'étape

In many respects a *gîte d'étape* is like a private youth hostel, with modestly priced dormitory accommodation, communal washrooms and, usually, meals provided. Almost exclusively aimed at walkers and trekkers, a few of these establishments exist within the area covered by this guide. Again, contact the local tourist office for specific addresses.

Dortoirs/Matratzenlager

Several Valaisian hotels provide low-cost communal dormitories in addition to standard bedrooms. Some have traditional two-tier bunk beds, others merely a supply of mattresses on the floor of a large room. Enquire at the local tourist office.

Bed and Breakfast

Similar to bed and breakfast establishments in the UK, private rooms (*Chambres d'hôtes* or *Gästezimmer*) are located in a number of villages and resorts throughout the Valais, and their details are usually available from the local tourist office. An annual booklet listing those in the Valais region is published in Sierre. Write to: Chambres d'hôtes VS13, Cathy Renggli, Route des Liddes 12, CH-3960 Sierre (e-mail: info@bnb.ch, website: www.homestay.ch or www.bnb.ch).

Mountain Huts

Since the majority of mountain huts (*refuge*, *cabane*, *hütte*) are located in spectacular surroundings, they usually

Located in a beautiful cirque walled by the Weisshorn and Zinalrothorn, the Cabane d'Ar Pitetta looks wintry after a summer snowstorm (Route 71)

provide a memorable experience for the first-time user. Although primarily intended as an overnight base for climbers, a number of Valaisian huts are accessible to walkers. Mostly owned by the Swiss Alpine Club, but open to all, mixed-sex dormitories are the norm for sleeping accommodation (take your own sheet sleeping bag) and washing facilities can be primitive, but where a guardian (hut keeper) is in residence for the summer, meals and refreshments are usually available. Basic details are given in the main section of this book, but further information is available at www.sac-cas.ch, which provides a list.

As a number of routes contained in this guide visit mountain huts, a note on hut etiquette may be useful for newcomers intending to stay. Upon arrival remove your boots and change into a pair of special hut shoes (clogs or slippers) found on racks in the boot room or porch. Locate the guardian to book sleeping space for the night and any meals required. Meal times are usually fixed, and a choice of menu is sometimes, but not always, available. Payment should be made in cash the night before your departure. Although you will be allocated a place in a dormitory, access to it may not be possible until the evening. Since the room may be unlit, keep your headtorch or flashlight handy.

Holiday Apartments
Giving a degree of freedom and flexibility, self-catering apartments are an option worth considering by families or groups of friends if you plan to base your holiday in one centre. A large number of villages mentioned in this book have apartments for rent, usually for a minimum of one week.

Hotels and Mountain Inns
As mentioned above, a wide range of hotels exist throughout the Valais region. In addition, some of the more popular areas have mountain inns that may not be star rated, but, being located in often remote or romantic sites, provide accommodation with appeal. A few mountain restaurants also offer good value overnight accommodation in bedrooms or dormitories. Enquire at the nearest tourist office for details.

Package Holidays
Holiday packages which provide both accommodation and travel can offer a useful service at a competitive rate for walkers looking for a base in a specific resort. The following tour companies have packages in Valais resorts: Crystal Holidays, Inghams Travel and Thomson Holidays – study their 'Lakes & Mountains' brochures available from high-street travel agents.

WEATHER
It's an old adage, but there's more than a ring of truth to it: 'Mountains make their own weather'. This is as true of the Valais as it is of any other region of the Alps, and from massif to massif, valley to valley, and even

Average monthly temperatures and precipitation figures (mm) for Sion in the Rhône valley, with the Bernese Alps to the north and Pennine Alps to the south

	Jan	Feb	Mar	Apr	May	Jun	Jul	Aug	Sep	Oct	Nov	Dec
min °C	-6	-3	1	3	8	10	11	10	9	4	0	-3
max °C	3	6	9	14	20	21	25	24	21	15	9	5
precip.	51	45	40	37	39	46	50	64	45	50	53	62

from one side of a valley to another and from the foot of a mountain to its summit, different influences come into play to create micro-climates and individual weather systems. On the whole, Valaisian valleys not only benefit from lying in the rain-shadow of the Bernese Alps, but enjoy a more settled and slightly warmer climate than their neighbours. However, generalisations are not to be taken too seriously, especially as Alpine weather patterns appear to be in a state of flux under the influence of global warming, and walkers who go there should be prepared for all eventualities.

If planning to walk reasonably high, June will normally be the earliest month to contemplate a holiday in the Alps, and even then there will probably be limitations because of low-lying snow or even avalanche danger. In the Valais, temperatures are at their highest in July, with the likelihood of electrical storms; rainfall is at its heaviest in August, while September can be utterly magical. Then the first night-frosts will be experienced in the mountains, and the days can often be luminescently clear. If the weather holds, October rewards with larchwoods turning gold and fresh powder snow on the summits, but many resorts will be closing down for a few weeks before the winter season begins.

When the *Föhn* blows there will be clear skies for several days, but in the wake of this warm, dry wind, rain should be expected. Snow can fall at any time of the year in the higher valleys, and sudden violent thunderstorms are not at all uncommon in summer.

The Swiss meterological service, MeteoSwiss, is challenged by the complex nature of forecasting the day-to-day weather for such a mountainous country, and while the published four-day forecast provides a general picture of trends, it can only be that – a general picture. The broadcast daily weather report is more helpful, and a local weather bulletin is usually posted in the window of tourist offices and mountain guides' bureaux. For an internet report in English, visit www.meteoswiss.ch/en – this provides a daily forecast as well as a five-day prediction. Current weather conditions throughout Switzerland can be checked on www.MySwitzerland.com.

NOTES FOR WALKERS

This book is intended to be used by casual walkers who may never have visited the Alps before, as well as by the more experienced mountain wanderer aiming for the snowline. There's something in the Valais to suit everyone, and each level – from valley bed to mountain summit – has its own very special charm.

Routes described in these pages have been chosen with a particular viewpoint, lake, alp hamlet, hut or pass as the goal, while the principal objective of each walk is to enjoy a day's exercise among some of Europe's most visually exciting scenery. But to gain the most from an active holiday in the Valais one needs to be in a reasonably good physical condition on arrival. That way you can face the initial uphill path without feeling daunted, and enjoy the first day of your holiday as much as the last.

Avoid being over-ambitious for the first few days, especially if you've never walked in the Alps before. It's worth remembering that some of the valley resorts are situated higher than Britain's highest mountain, and the altitude may demand a few adjustments, so plan your programme of walks to increase gradually both in distance and height-gain over the period of your stay. A range of walks has been chosen for this book, and there should be sufficient routes on offer to enable most walkers to enjoy a good day out at a level to suit their particular ability and ambition.

Walks fall into three categories, graded 1–3, with the highest grade

Typical Swiss efficiency ensures that most walks are well signed

Ibex can often be seen on the Sentier des Chamois near Col Termin (Route 99)

given to the more challenging routes. This grading system is purely subjective, but is offered to provide a rough idea of what to expect. There are moderate walks (Grade 1) that would appeal to most active members of the family, while the majority of routes are graded 2 or 3, largely as a result of the very nature of the landscape, which can be pretty challenging. A full definition of these grades is given at the end of this Introduction.

Most of the paths adopted for these routes are well maintained, waymarked and signed at junctions with typical Swiss efficiency. Apart from a few districts where the local tourist office has put its own stamp of individuality on signposts, the majority of path signs are painted yellow and contain the names of major landmark destinations, such as

a pass, lake, hut or village, with estimated times given in hours (Std – *Stunden* – in German-speaking districts; h – *heures* – in French) and minutes (min). A white plate on these yellow signs gives the name of the immediate locality, and often the altitude too. Rarely do described routes stray onto unpathed territory, but where they do, occasional cairns and/or waymarks guide the route. In such places it is essential to remain vigilant to avoid becoming lost – especially if visibility is poor. If in doubt about the onward route, return to the last point where you were certain of your whereabouts and try again. If you consult the map frequently during your walk, it should be possible to keep abreast of your position and anticipate junctions before you reach them.

33

For safety's sake, never walk alone on remote trails, on moraine-bank paths or glaciers. If you prefer to walk in a group but have not made prior arrangements to join an organised holiday, the staff of several tourist offices arrange day walks in the company of a qualified leader. These take place throughout the summer months and are often free of charge to those staying in the organising resort. Enquire at the local tourist office for specific details.

SAFETY CHECK-LIST

- Before setting out, check the weather forecast (see above) and be aware that all Alpine areas are subject to rapidly changing conditions; throughout the day you should watch for tell-tale signs and be prepared for the worst by having adequate clothing.

- Study route details beforehand, noting any particular difficulties and the amount of time needed to complete the route. Make sure you can be back safely before nightfall.

- On a full-day's walk carry food (and emergency rations such as chocolate or dried fruit), and at least one litre of liquid per person to avoid dehydration.

- Leave details of your planned route and expected time of return with a responsible person.

- Be vigilant when crossing wet rocks, scree, snow patches and mountain streams. If you come to a section of path safeguarded by fixed ropes or chains, check that they have not worked loose before relying on them.

- Do not stray onto glaciers unless you have experienced companions and the necessary equipment to deal with crevasse rescue. Keep away from icefalls and hanging glaciers.

- Avoid dislodging stones onto others who might be below.

- Never be reluctant to turn back in the face of deteriorating weather or if the route becomes hazardous. In the event of your being unable to reach the place where you are expected, try to send a message.

- Carry map and compass (and GPS if you have one) with you – and know how to use them.

- Always carry some first aid equipment, as well as a whistle and torch for use in emergencies. The emergency telephone number for mountain rescue is 144. Try not to use it!

- Make a note of the International Distress Signal printed at the front of this guide: six blasts on a whistle (and flashes of a torch after dark) spaced evenly for one minute, followed by a minute's silence. Then repeat until an answer is received and your position located. The answer is three signals followed by a minute's pause.

- Be insured against accidents (rescue and subsequent medical treatment), for although mountain rescue is highly organised and efficient in Switzerland, it can be extremely expensive for the casualty.

- Finally, please help keep the mountains and their valleys litter-free.

SUGGESTED EQUIPMENT LIST

Whilst experienced hill walkers will no doubt have their own preferences, the following list is offered as a guide to newcomers to the Alps. Some items will clearly not be needed if you envisage tackling only low valley routes.

Clothing

- Walking boots – must be comfortable, a good fit, have ankle support and plenty of grip in the soles
- Trainers or similar for wear in huts, hotels and villages
- Wind- and water-proof jacket and overtrousers
- Woollen hat and sunhat
- Gloves
- Fleece or woollen sweater
- Shirts – 2 or 3 for a fortnight's holiday
- Warm long trousers, slacks or breeches – not jeans, which are very cold when wet and take ages to dry
- Shorts (optional)
- Long woollen socks
- Underwear

Miscellaneous

- Rucksack – with waterproof liner and/or cover
- Sheet sleeping bag (if you intend to sleep in huts)
- Bivvy bag – in case of emergencies
- Umbrella – excellent rain protection; especially useful for spectacle wearers
- Trekking pole(s) – highly recommended
- Headtorch plus spare batteries and bulbs
- Water bottle (1 litre minimum)
- Sunglasses, suncream/sunblock and lip salve
- First aid kit
- Map and compass (and GPS if available)
- Whistle
- Watch
- Guidebook
- Penknife
- Camera and films
- Altimeter
- Binoculars

RECOMMENDED MAPS

The *Landeskarte der Schweiz* (LS) series of maps that cover the Valais region are magnificent works of art. Open any sheet and a picture of the country immediately leaps from the paper – for by clever use of shading, contours and colouring, the line of ridges and rock faces, the flow of glaciers and streams, the curve of an amphitheatre, narrow cut of a valley, expanse of a lake, and the forest cover of a hillside all announce themselves with great clarity. They are a source of inspiration prior to setting out and a pleasure to use day by day.

At the head of each valley section in this book, a note is given in regard to the specific map recommended for use. In every instance the 1:50,000 series of *Wanderkarten*, produced in collaboration with the Swiss walking organisation the SAW (Schweizerischen Arbeitgemeinschafter für Wanderwege), has been chosen. Although more detail is presented on the 1:25,000 sheets, the *Wanderkarten* – distinguished by their orange covers and with the letter 'T' after their official number – should be adequate for most, if not all, the walks described. These maps are available in the UK from Edward Stanford's in London (see Appendix A for the address) or locally in the Valais from bookshops or tourist offices.

The commercial publisher Kümmerly + Frey also covers the Valais with a series of maps based on the LS

The Balfrin is on show for much of the early part of the Gspon Höhenweg (Route 12)

sheets, and these are mostly available in local resorts. Their 1:120,000 sheet *Wallis* covers the entire canton and is a useful locator, with a number of major long walking routes outlined in red.

Some regional tourist authorities also produce their own *Wanderkarten* to show walking routes based on specific resorts or valleys, and these are on sale at the local tourist offices.

USING THE GUIDE

The layout of this guide follows an east–west convention, beginning on the north side of the Rhône valley and describing routes from Bettmeralp and the Lötschental, then moving to the Pennine Alps south of the Rhône. The most easterly valley to be described here is the Saastal, after which the guide moves west into the Mattertal, before visiting the Turtmanntal, Val d'Anniviers and so forth.

Each valley system is treated as a separate unit (or chapter), for which a map is provided as a locator. The walks themselves should be followed on the recommended topographical map of the area. Within each valley chapter details are given in regard to the various villages or resorts, their access, facilities, tourist offices, huts, etc, and a number of walks of various grades are then described. All the walks are listed in an index at the back of this book, and an explanation of the grading system is found below.

Distances and heights are quoted throughout in kilometres and metres.

These details are taken directly from the map, where possible, but in attempting to measure the actual distance of each walk it has been necessary to make an estimation, for with countless zigzags on many of the routes, it's impossible to be precise.

Times quoted for each route are approximations only. They refer to **actual walking time and make no allowances for rest stops or interruptions for photography** – such stops can add considerably (25% or more) to the overall time you're out during the day, so bear this in mind when planning your day's activity. Although such times are given as an aid to planning they are, of course, subjective, and each walker will have his or her own pace which may or may not coincide with that quoted. By comparing your times with those given here, you should soon gain an idea of the difference and be able to compensate accordingly.

In route descriptions 'left' and 'right' apply to the direction of travel, whether in ascent, descent or traverse. However, when used with reference to the banks of glaciers or streams, 'left' and 'right' indicate the direction of flow, ie: looking downwards. Where doubts might occur, a compass direction is also given.

Abbreviations are used sparingly in the guide, but some have of necessity been adopted. While most should be easily understood the following list is given for clarification:

Lac de Chanrion, a small tarn caught in a hollow of pastures below the Chanrion Hut (Route 101)

C–Z	Chamonix to Zermatt, the Walkers' Haute Route
hrs	hours
km	kilometres
LS	Landeskarte der Schweiz (maps)
m	metres
mins	minutes
PTT	Post Office (Post, Telephone & Telegraph)
SAC	Swiss Alpine Club
VTT	Trains à Grande Vitesse
TMB	Tour of Mont Blanc

GRADING OF WALKS

The walks in this book have been chosen with the express aim of helping you to make the most of your holiday in the Valais, and since it is hoped that walkers of all degrees of

commitment will find something useful here, a grading system has been used to direct readers to the standard of outing that might best suit their requirements. As mentioned above, the walks have been graded into three categories, but since the grading of walks is not an exact science, each of these categories will cover a fairly wide spectrum. There will inevitably be variations and, no doubt, a few anomalies which may be disputed by users of this book, but they are offered in good faith and as a rough guide only.

Grade 1: Suitable for family outings; mostly short distances or walks along gently graded paths or tracks with little altitude gain.

Grade 2: Moderate walking, mostly on clear footpaths with a reasonable amount of height gain. Walkers should be adequately shod and equipped.

Grade 3: More strenuous routes on sometimes rough or unclear paths. Some modest scrambling or use of ladders, fixed ropes, etc, may be involved in rare instances. A head for heights may be called for. On some of these routes there will be passes to cross, some glacial travel (individual sections will be marked in the text) and possibly screes to contend with. In short, true Alpine walking. There will be steep ascents and descents, and fairly long distances involved. Walkers attempting these should be fit and well equipped.

INFORMATION AT A GLANCE

Currency: The Swiss franc (CHF); 100 centimes/rappen = 1CHF. Although Switzerland is not in the Euro zone, some hotels and retail outlets accept payment by Euro. Change will be given in Swiss francs.

Formalities: Holders of a valid UK passport or the national identity card of a Western European country do not need a visa to enter Switzerland. Citizens of the USA, Canada, Australia, New Zealand and South Africa can stay for up to three months without a visa.

Health precautions: At the time of going to press, there are neither major health concerns to consider nor vaccinations required by visitors entering Switzerland from Europe or the West. However, as there is no state health service and all medical treatment must be paid for, it is advisable to take out insurance cover that includes personal accident and sickness. Should you plan to tackle walking routes that stray from habitation, rescue cover in the event of an accident ought to be included.

International dialling code: When dialling Switzerland from the UK: 0041. To phone the UK from Switzerland the code is 0044, then ignore the initial 0 of the area code which follows. Cashless Swiss public call boxes are operated by a phonecard (Taxcard) on sale at post offices, newsagents and railway stations for CHF 5, CHF 10 and CHF 20.

Language: French and German in the Valais, but English is widely spoken.

Tourist information: Valais Tourism, Rue Pré-Fleuri 6, 1951 Sion, Switzerland (☎ 0041/(0)27 327 35 70, e-mail: info@valaistourism.ch, website: www.valaistourism.ch or www.matterhornregion.com) Switzerland Travel Centre Ltd, Swiss Centre, 30 Bedford St, London WC2E 9ED (☎ 00800 100 200 30, e-mail: info.uk@myswitzerland.com, website: www.MySwitzerland.com)

The ladder route below the Pas de Chèvres (Route 91)

BETTMERALP

Isolated upon a broad and sunny hillside terrace 1100m above the Rhône, the old alp settlement of Bettmeralp, now a neat resort, gazes south into a wide panorama that contains some of the finest snowpeaks in the Valais. However, one of the main reasons for visiting this terrace is to gain access to its backing ridge, on the far side of which lies the longest glacier in the Alps – the 22km Grosser Aletschgletscher, a highway of ice that ploughs a furrow through the high mountains of the Bernese Alps. Flanking the tongue of this glacier is the unspoilt Aletschwald, one of the highest pine and larch forests in Europe, set above the Massa gorge. Scenic paths cut along both sides of Bettmeralp's ridge and reward the visitor with views of great beauty and contrast: the moraine-banded glacier on one side, a dreamy sea of peaks on the other. The neighbouring resort of Riederalp, which shares the Bettmeralp terrace, enjoys similar views and the same walks, while Fiesch, in the Goms valley below, has cablecar access to Kühboden (Fiescheralp) – a tiny resort northeast of Bettmeralp – and the popular vantage point of the Eggishorn.

ACCESS AND INFORMATION

Location:	On the north slope of the Rhône valley, about 12km northeast of Brig. The Bettmeralp terrace is situated at the western end of the Goms valley, in effect the upper reaches of the Rhône's valley above Brig.
Map:	LS 264T *Jungfrau* 1:50,000. Also available: *Wanderkarte Aletschgebiet und Untergoms* 1:25,000
Bases:	Bettmeralp (1957m), Riederalp (1930m), Fiesch (in the valley at 1049m)
Information:	Bettmeralp Tourismus, CH-3992 Bettmeralp (☎ 027 928 60 60, e-mail: info@bettmeralp.ch, website: www.bettmeralp.ch)
	Riederalp Tourismus, CH-3987 Riederalp (☎ 027 928 60 50, e-mail: info@riederalp.ch, website: www.riederalp.ch)
	Tourismusbüro, CH-3984 Fiesch (☎ 027 970 60 70, e-mail: info@fiesch.ch, website: www.fiesch.ch)
Access:	By rail or road to Betten-FO, then cablecar direct to Bettmeralp – or cablecar via Betten. For Riederalp take rail or road to Mörel, then cablecar direct to Riederalp – or cablecar via Ried. Both Bettmeralp and Riederalp are car-free resorts. Parking is at Betten-FO and Mörel. Located at the mouth of the Fieschertal, Fiesch is reached by both road and rail.

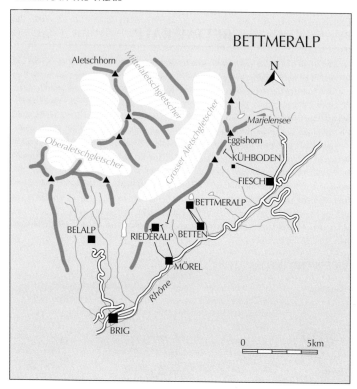

Well over 100km of footpaths meander along the Bettmeralp terrace and the slopes both above and below it. On the south side of the protective ridge wall that backs the terrace small mountain lakes, such as Blausee, Bettmersee and one or two others without names, reflect some of the beauty of the area, while from rock slabs above the fabled Märjelensee you gaze north across the impressive Grosser Aletschgletscher to the Jungfraujoch at its head. Often dotted with mini iceflows, the Märjelensee lies in a glacial hollow between two sections of ridge. The northern half of this ridge extends as a high and narrow crest containing a series of peaks collectively known as the Walliser Fiescherhörner, while above and to the south of the lake stands the more modest 2927m Eggishorn, whose lower, secondary summit at 2893m is crowned by a cablecar station, and from which paths lead to the main summit as well as descending to a variety of locations. From the

Eggishorn the ridge runs in a rough southwesterly direction to cross the Bettmerhorn, and continues above Bettmeralp and Riederalp before dropping into the Massa gorge below the snout of the Aletschgletscher.

Bettmeralp itself is a spruce, modernised resort without motorised traffic. With no access road from the valley, visitors must either travel up by cablecar or on foot – a climb of well over 1100m. The resort is as popular with skiers as it is with walkers, as a consequence of which a number of mechanical aids rise above the village. These rather detract from the visual splendour of the area, although there are plenty of paths that lead to uncluttered vantage points that are its greatest asset.

Riederalp is even smaller than its neighbour, but it too has a glorious outlook across the Rhône to 4000m giants of the Pennine Alps, and in addition boasts plenty of walking opportunities along the terrace/plateau as well as having easy access to the Aletschwald conservation area. It is linked with Bettmeralp by clear footpaths and a service road.

The chapel of Maria zum Schnee at Bettmeralp

MAIN BASES

BETTMERALP (1957m) is the best-known base for walks along the high meadowland terrace. With a picturesque white-walled chapel (Maria zum Schnee) being something of a symbol of the village, its situation is idyllic. For accommodation there are 9 hotels, 700 apartment beds and a total of 150 dormitory places (*touristenlager*). Bettmeralp has shops, restaurants, PTT and banks, and guided mountain trips are organised from the local Bergsteigerzentrum (☎ 027 927 24 82).

For further information or accommodation lists, contact the tourist office whose details are given at the head of this section.

RIEDERALP (1930m) lies at the western end of the backing ridge. It has several two- and three-star hotels, apartments, restaurants and shops, an Alpine museum and, in the Villa Cassel, a nature conservation centre. The tourist office can supply accommodation lists on request.

FIESCH (1049m) is a small resort standing at the entrance to the minor tributary valley of the Fieschertal, whose upper reaches are blocked by the Fieschergletscher. As the main resort in the Goms valley section of the Rhône, Fiesch is a mixture of modern, white-fronted buildings and characteristic dark-timbered Valaisian chalets. A cableway swings visitors to Kühboden and the Eggishorn for unrivalled views of the Grosser Aletschgletscher. In addition to a handful of hotels, the village also has some 3600 beds in chalets and apartments. There are restaurants, shops and a guides' office (Bergsteigerzentrum Aletsch: ☎ 027 971 17 76), as well as the tourist office whose contact details are listed above.

OTHER BASE
KÜHBODEN (2212m) Also known as Fiescheralp. A tiny resort accessed by cableway from Fiesch, it lies northeast of Betmeralp on the mid-height slopes of the Eggishorn. Dormitory beds and standard rooms available in four hotels.

MOUNTAIN HUT
MÄRJELEN HUT (2360m) is also known as the Gletscherstube Märjela. This privately owned two-storey timber building stands in the little Märjela valley below the Eggishorn. It has 36 dormitory places and is open from July to the end of October. Meals and refreshments provided (☎ 027 971 47 83).

ROUTE 1

Bettmeralp (1957m) – Hohbalm (2482m) –
Blausee (2204m) – Bettmeralp

Grade:	2
Distance:	8km
Height gain:	525m
Height loss:	525m
Time:	3hrs
Location:	Northeast of Bettmeralp

Since a close view of the Grosser Aletschgletscher is one of the prime reasons for visiting Bettmeralp, this walk makes a near perfect introduction. Both the length of the walk and the amount of height gain are modest, but the views are not. Although the initial ascent to the Hohbalm high point is overhung with cableways, arrival on the ridge has a powerful impact, for the sudden great sweep of the glacier is enough to stop you in your tracks. This is not all. Contrasts between one side of the ridge and the other give the walk a special quality: on one side there are the plunging depths of the Rhône valley; on the other a vista of icefields and abrupt rock walls. There are contrasts, too, of grass slopes and shrubbery pitted against a world of snow, ice and apparently barren rock.

From the cablecar station at the lower end of Bettmeralp's street, bear right and walk through the village following signs to Hotel Bettmerhorn and Kühboden (or Fiescheralp). A dirt road heads northeast, passes beneath the Schönbiel chairlift, continues through pastures and comes to the white-walled **Hotel Bettmerhorn** (*accommodation, refreshments,* ☎ 027 927 40 50) after about 50mins. Turn left onto a rising footpath, soon to reach the western end of a narrow lake and a path junction (2228m). Bear left again on a continuing path angling up the hillside to gain the upper terminus of the chairlift passed earlier.

Take the upper route (direction Hohbalm), which climbs steeply in places beneath the Bettmerhorn gondola lift and eventually emerges onto the rock-strewn ridge of the Bettmergrat at the **Hohbalm** saddle (2482m:

1hr 40mins). The saddle marks another junction of tracks: the right-hand path climbs to the Bettmerhorn gondola lift station (*refreshments*), straight ahead is a path to the Märjelensee (see Route 2), while the left-hand trail goes to Riederfurka and the Aletschwald.

Take a few paces ahead to enjoy magnificent views onto the glacier, which comes sweeping from the hidden Konkordiaplatz and multi-buttressed Walliser Fiescherhörner. The long stripes of central moraine are formed by the confluence of feeder glaciers at the Konkordiaplatz several kilometres away. On the western side of the icefield, jagged ridges mount to the Grosser Fusshorn and Geisshorn, themselves plastered with hanging glaciers. Snow peaks, rocky crests and ice-clad walls cluster for attention in a highly photogenic view.

Take the left-hand path along the crest of the broad Bettmergrat among boulders and shrubs of alpenrose, juniper and bilberry. It's an easy, undulating and scenic path which leads to **Mossfluo** (2333m) and the head of a chairlift (*refreshments*). Continue ahead for another 5mins to find a footpath slanting left, with red waymarks guiding the way down through a series of miniature landscapes consisting of hillocks, hollows and more shrubs, now moving away from glacier views to reach another signposted junction. Follow the left-hand path down to the Blausee (2204m), an attractive tarn in an idyllic setting. Continue down to the larger Bettmersee (2006m) through a hillside thick with shrubbery. From this lake it is only a short walk back to Bettmeralp.

An alternative to the descent from Blausee would be to continue along the ridge as far as the Riederfurka (2065m), then wind down to Riederalp and return to Bettmeralp on the linking service road. See Route 3.

ROUTE 2

*Bettmeralp (1957m) – Hohbalm (2482m) –
Märjelensee (2300m) – Märjelen Hut (2363m)*

Grade:	3
Distance:	9km
Height gain:	588m
Height loss:	182m
Time:	3¼–3½hrs
Location:	Northeast of Bettmeralp
Accommodation:	Märjelen Hut

As with Route 1, the highlight of this walk is the close proximity of the Grosser Aletschgletscher and the wonderful views gained along it. However, this time the route provides a different aspect – looking towards the head of the glacier on the way to the Märjelensee. This little lake has a chequered history. Once much more extensive than it is now, several times the pressure of water contained by its ice wall forced a breach in that wall, resulting in a flood that swept down-valley bringing devastation to Rhône valley villages.

Follow directions as for Route 1 as far as the saddle of **Hohbalm** (2482m: 1hr 40mins). Take the path ahead which angles down towards the glacier. This eventually joins another route coming from the Bettmerhorn gondola station, at Roti Chumma (2349m), and continues below the Eggishorn. This is a dramatic, well-made path overlooking the crevassed glacier and with splendid rock scenery to back it. The way turns the Eggishorn's northwest ridge and slopes down to the **Märjelensee** (2300m: 3hrs).

Walk along the south side of the lake on the continuing path which leads to several more lakes lying in the little Märjela valley, and come to the **Märjelen Hut** (2363m *accommodation, refreshments*) near the Vordersee.

**From the Märjelen Hut
you're faced with several possibilities:**
* return to Bettmeralp by the same path in 3hrs

The Grosser Aletschgletscher is the longest icefield in the Alps

- make an ascent of the Eggishorn in 2½hrs and then ride the cablecar down to Kühboden
- return to Bettmeralp via Kühboden on an obvious path in about 3hrs
- take the trail alongside the Seebach stream which drains the Märjelen lakes, and descend through the Fieschertal to Fiesch.

Other walk options from Bettmeralp and Kuhboden

- Ride the Bettmerhorn gondola lift to the Bettmergrat ridge (2643m) above Hohbalm, then take a well-made path which descends on the north side towards the Grosser Aletschgletscher. This joins the path from Hohbalm taken by Route 2 at Roti Chümma, at which point you follow that route round to the Märjelen Hut – a walk of about 1½hrs.

- From Kuhboden take the Eggishorn cablecar to the top station, and make the easy but scenically rewarding ascent to the main summit in 30mins.

- Follow the dirt road from Bettmeralp to Kuhboden, and continue heading northeast on a signed route across the Tälligrat to the Märjelensee, where you then reverse Route 2 round the lower slopes of the Eggishorn back to Hohbalm and Bettmeralp – 6–7hrs in all.

ROUTE 3

*Riederalp (1930m) – Riederfurka (2065m) –
Hoflüe (2227m) – Riederalp*

Grade:	1
Distance:	5km
Height gain:	320m
Height loss:	320m
Time:	2½hrs
Location:	North of Riederalp

This short and easy walk crosses the Riederfurka, eases along the top boundary of the Aletschwald, overlooks the tongue of the Grosser Aletschgletscher, then mounts the ridge for a return to Riederalp.

Leave Riederalp heading west on an obvious broad path that winds easily up to the **Riederfurka** (2065m: 30mins), where you'll find the Villa Cassel nature conservation centre and the Hotel Riederfurka (*accommodation, refreshments,* 14 beds, open mid-April to Oct, ☎ 027 927 21 31).

Cross to the north side and briefly descend on a good path curving right (northeast) along the edge of the Aletschwald forest. The trail is on the old glacial moraine, with increasingly fine views of the huge trench bulldozed through the mountains by the Aletschgletscher. On coming to the Breite Bode junction turn right and ascend the slope to gain the ridge crest near the Blausee (2204m). A very fine view here takes in the line of the Pennine Alps across the Rhône valley, with the unmistakable shape of the Matterhorn catching one's attention. Turn right and wander along the near-level ridge, passing the Hoflüe chairlift (2227m) before sloping down to Riederfurka for the return to Riederalp.

THE LÖTSCHENTAL

The longest of the valleys draining into the Rhône from the north, the glacier-carved Lötschental is one of the loveliest in the Valais. In its bed a string of small villages line the true right bank of the Lonza river, with meadows dotted with hay barns on the opposite bank, and glacier-hung peaks leading the eye to the retreating Langgletscher, which tumbles from the icy saddle of the Lötschenlücke at its head. Pools and tiny lakes add to the scenic pleasures of this valley on the edge of the Bernese Alps, and the walking potential offers something for everyone.

ACCESS AND INFORMATION

Location:	On the north side of the Rhône valley, between Sierre and Visp.
Map:	LS 264T *Jungfrau* 1:50,000. Also available from the local tourist office: *Wander- und Skitourenkarte Lötschental* 1:25,000
Bases:	Kippel (1376m), Wiler (1419m), Blatten (1540m)
Information:	Lötschental Tourismus, CH-3918 Wiler (☎ 027 938 88 88, e-mail: info@loetschental.ch, website: www.loetschental.ch)
Access:	By train to Goppenstein at the southern end of the Lötschberg tunnel on the Bern–Brig railway, and bus from there. For access by road turn north from the main Rhône valley highway 10km west of Visp.

The Lötschental retains an air of isolation. Approached through the once forbidding, avalanche-prone narrows of the Quertalschlucht, some of the charms of this splendid valley are the result of the fact that it was slow to respond to commercialisation – before the Second World War the only motor road ran for just 4km between Goppenstein and Kippel. It offers little to the downhill skier, and as such remains virtually uncluttered today. On the hillsides the only mechanical aid rises above Wiler and the Lauchernalp. There's a sense of 'unworldliness' about some of its villages – an air of primitive antiquity aided by a folklore represented by grotesque masks made of wood and animal hair, with cows' teeth fixed to gaping mouths. These hideous demons – *Tschaeggaetten* – appear in local carnivals, where they are paraded through the village streets, a custom dating back hundreds of years.

Draining southwest from the Lötschenlücke, the Lötschental is a sunny U-shaped valley cradled between a 3000m wall of mountains on the north side and a higher, more severe line of peaks culminating in the graceful Bietschhorn on the south. The north wall supports the Petersgrat, one of the last remaining vestiges of a great ice sheet that covered much of the Bernese Alps during the last Ice Age.

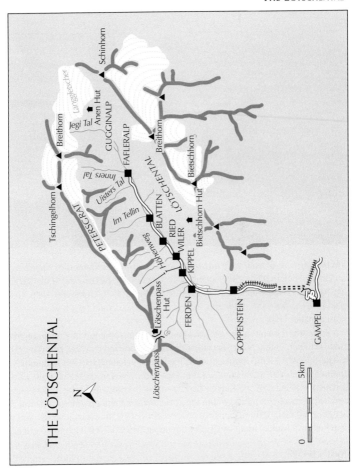

On its far side the Petersgrat spills via the Kanderfirn into the Gasterntal above Kandersteg, but on the Lötschental flank it lightly overhangs a succession of small tributary glens. The Lötschenpass at the head of one of these carries an old trading route across the mountains to Kandersteg, and has a small hut nestling just below it. Nearby one can gaze south to the Pennine Alps across the Rhône valley, while a shallow lake turns the Bietschhorn on its head. Below peak and glacier

51

Faldumalp, overlooking the Lötschental

the hillsides are dressed with forests of larch and pine interrupted by meadows, and at mid-height on the Petersgrat slope a magnificent balcony path links seven alp hamlets before sloping into the bed of the valley at an eighth, Fafleralp. This path gives as pleasant and scenic a day's walk as you could possibly wish – the Lötschentaler Höhenweg.

Fafleralp is as far as the postbus goes (summer services between June and mid-October), but there are two more alp hamlets beyond in what's known as the Gugginalp, the valley's upper reaches leading to the Langgletscher and another mountain hut, the Anen Hut, at 2358m. Apart from the Lötschen Hut, built virtually on the Lötschenlücke and reached by way of the crevassed Langgletscher, the only other mountain refuge within the Lötschental is the Bietschhorn Hut, which stands amid rocky terrain at 2565m on the slopes of the mountain it serves, and is reached by a walk of about 3–3½hrs from either Wiler or Ried.

MAIN BASES

KIPPEL (1376m) is an attractive village with narrow cobbled alleyways dropping steeply towards the river. Dark-timbered buildings and hay barns crowd these alleys, and there are fine views to the head of the valley. Accommodation may be found in a handful of hotels (the Bietschhorn, Sporthotel and Lötschberg), while there are several holiday apartments and chalets to rent. The valley's only official campsite is located on the south side of the river, reached by a steep and narrow road whose entrance is at the eastern end of the village. Kippel has restaurants, post office, a bank and limited shopping facilities. The Lötschental museum is near the church.

WILER (1419m) is bypassed by the main valley road, and is growing faster than any other village in the Lötschental. The Lauchernalp cableway serves the modest ski slopes of the Hockenhorn, and (of more interest to walkers) it provides access to the Lötschentaler Höhenweg. Wiler has a range of accommodation (contact the local tourist office for details), restaurants, shops, post office, banks and a mountain guides' bureau. The valley's only tourist office is also located in the village.

BLATTEN (1540m) is another attractive village, and one of the most important valley bases. It stands on the north bank of the river, and there is a large square in the village by the church. Blatten has a post office, limited shopping facilities and accommodation in the three-star Hotel Edelweiss, but there are numerous apartments and chalets available for let.

OTHER BASES

Most Lötschental villages have accommodation in varying amounts. **FERDEN** has apartments, **RIED** has a hotel, while at the roadhead at **FAFLERALP** Hotel Fafleralp offers both standard beds and dormitory accommodation. On the hillside above Wiler both **LAUCHERNALP** and **FIESCHBIEL** have accommodation in chalets and apartments, with dormitory spaces at Berghaus Lauchern. The three-star Zur Wildi in Lauchernalp has 30 beds. **GASTHAUS KUMMENALP** also has 26 dormitory places and 10 beds. Contact the Lötschental tourist office (see above) for current details.

MOUNTAIN HUTS

ANEN HUT (2358m) Reached by a walk of about 2½hrs from Fafleralp, the Anen Hut stands on the north bank of the Langgletscher, has 50 places (8 in the winter room) and is manned from mid-June to mid-October (☎ 027 939 17 64, www.henzen.com/anen).

BIETSCHHORN HUT (2565m) Owned by the Academic Alpine Club of Bern, has 26 places. The hut is manned at weekends from July to end of September (☎ 027 305 85 94). For reservations ☎ 027 934 22 81.

LÖTSCHENPASS HUT (2690m) This privately owned hut faces across the Lötschental from a high vantage point and has a splendid view of the Bietschhorn. It has 40 places and is manned from June to the end of October (☎ 027 939 19 81, website: www.loetschenpass.ch).

ROUTE 4
Ferden (1375m) –
Faldumalp (2037m) – Kummenalp (2083m) –
Lauchernalp (2106m) – Fafleralp (1787m)

Grade:	2
Distance:	18.5km
Height gain:	731m
Height loss:	319m
Time:	6½–7hrs
Location:	On the west and north flank of the valley

This is *the* classic walk of the valley – the Lötschentaler Höhenweg. Unquestionably one of the loveliest walks in the Valais, it's a truly delightful outing with picturesque views all the way. Although nowhere difficult, it is given a Grade 2 on account of its length and the steepness of the path leading from the valley to Faldumalp, where the höhenweg begins. However, many walkers break this route into two distinct sections, and make use of the Lauchernalp cableway to relieve the effort of the initial climb from the valley. This alternative method of tackling the walk is offered below as Routes 4a and 4b – both graded 1.

Several aspects of the walk ensure its classic status. There are the views that encompass the whole valley and reveal its splendour in a single glance. There are the alp hamlets that enliven the route with variety and interest. And there is the path itself, a splendidly graded trail that undulates along a vague terrace, in and out of tree shade, cutting back here and there to cross a stream, rising now and then over a green bluff or passing across meadows far above the valley. Refreshments are available along the way, and in a number of places it would be possible to descend to the valley by footpath, should it be necessary.

The walk begins in Ferden village square by the church, where a signpost directs the way to Faldumalp. Soon above the village, another sign points to a path climbing among trees and up a steep grassy hillside. This rapidly gains height with steep windings, and when it emerges from forest to pasture, spectacular views are gained to the head of the valley. In 1½hrs arrive at the alp hamlet of **Faldumalp** (2037m), with its tiny chapel.

Retrace the approach path a short distance to where it crosses the Faldum stream and divides. Now take the left-hand option towards Restialp. This is a splendid belvedere, narrow and a little exposed in places, leading among larches and along slopes of bilberry and alpenrose. Just below **Restialp** come to a junction of tracks and take the path heading left up the slope to the hamlet, where refreshments are available.

A track continues to **Kummenalp** (in 30mins), with fine views throughout. Accommodation and refreshments are also available here, and behind the hamlet an alternative path climbs to the Lötschenpass (see Route 7). The *höhenweg* maintains its journey along the hillside, heading roughly eastward for another 40mins to **Hockenalp** (2048m: *refreshments*), with views dominated by the Bietschhorn. Hockenalp is a cluster of timber chalets and hay barns, and from it the path continues across hillsides seething with crickets in summer to reach the slopes of **Lauchernalp** in 20mins. The valley's only ski tows and chairlifts run across the open bowl of hillside; Lauchernalp also has both refreshments and accommodation. ▶

The Bietschhorn is clearly seen from the Lötschentaler Höhenweg

Note: It's possible to descend by cablecar to Wiler from here.

The continuing path descends a little (follow waymarks), then contours to **Weritzalp** (Werizstafel: 2099m: *refreshments*), a hamlet of red-shuttered chalets, in a further 45mins. Beyond it the *höhenweg* path begins to slope down through forest to the few hay barns and alp huts of **Tellialp** (Tellistafel: 1865m), then crosses a stream and follows an undulating course along the hillside, passes the little Schwarzsee tarn and comes to **Fafleralp** (1787m: *accommodation, refreshments*), which has a charming modern chapel in the woods behind the hotel. About 10mins from Hotel Fafleralp the *höhenweg* ends when the path reaches a large car park at the roadhead and a bus stop.

ROUTE 4A

Lauchernalp (1922m) –
Kummenalp (2083m) – Restialp (2098m) –
Faldumalp (2037m) – Ferden (1375m)

Grade:	1
Distance:	10.5km
Height gain:	176m
Height loss:	723m
Time:	3hrs 40mins
Location:	North of Wiler, heading southwest

As mentioned above, by judicious use of the cablecar from Wiler, the Lötschentaler Höhenweg can be tackled as two individual sections. This is the westward section, a walk of considerable charm – see introductory paragraphs to Route 4 above.

From **Wiler** take the cablecar to **Lauchernalp**, where the *höhenweg* rises, then curves round the hillside aiming for **Hockenalp** (2048m: *refreshments*), the first of several alp hamlets linked by this path, whose waymark is a yellow diamond with black edging. All hamlets visited on this walk, except Faldumalp, have refreshment facilities.

With signposts at strategic footpath junctions, and waymarks at intermediate points, it would be difficult to lose the way. From Hockenalp the path continues to **Kummenalp** (2083m), then to **Restialp** (2098m) and round the slopes of the Alplighorn to **Faldumalp** (2037m). The final leg of the walk is a steepish descent to **Ferden** in the valley. The village is served by postbus for a return to your valley base.

ROUTE 4B

Lauchernalp (1922m) – Weritzalp (2099m) –
Tellialp (1865m) – Fafleralp (1787m)

Grade:	1
Distance:	8km
Height gain:	177m
Height loss:	312m
Time:	2½hrs
Location:	North of Wiler, heading northeast

This eastern section of the Lötschentaler Höhenweg is the least taxing of the high routes, but is a worthwhile outing nonetheless.

As with Route 4a, begin by taking the cablecar from **Wiler** to **Lauchernalp**, then head to the right along the signed and waymarked footpath described more fully under Route 4. Hamlets visited on this walk after leaving Lauchernalp are: **Weritzalp**, **Tellialp** and **Fafleralp**. Across the valley views take in the high peaks of Bietschhorn, Breitlauihorn, Lötschentaler Breithorn and the Schinhorn. The big Gletscherstafel wall that buttresses the Breitlauihorn and Breithorn is plastered with small hanging glaciers and is an impressive feature of the valley. On arrival at Fafleralp make your way to the road-head car park for the postbus back to your base.

ROUTE 5

Ferden (1375m) –
Faldumalp (2037m) – Kummenalp (2083m) –
Lötschenpass Hut (2690m)

Grade:	2–3
Distance:	10km (one way)
Height gain:	1315m
Time:	5–5½hrs
Location:	Northwest of Ferden
Accommodation:	Lötschenpass Hut

The location of the Lötschenpass Hut is idyllic, resting as it does high above the valley, with a few small tarns below and a magnificent outlook to the Bietschhorn to the east. It makes a convenient overnight lodging for trekkers crossing the mountains on the way to or from Kandersteg (see Route 6), or as a lunch stop during a day's hike. The route described here is not the shortest or most direct approach from the Lötschental, but adds to the variety by adopting a short stretch of the höhenweg before climbing to the pass. To make a more direct route, follow signed ways from either Ferden or Kippel to Kummenalp, where you join the walk described as follows. Alternatively, an even more direct route can be achieved by riding the Wiler–Lauchernalp cablecar, then walking up to the highest part of the hamlet, where a signed path makes a long rising westward traverse to the Lötschenpass in about 2½hrs. This route is clearly marked on the LS map.

The **Lötschenpass Hut** is usually manned from June to the end of October, when food and drinks are available. See hut details in the introduction to the Lötschental section, should you intend to spend the night there.

For our longer route, however, take the path from **Ferden** to **Faldumalp** as described at the beginning of Route 4, and continue along the Lötschentaler Höhenweg to **Restialp** and **Kummenalp** in about 3hrs. Refreshments are available at both Restialp and Kummenalp. At Kummenalp a clear, signposted trail eases into the hanging valley behind the hamlet, and heads up rough slopes and past a few little tarns without any difficulty or diversion to reach the **Lötschenpass Hut** (2690m: *accommodation, refreshments*) in another 2–2¼hrs. ◀

Shortly before gaining the hut it's worth pausing to admire the panorama, which not only includes the

Bietschhorn but the Mischabel group of mountains making a wall across the Rhône valley, with the distinctive Weisshorn and snowy Monte Rosa on the far horizon. From the Lötschenpass, the northward view looks to the Doldenhorn rising out of the Gasterntal, and northeast to the Blüemlisalp.

Dominating the Lötschental, the Bietschhorn is seen reflected in a small lake below the Lötschenpass Hut

ROUTE 6
*Lötschenpass Hut (2690m) –
Selden (1552m) – Kandersteg (1176m)*

Grade:	3
Distance:	10km
Height loss:	1514m
Time:	4½hrs
Location:	North and northwest of the Lötschenpass
Accommodation:	Gfällalp (*berghaus*), Selden (hotels), Kandersteg (hotels)
Return transport:	Train, Kandersteg–Goppenstein via the Lötschberg Tunnel
Additional map:	LS 263T *Wildstrubel* 1:50,000

The Lötschenpass has been used as a trading route between the Valais and canton Bern since at least medieval times, and this walk follows a section of that route. On the north side of the pass the way is exposed in places, and there's a glacier to cross. The route over this is usually marked in summer and is fairly obvious. Even so, caution is advised.

Kandersteg has all the usual amenities for summer and winter visitors, with plenty of accommodation, restaurants, shops, banks, PTT, etc. The tourist office is located in the centre of the village (☎ 033 675 80 80, e-mail: info@kandersteg.ch, website: www.kandersteg.ch). For walks in the Kandersteg region see *The Bernese Alps, a walking guide*, by Kev Reynolds, published by Cicerone Press.

From the hut cross the pass and follow the marked way as it descends a series of rock terraces before getting onto the Lötschengletscher. Study the route across and follow the marker poles. There may be a few crevasses, but these should be easily stepped across. On reaching the far side the path then descends steeply, keeping well to the left of the Leilibach stream, and leads directly to **Berghaus Gfällalp** (1847m: *accommodation, refreshments*, ☎ 033 675 11 61), from where you gain a very fine view of the Gasterntal's upper reaches and of the Kanderfirn at its head. Continue down the slope, the path edging closer to the stream, and eventually reach the bed of the unspoilt Gasterntal beside the Kander river. A Himalayan-style suspension bridge takes you across the river to the hamlet of **Selden** (1552m: 2hrs: *accommodation, refreshments*). There are two inns here, both of which have dormitory accommodation as well as standard bedrooms: Hotel Steinbock (☎ 033 675 11 62) and Hotel Gasterntal-Selden (☎ 033 675 11 63).

Turn left and walk down the valley to the Chluse gorge at its entrance, where the Kander river thunders in a series of cascades, then through this gorge, curving down the main Kandertal to **Kandersteg** (1176m: *accommodation, refreshments*), passing close to the railway station. ◀

ROUTE 7

Fafleralp (1787m) – Petersgrat (3206m) –
Selden (1552m) – Kandersteg (1176m)

Grade:	3
Distance:	18km
Height gain:	1419m
Height loss:	2030m
Time:	11hrs (2 days)
Location:	Northwest and west of Fafleralp
Accommodation:	Mutthorn Hut, Selden (hotels), Kandersteg (hotels)
Return transport:	Train, Kandersteg–Goppenstein via the Lötschberg Tunnel
Additional map:	LS 263T *Wildstrubel* 1:50,000

This long, demanding, but delightful traverse of the icy Petersgrat should be attempted only by those familiar with glacier crossings, as much of the route lies over snow- and icefields. It is essential, too, that the necessary equipment for safe travel over crevassed glaciers is taken (rope, ice axe, etc). There are no major difficulties, but caution should be exercised at all times, and it is advisable to make an early (pre-dawn) start in order to avoid the worst effects of the sun on the Kanderfirn glacier.

From the pond in the hamlet of **Fafleralp** take the track left which gains height and swings round into the mouth of the Uisters Tal (also known as the Äusseres Faflertal). On reaching the stream at 1860m leave the track and take the path which strikes through the glen along the east bank. At the head of this little valley the path climbs steeply to the north of the Krindelspitz (Chrindelspitza) to gain the shrinking Üssertal glacier, with the long snow ridge of the Petersgrat directly above. Make for the lowest point on the ridge, a little west of north from the point at which you joined the glacier. The broad, flat Petersgrat arête affords magnificent views in all directions, but especially to the big peaks of the Pennine Alps to the south, across to the Bietschhorn guarding the Lötschental

Below the Petersgrat, the Uisters Tal spills into the Lötschental with views that include the Bietschhorn

The **Mutthorn Hut** (2898m) is found a short distance below this to the right. With 100 places, it is manned from July to the middle of September (☎ 033 853 13 44).

and the Blüemlisalp ahead. Now descend the easy glacier heading north towards the obvious saddle which lies below the rocky lump of the Mutthorn. ◀

From the saddle, or close enough to it to get a clear perspective through it, take in the view of the west face of the Jungfrau, then return to the descent. Bear left (south-west) and go down the Kanderfirn glacier, keeping to its left-hand side. On reaching the end of the icefield you should come to a marked path which leads steeply down to the Gasterntal. At the first opportunity cross the stream to the right bank and wander down-valley through natural rock gardens to reach **Berghaus Heimritz**, the first of the Selden buildings (☎ 033 675 14 34), which has bedrooms and dormitory accommodation. Continue along the dirt road to the other atmospheric buildings of **Selden** (1552m: 8½hrs: *accommodation, refreshments* – see details under Route 6).

It will take another 2½hrs to reach Kandersteg from Selden by a straightforward valley walk – see Route 6 for information. ▸

ROUTE 8

Fafleralp (1787m) –
Krindeln (Chrindellun) (2230m)

Grade:	2
Distance:	4km (one way)
Height gain:	443m
Time:	1½hrs
Location:	North of Fafleralp

This relatively short walk could make good use of a half-day, with some rewarding views from the high point. Bear in mind that you will need about 1hr for the descent.

From the roadhead car park head back towards a tree-clothed bluff by crossing a bridge and bearing right along a broad track. Follow the track as it swings to the left and, shortly after, bear right when it forks. This brings you to the hamlet of Fafleralp by a small pond, where you will find a signpost for Krindeln. The way now heads off to the right and enters larchwoods. Climbing easily by way of lengthy zigzags, the route gains height above the Inners Tal, becomes a little steeper and brings you to a grassy knoll (avalanche fences) offering magnificent views to the snowy saddle of the Lötschenlücke in the east, of the main valley sweeping below, and across to the wall of peaks dominated by the Bietschhorn.

Note: Instead of walking down-valley to Kandersteg, a splendid circuit could be created by crossing the Kander stream at Selden and reversing Route 6 to the Lötschenpass, and descending from there back into the Lötschental – allow 6–6½hrs for this.

ROUTE 9
Fafleralp (1787m) –
Anen Hut (2358m) – Fafleralp

Grade:	2
Distance:	9.5km
Height gain:	571m
Height loss:	571m
Time:	4hrs
Location:	ENE of Fafleralp

The Anen Hut stands in the upper reaches of the Lötschental near the little Ananensee tarn, with a close view of the Langgletscher. Thousands of years ago this glacier was responsible for gouging out the valley, but it's retreating fast now towards the Lötschenlücke (birthplace of the Grosser Aletschgletscher, seen to good effect on walks from Bettmeralp – see Routes 1–3) and leaving in its wake a turmoil of old moraines in a progressive state of rejuvination. On this lozenge-shaped route walkers visit two alp hamlets and three small lakes, pick a way across the moraines, view the glacier's snout, and have an opportunity for refreshment at the hut.

Leave the roadhead car park (postbus terminus) and pass through the gate leading up-valley on a marked footpath (Grundsee, Gletschertor, etc) that goes through pastures, with the chalets and hay barns of **Gletscherstafel** off to the left. Cross a bridge over the Lonza torrent and turn left on a well-worn footpath that winds uphill, then crosses another stream, after which you bear half-right to reach the little green tarn of Grundsee (1842m). Continue up-valley through bouldery pastures and open meadows, then across a slightly marshy area fluffed with cotton grass to a bridge at its northern end. After the meadowland the way climbs between stands of larch in view of the Langgletscher, goes through a rough boulderscape, then swings left over a substantial bridge spanning the glacial torrent.

Now on the north side of the valley, continue to gain height over a wild and somewhat chaotic hillside that suddenly gives way to slopes of alpenrose (afire with bloom in early summer) and dwarf alder, and this in turn is exchanged for soft, springy turf in a splendid glacial combe at the entrance to the little Jegital. Ahead now the Lauterbrunnen Breithorn (just a few centimetres higher than the Lötschentaler Breithorn on the opposite side of the valley) rises above the Jegi glacier. With the Jegital's stream pouring down to your left, come to a path junction. ▶

Branch right into a region of alpenrose, juniper and dwarf willow (note the little tarn nearby fed by a cascading stream), then climb steeply up an old moraine wall to reach the **Anen Hut** (2358m: 2½hrs: *accommodation, refreshments*). ▶

Return to the path junction in the mouth of the Jegital, cross the footbridge over a mini-gorge (2108m) and continue down-valley on the trail which remains above the river. The way leads through the pastures of the Gugginalp, beside the tiny **Guggisee** (2007m) and down across alpenrose and bilberry slopes to the chalets of **Guggistafel** (1933m). After this the descent winds down to cross the stream draining from the Inners Tal, and finally reaches **Fafleralp** and the car park.

A diversion into the **Jegital** is recommended if you have time. A waymarked route with an easy gradient follows the stream into the glen's innermost recess, where several waterfalls pour down the great cliffs of the amphitheatre.

The **Anen Hut** is usually manned from June to October, with 50 dormitory places – 8 in the winter room (☎ 027 939 17 64). The snout of the Langgletscher (the Gletschertor) can be visited from here by a short diversion.

ROUTE 10

*Fafleralp (1787m) –
Blatten (1540m) – Goppenstein (1216m)*

Grade:	1
Distance:	13km
Height loss:	571m
Time:	3hrs
Location:	Southwest of Fafleralp

An easy, gentle valley stroll, an ideal family outing that wanders downstream with plenty of opportunities to divert for refreshment. The paths are mostly clear and well trodden; in summer the meadows are bright with wild flowers, and in autumn the golden tint of the larches adds another dimension.

From the roadhead car park take the track to Fafleralp on the right bank of the Lonza river. A signpost here directs the route down-valley on a clear path to **Eisten** (1580m), and shortly after to **Blatten** (1540m: *refreshments*). Now go down below the village to cross the river where a footpath on the left bank leads through pastures and patches of woodland, past attractive hay barns and old farms and chalets, all the way to **Goppenstein** (*refreshments*). Take the postbus back to the main valley.

ROUTE 11

Ried (1486m) – Bietschhorn Hut (2565m)

Grade:	3
Distance:	4.5km (one way)
Height gain:	1079m
Time:	3–3½hrs
Location:	South of Blatten

A steep climb to a small mountain hut perched on the flanks of the most distinctive of Lötschental peaks, this route experiences a variety of terrain. There are no notable difficulties, other than the possibly problematic crossing of the torrent draining the Nestgletscher. There is no bridge, and under normal summer conditions it should be easy enough to cross. But during early summer snow-melt or following heavy rain, the water level could be sufficient to demand caution. Note that the hut is infrequently manned, so do not automatically expect refreshment on arrival. Check at the Wiler tourist office for the current situation.

A short distance along the road between Ried and Blatten turn right, cross the Lonza river on a bridge and take the right fork across the Birchmatte meadows. At a junction turn left, then right to enter forest, where the climb begins in earnest. Twisting quite steeply up among the trees, the way rises through the gorge-like narrows cut by the Nestbach and emerges to a more open hillside of bilberry and alpenrose in the Nestalp. Continue to climb until the path veers right to cross the stream on stepping stones. Shortly after this come to a junction with the path from Wiler (about 1½hrs).

The path improves as you climb up the west side of the Nestbach into a more typically alpine landscape. A series of zigzags then leads to a rising traverse right (west) to gain the prominent **Howitzen** spur, which makes an excellent viewpoint. The Bietschhorn Hut can now be seen above, and is gained by a route up the west side of the spur over moraine debris and grass.

Allow at least 2½hrs for the descent by the same route.

Owned by the Academic Alpine Club of Bern, the old timber-built **Bietschhorn Hut** is set among wild country with the precise aim of giving overnight shelter to climbers tackling the Bietschhorn. Falling a little short of the magical 4000m mark, the **Bietschhorn** (3934m) is generally reckoned to be the most difficult of peaks in the Bernese Alps. It was first climbed in the summer of 1859 by Leslie Stephen with his guides.

THE SAASTAL

This long trench of a valley, draining northwest from the Monte Moro pass which looks across to the Italian face of Monte Rosa, provides a fabulous range of walking prospects amid scenes of dramatic beauty. From lush alpine meadows to grim boulderscapes, from tranquil lakes to hanging glaciers, and from birch-lined streams to dazzling snow-fields, the Saastal refuses simple definition. In its upper reaches, hemmed in by an arc of lofty ridges that either carry the Swiss/Italian border or are hung about with glaciers, three feeder valleys add to its charm and increase opportunities for the eager walker, while high trails have been created at mid-height along both flanks of the valley and provide challenging routes and exquisite views. Directly below Switzerland's highest mountain, the important resort of Saas Fee lies in a stupendous glacial amphitheatre nearly 300m above the Saaser Vispa river, while the remainder of Saastal villages and hamlets either hug the river's bank or stand a short way from it, one after another: Saas Almagell, Saas Grund, Tamatten, Bidermatten, Saas Balen and Eisten.

ACCESS AND INFORMATION

Location:	On the south side of the Rhône valley, west of the Simplon pass.
Maps:	LS 274T *Visp* & 284T *Mischabel* at 1:50,000 Also available, and covering the whole valley on one sheet, Kümmerly + Frey publish *Wanderkarte Saastal* at 1:40,000 with accompanying booklet in four languages.
Bases:	Saas Grund (1559m), Saas Almagell (1673m), Saas Fee (1809m)
Information:	Tourist Office Saas Grund, Dorfplatz, CH-3910 Saas Grund (☎ 027 957 24 03 e-mail: to@saas-grund.ch website: www.saas-grund.ch)
	Verkehrsbüro, Dorfplatz, CH-3905 Saas Almagell (☎ 027 957 26 53) Tourismusorganisation Saas Fee, CH-3906 Saas Fee (☎ 027 958 18 58, e-mail: to@saas-fee.ch, website: www.saas-fee.ch)
Access:	By train to Visp or Stalden, then postbus to all Saastal villages.

The popularity of the Saastal (Saas valley) dates back to the pioneers of mountaineering, who in the 19th century were drawn there by the magnificent array of peaks that curve in a dazzle of ice and snow above Saas Fee, by the huge wall of the Mischabel group that separates the valley from that of Zermatt (and which includes among its summits the 4545m Dom), and by the glacier passes by which access with Zermatt to the west was made possible for the Victorian mountaineers and their guides, and offered scenically spectacular routes.

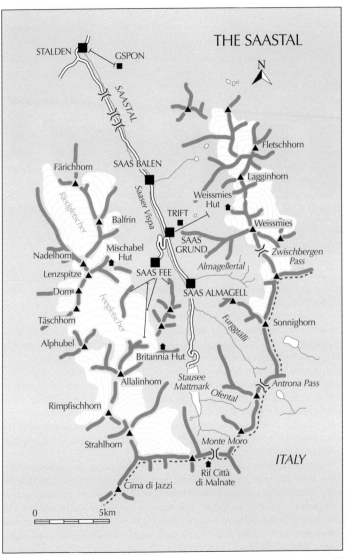

THE SAASTAL

N

STALDEN GSPON

SAASTAL

Färichhorn

Riedgletscher

SAAS BALEN

Saaser Vispa

Fletschhorn

Lagginhorn

Weissmies Hut

TRIFT

Balfrin

Weissmies

SAAS GRUND

Mischabel Hut

Zwischbergen Pass

Nadelhorn

SAAS FEE

Almagellertal

Lenzspitze

Feegletscher

Dom

SAAS ALMAGELL

Täschhorn

Furggtälli

Sonnighorn

Alphubel

Britannia Hut

Allalinhorn

Stausee Mattmark

Antrona Pass

Rimpfischhorn

Ofental

Strahlhorn

Monte Moro

ITALY

Rif Città di Malnate

Cima di Jazzi

0   5km

Saas Fee, one of the major resorts of the Valais

Yet centuries before these mountains became absorbed into the Playground of Europe, the Saastal was on an important trade route with Italy by way of the Monte Moro and Antrona passes. The first of these, at the southern end of the valley above the Mattmark lake, has been in use since at least the 13th century; while the Antrona pass, linking the Furggtälli behind Saas Almagell with the Valle d'Antrona which flows down to Villadossola and the Italian lakes, was used in Roman times. Stretches of medieval paving are still visible near the pass.

The old mule trail that was the Saastal's historic link with the Rhône valley was not replaced with a motor road until the 1930s. It reached Saas Grund in 1938, while the first motor vehicles arrived in Saas Fee only in 1952. But while the Saastal took a long time to be properly opened up to the outside world with an accessible road, Saas Fee had a hotel as early as 1850 in recognition of the great potential for tourism there. By the dawn of the 21st century that potential had been exploited almost to the limit.

Entering from Visp, the visitor approaches for 7km along the Vispertal, which forks at the village of Stalden. The southwest branch becomes the Mattertal, leading to Zermatt; the southeastern stem is the Saastal. It's a narrow, rock-girt valley at first (Saas comes from the Italian *sasso* meaning 'rock'), the road clinging to the mountain wall as it squeezes through Eisten, but by the time Saas Balen is reached the valley begins to open out, with dramatic peaks gradually revealed. Four kilometres beyond Balen, at the foot of the Weissmies (4023m) and Lagginhorn

(4010m), nestles Saas Grund, formerly the valley's main village, but now over-shadowed by the popularity of Fee. In some ways that is to Grund's advantage.

Upstream of Grund the valley continues towards the south, narrowing on the approach to Saas Almagell, which has a brace of minor valleys nearby eating into the eastern wall of mountains. Beyond Almagell the Saastal opens once more as the road finishes at the large dammed Mattmarksee. Fed by glaciers and streams draining the head of the valley, this lake, now safely contained by a huge retaining wall, was responsible for a series of disastrous floods that brought devastation to buildings and the deaths of villagers when it burst its moraine banks. During construction of the barrage in August 1965, 88 workmen lost their lives when a mass of ice from the overhanging Allalin glacier crashed down upon their building site. This loss of life is commemorated in the chapel at Zer Meiggeru near Saas Almagell.

Above and to the southwest of Saas Grund, Saas Fee is approached by a fine road that climbs in two long loops up the wooded hillside to emerge into a sunny bowl of an amphitheatre scooped out by the curtain-like Feegletscher that hangs from the headwall. Looking up from Fee, that headwall of peaks begins on the left (east) with the snow dome of the Allalinhorn (4027m), then the Alphubeljoch saddle which rises to the flattened crest of the Alphubel (4206m), the sharp rock wall of the Täschhorn (4491m), followed closely by Dom (4545m), Lenzspitze (4294m) and Nadelhorn (4327m). It is a magnificent collection of peaks, compelling to the climber interested in routes of a classical nature, while the mountain walker has a wonderland of trails to explore with those shining summits as a backdrop.

With over 300km of paths to explore throughout the Saastal, there should be more than enough to suit walkers of all ambitions. In addition, guided glacier tours are offered each week in summer – for current details contact one of the valley's tourist offices.

MAIN BASES

SAAS GRUND (1559m) is located in the bed of the valley below the Weissmies massif on the right bank of the river at the junction of the road to Fee. Its old traditional buildings have been outnumbered by those of more recent construction, but to all intents and purposes Saas Grund remains a low-key resort with good access to the rest of the valley. There are plenty of apartments, four campsites open in summer, and hotels of all grades, some of which have dormitories. There's a PTT, a fair range of shopping facilities, banks, restaurants, a climbing school (Bergsteigerschule Weissmies, ☎ 027 957 14 44) and a gondola lift to Kreuzboden and Hohsaas. For accommodation lists, contact the tourist office.

SAAS ALMAGELL (1673m) is the valley's southernmost village. Smaller than Grund or Fee, it nonetheless has a number of one-, two- and three-star hotels, and at least four pensions. The village has limited shopping facilities, but several restaurants, a PTT, tourist office in the main square, and a chairlift to the alp hamlet of Furggstalden.

SAAS FEE (1809m) Despite a rapid increase in size and facilities, Saas Fee somehow manages to retain the character of a mountain village without being totally submerged by its international appeal. Few alpine villages have a more dramatic setting, and the fact that motor vehicles are banned from it (there's a large and expensive car park at the entrance) adds to its charm. There is no shortage of hotel, chalet or rented apartment accommodation available, ranging from modest dorm beds to four-star luxury, and the shop-lined streets offer everything from postcards and ice cream to extravagently expensive Swiss watches. There are banks, bars and restaurants, PTT next to the bus station, tourist office nearby and several mechanical lifts by which to access high points to begin a variety of walks. Local mountain guides not only lead top-grade climbs on neighbouring peaks, but also organise mountaineering courses and walking tours (contact the Bergführerbüro, ☎ 027 957 44 64, website: www.rhone.ch/mountainlife).

OTHER BASES

SAAS BALEN, the smallest of the main Saastal villages, noted for its attractive circular church and a fine waterfall, has about 600 beds to rent in apartments and local houses. Contact the tourist office for a list: Verkehrsverein, CH-3908 Saas Balen (☎ 027 957 16 89). Elsewhere in the Saastal and on the hillsides above it, overnight accommodation of one sort or another is available. In the Almagellertal east of Saas Almagell, for example, **BERGHOTEL ALMAGELLERALP**, which has dormitory places as well as standard beds, is a romantically situated inn with neither road nor cableway access (☎ 027 957 32 06). The tiny alp hamlet of **TRIFT** above Saas Grund has rooms at Restaurant Triftalp (☎ 027 957 23 74), while at the top of the **KREUZBODEN** gondola lift Panoramarestaurant Kreuzboden has dormitory beds (☎ 027 957 29 45). Above Saas Balen on the valley's east flank, **RESTAURANT HEIMISCHGARTEN**, on a linking path from the Gspon Höhenweg (see Route 12), also provides bed and breakfast. **GSPON** is a small hamlet perched high above the valley's northern end, reached by cablecar from Stalden via Staldenried (no motor access). It has one hotel with 25 beds, the Alpenblick (☎ 027 952 22 21). For further information contact the Verkehrsverein, CH-3933 Staldenried/Gspon (☎ 027 952 16 46).

MOUNTAIN HUTS

ALMAGELLER HUT (2894m) Owned by the SAC and built high in the Wysstal stem of the Almagellertal about 4hrs from Saas Almagell, this hut makes a useful overnight stop in advance of crossing the Zwischbergen pass. It has places for 120, and is fully manned from the end of June to end of September (☎ 027 957 11 79, website: www.almagellerhuette.ch).

BRITANNIA HUT (3030m) Partly financed by the ABMSAC (Association of British Members of the Swiss Alpine Club), the Britannia Hut sits in a cleft between the Klein Allalin and a ridge of the Hinter Allalin, with glaciers on either side. It's a large hut, with 134 places and a guardian in occupation from early March until the end of September (☎ 027 957 22 88, website: www.britannia.ch). It can be reached easily in 40–45mins from the Felskinn cableway on a marked glacier route, or by way of a splendid 2hr walk on a high-level path from the Plattjen gondola.

MISCHABEL HUT (3329m) There are, in fact, two Mischabel huts built on a spur of the Lenzspitze more than 1500m above Saas Fee. The approach route of 4hrs from Fee (3hrs from Hannig) is unremittingly steep, but scenically rewarding. Owned by the Academic Alpine Club of Zürich, there are dormitory places for 130 and a resident guardian from July to the end of September (☎ 027 957 13 17, website: www.ssf.ch).

WEISSMIES HUT (2726m) Reached by a walk of a little under an hour from the Kreuzboden gondola above Saas Grund, the Weissmies Hut stands on the slopes of the Lagginhorn. With places for 150, the hut is manned from mid-June until the end of September (☎ 027 957 25 54).

The well-appointed Britannia Hut, partly financed by British members of the Swiss Alpine Club

ROUTE 12
Gspon (1895m) – Kreuzboden (2400m)
(the Gspon Höhenweg)

Grade:	2
Distance:	13km
Height gain:	645m
Height loss:	135m
Time:	5hrs
Location:	High on the east flank of the Saastal, from the northern end heading south

The Gspon Höhenweg is one of the great walks of the Saastal, a belvedere of a trail that runs high above the valley bed across pastures, through woodland, and from alp to alp, with glorious views virtually from start to finish. This is a fine-weather route, for it's a committing walk, and although there are a few escape options in the event of bad weather or accident, most of the descending paths are long and steep. So choose a good day with a settled forecast, carry plenty of liquid and food, and the glories of the Saastal will be revealed.

To get to the start of the höhenweg, make your way to Stalden railway station at the junction of the Saastal and Mattertal. The station is, of course, on a postbus route from all Saastal villages. From there take an early cablecar (a two-stage lift via Staldenried) to Gspon. This little hamlet is set upon an open hillside with a panoramic view that includes the Bietschhorn across the Rhône valley and the top of the Weisshorn towards the head of the Mattertal, but is dominated by the Balfrin – as is much of the early stage of this walk – a glacier-clad mountain to the south, forming part of the dividing wall between Mattertal and Saastal.

From the cablecar station take a path sloping below the village chapel to a group of *mazots* (hay barns) and a junction whose sign gives Kreuzboden as Chrizbode. Choose the left-hand option, which soon goes through larchwoods and comes to another junction (Oberfinilu: 2039m) about 50mins from Gspon. Again, take the left-hand path climbing to the huddled buildings of **Finilu**, and continue rising into more larchwoods until the way eases on a contour beside a *bisse* (an irrigation channel).

Gspon, above the Saastal's entrance, with the Bietschhorn as a backdrop

Leaving this the path climbs again and comes to a solitary house at **Obere Schwarzwalde** (2200m: 1½hrs). During research it was possible to buy tea and coffee from the owner, a wood carver. There are very fine views of the Balfrin, while the Allalinhorn begins to appear up-valley.

About 10mins beyond the house the *höhenweg* crosses an open rocky slope before entering larchwoods once more. This eventually brings you to a high pasture-land with a small hut standing just above the path (Färiga: 2271m). After this the trail angles down to cross the Mattwaldbach, which drains the Mattwald glacier on the Fletschhorn then mounts steeply to Siwibode, a high shoulder of pastureland at 2244m, where there's yet another junction. ▶

Keep ahead and briefly join another *bisse* among trees. About 15mins from the last junction come to another at Linde Bodu (another opportunity to descend to Saas Balen and Saas Grund). Maintain direction, and shortly after the path joins a track. Follow this uphill, and 4mins later you will see another path breaking to the right. ▶

As far as this walk is concerned, the destination lies another 1¾hrs ahead. Remain on the track, and when it forks 3mins later bear right. After 100m you reach another junction and go straight ahead to the buildings of **Hoferälpji**, beyond which you cross a stream and

Note: If an escape route is needed, it's possible to descend to Saas Balen from here in 1½hrs.

Note: This is the official *höhenweg* descent to Saas Grund via Restaurant Heimischgarten, which offers accom-modation and refresh-ments just 10mins from this junction. Saas Grund is reached in 1hr 25mins from the junction.

climb to Grüebe (2300m). The gradient steepens on the way to the next junction, where you then bear right to contour for 40mins or so across a rough slope of rocks and bouders to gain the highest part of the walk at **Hannig** (2445m), a path junction with bench seats. Slanting left the path angles down the hillside, then turns into the **Kreuzboden** basin with its man-made tarn, excellent views across the valley and the gondola lift to Saas Grund.

Notes

• Accommodation and refreshments are available here at the Panorama Restaurant.

• An alternative descent by footpath to Saas Grund via Trift takes about 2hrs. See Route 14.

• Given sufficient energy, a splendid natural extension to the Gspon Höhenweg continues on a high path known as either the Höhenweg Kreuzboden or Höhenweg Allmagelleralp. Taking around 2½hrs to reach Berghotel Almagelleralp, or 4–4½hrs to Saas Almagell, this walk is described as Route 15.

ROUTE 13
Kreuzboden (2400m) – Weissmies Hut (2726m)

Grade:	2
Distance:	1.5km (one way)
Height gain:	326m
Time:	45–50mins
Location:	Northeast of Saas Grund

This short but strenuous walk takes a steep path from the Kreuzboden gondola station up the lateral moraine of former glaciers to reach the Weissmies Hut. Standing on a lofty shelf, a splendid view is gained of the Mischabel peaks and icefields above Saas Fee across the valley to the southwest.

The Kreuzboden/Hohsaas gondola lift is found a short distance down-valley from the village square in Saas Grund. Only the first stage of the lift is required for this walk, and on arrival at Kreuzboden you take the signed path behind it, heading northeast up a steep cone of moraine that leads directly to the **Weissmies Hut** (*accommodation, refreshments*). ▶

A small man-made tarn near the Kreuz-boden lift system high above Saas Grund

With places for 150 the **Weissmies Hut** is usually manned from mid-June until the end of September (☎ 027 957 25 54).

ROUTE 14
Kreuzboden (2400m) –
Trift (2072m) – Saas Grund (1559m)

Grade:	1–2
Distance:	5km
Height gain:	45m
Height loss:	886m
Time:	2–2½hrs
Location:	Northeast of Saas Grund

With magnificent views accompanying almost every step of the way, the path to Triftalp from the Hannig Panoramaweg is very steep in places and requires concentration. In other words, don't get too carried away with the scenery unless you are stationary!

Having taken the gondola from Saas Grund to Kreuzboden, leave the lift and turn left onto the Hannig Panoramaweg, which forks 2mins later. On the left a small man-made lake makes a photogenic foreground to the panorama of high mountains and glaciers. Take the right branch, cross a bridge over a stream, then angle up the hillside across a rough rocky section to the **Hannig** vantage point at 2445m, where there are bench seats on which to relax and enjoy the view.

Take the descending path signed to Triftalp. It leads down in numerous zigzags over grass slopes, sometimes steeply, and comes onto a track below a chairlift. Bear left up the track to the meadows of Triftalp (2090m). After crossing a stream the track forks. Bear right and soon arrive at the pretty hamlet of **Trift** (2072m: 1hr 10mins), which consists of a picturesque white-walled chapel, a

The attractive Trift alp above Saas Grund

few houses and hay barns. Wander past the chapel and
continue along the track as it winds among trees and
3mins later come to Restaurant Trift (2035m: *accommodation, refreshments*), where the track ends.

Continue ahead on a footpath through larchwoods
and down to another track which leads past the hamlet
of **Brunnen** (1893m). A path now carries the descent
through more larchwoods in steady zigzags and comes
to another junction, both of whose options lead to Saas
Grund. Take the left-hand path, which crosses an open
hillside with views over the village then continues as a
dirt road/track, which you cross straight ahead to enter
Saas Grund by an attractive pathway among barns and
houses near the centre of the village.

ROUTE 15

*Kreuzboden (2400m) –
Berghotel Almagelleralp (2194m) – Saas Almagell
(1673m) (Höhenweg Almagelleralp)*

Grade:	2
Distance:	10km
Height gain:	165m
Height loss:	892m
Time:	4–4½hrs
Location:	Northeast of Saas Grund, heading south

In the same vein as the Gspon and Balfrin Höhenwegs (see Routes 12 and 32),
this is another splendid balcony path which contours along the mountainside
high above the valley before descending into the Almagelleralp. There are no
major difficulties, but anyone tackling it should have a reasonably good head for
heights. Refreshments are available at the Berghotel Almagelleralp.

On leaving the Kreuzboden gondola station go to the
path junction by the Hohsaas section of the cableway,

Linking Kreuzboden with the Almagelleralp, a high path gives splendid long views towards the head of the Saastal

where a sign suggests 2hrs 45mins to Almagelleralp. The path goes beneath the gondola lift and heads across the hillside in a southerly direction, with Saas Fee and its walling mountains in view. After an initial contour, the path rises gently across flowery slopes which have given rise to this section being named the Alpenblumen Promenade. Identification plaques have been fixed beside the path, and for a while the hamlet of Trift, with its white chapel, can be seen 400m below.

After about 30mins you come to a rocky area where red–white waymarks guide the route across, and then begin to lose height as you turn the Triftgrätji spur at 2480m. Once around the spur the view extends to the head of the valley, to the Mattmarksee and Monte Moro pass in the headwall. The trail descends towards avalanche fences, then levels off and comes to a track which you follow until it ends below a wooden hut. A traversing path continues from it, crosses another spill of rocks and boulders, then climbs again with a twist or two on the approach to the Almagellertal.

Throughout the walk views have been changing and rearranging: the Rimpfischhorn now joins the Strahlhorn across the Saastal to the southwest, and the Britannia

Hut may also be seen with the crisp white mountains as a backdrop, while the rooftops of Saas Almagell lie some 800m below. On coming to a high point (Weissflue) at about 2505m, descent towards the Almagellertal begins. Across the glen the Almagellerhorn is the most conspicuous of its walling peaks, and the handsome Portjengrat ridge with its glacial scarf marks the eastern end of the glen, with the little Wysstal draining its upper limits.

The trail slopes down into the Almagellertal with long winding zigzags across flower-rich slopes in early summer, and with backward views to the Mischabel peaks which now assume an almost Himalayan scale. Then, in the bed of the valley, the way tracks through natural alpine flower gardens to reach **Berghotel Almagelleralp** (2194m: 2½hrs: *accommodation, refreshments*).

The continuing path to Saas Almagell is clear, well-marked and easy. At first along the right bank of the Almagellerbach, on reaching a bridge about 20mins from the *berghotel,* you cross to the left bank and descend through open larchwoods. On the zigzag descent there are several junctions, but each time signs indicate the way to Almagell. However, when you reach a junction just above the village you have a choice between the upper part (Ober Dorfteil) or the lower end of **Saas Almagell** (Unterer Dorfteil). For the village centre and postbus stop, go straight ahead (direction Unterer Dorfteil).

ROUTE 16

*Saas Almagell (1673m) – Berghotel
Almagelleralp – Almageller Hut (2894m)*

Grade:	3
Distance:	6.5km
Height gain:	1221m
Time:	4hrs
Location:	East of Saas Almagell

Built in 1982 halfway up the little Wysstal under the Portjengrat and on the way to the Zwischbergen pass, the Almageller Hut is used by climbers tackling such peaks as the Weissmies, Sonnighorn and Mittelrück, as well as by wild-country trekkers heading over the pass to the Zwischbergental and Gondo (a serious route for experienced trekkers only). The hut enjoys splendid high mountain views. The first part of this route as far as the Almagelleralp reverses the last section of Route 15.

Berghotel Almagelleralp enjoys a secluded location deep within the Almagellertal

From the village square follow signs for the Almagelleralp, going along an alleyway to the left of the post office on a tarmac path between houses, and soon rising above the village through a steep meadow to larchwoods. At a path junction (left to Unterer Dorfteil) continue uphill to another junction. (The right-hand path goes to Furggstalden.) Take the left branch, twisting up into the mouth of the Almagellertal. The gradient eases, and coming to a bridge you cross to the left (north) side of the Almagellerbach. The good clear path now follows alongside the stream, and about 1½hrs from Almagell reaches **Berghotel Almagelleralp** (2194m: *accommodation, refreshments*), with its splendid outlook to the Mischabel wall of mountains above Saas Fee.

Pass in front of the inn and continue up-valley, rising to cross first the Rottal stream, then that of the Wysstal, after which the way loops up into the Wysstal itself under the looming Portjengrat. Now climbing northeast, the gradient steepens and you meet another path also coming from the Almagelleralp, but on a steeper route. Above to the left rises the rocky three-pronged Dri Horlini. Continue rising, and about 2½hrs from Almagelleralp reach the **Almageller Hut**. ▶

Owned by the SAC, the **Almageller Hut** has places for 88 and is manned during the summer (☎ 027 957 11 79). Allow at least 2½hrs for a return to Saas Almagell by the same path used on the ascent, while the Zwischbergen pass may be gained in 1hr by a very rough route.

ROUTE 17
Saas Almagell (1673m) –
Saas Grund (1559m) – Saas Balen (1483m)

Grade:	1
Distance:	8km
Height loss:	190m
Time:	2hrs
Location:	North of Saas Almagell

The easiest walk in the Saastal, this riverside stroll links a string of villages and hamlets, and is an ideal outing for families with young children.

From the centre of Saas Almagell go down to the Saaser Vispa river, cross to the west bank and walk downstream on a tarmac path which takes you between meadows. About 10mins from the start the path forks. The two paths rejoin further down, so take whichever suits: the right-hand option remains beside the river, while the left fork continues between meadows and rises a little to pass a lone house (Biel) in a meadow on the right, and soon after rejoins the riverside path. In another 10mins or so come to **Unter den Bodmen** (1593m: *refreshments*), a hamlet with a curious little chapel and views up to the Mischabel peaks high above to the left.

Shortly after leaving Bodmen cross a side stream and walk ahead along the edge of a campsite and past the start of the Kapellenweg, which climbs to Saas Fee (see Route 23). The riverside path leads to **Saas Grund** (1559m: 1hr: *refreshments*) via the bridge that carries the Saas Fee road across the river. Remain on the left bank, and on the northern outskirts of the village the path forks once more. The left branch climbs to Saas Fee via Sengg (see Route 24), while you stay on the riverside path through more meadows. On coming to a bridge crossing the Saaser Vispa to Saas Tamatten and Unter den Berg, keep left to yet another junction. Continue ahead through open meadows to **Bidermatten** (1565m), the most attractive and unspoilt settlement on the walk.

The way goes through the hamlet via alleyways, then on a narrow road to a row of traditional hay barns. At the bridge keep to a track on the left bank which takes you down to **Saas Balen** (1483m: *refreshments*), where you can catch a postbus back up-valley. (The bus stop is found across the river.) The village has several attractive buildings and two churches.

Furggalp in the little Furggtälli above Saas Almagell

ROUTE 18

Saas Almagell (1673m) –
Furggalp (2075m) – Saas Almagell

Grade:	2
Distance:	6km
Height gain:	402m
Height loss:	402m
Time:	2½hrs
Location:	Southeast of Saas Almagell

The Furggtälli, which digs into the mountains above Saas Almagell, is a delight-fully peaceful and lonely glen. At its head lies the historic Antrona pass, visited on Route 20, but the walk described here is a much shorter circuit which visits an alp hamlet (Furggstalden), an isolated farm and the lower reaches of the valley itself. Furggstalden is also reached by chairlift from Almagell.

The start of this walk is the same as that for the Almageller Hut (Route 16). From the village square go along an alleyway to the left of the post office, and on the eastern outskirts climb a steep meadow and enter larchwoods. About 12mins from the start come to a path junction and continue uphill for another 8mins to another junction at 1760m. The Almagelleralp is the left-hand option, but for Furggstalden bear right, still climbing through woods to a service road. Cross this to the continuing path which enters **Furggstalden** (1893m: *refreshments*) shortly after. The hamlet has two restaurants and a chairlift.

There are two signed ways into the Furggtälli from here, but they reunite above the hamlet. One rises above Restaurant Alpina, the other leaves from the chairlift, and they come together a few minutes later after crossing meadows. On reaching a track turn right along it, and about 3mins later take an unmarked path rising above the track, among trees, then over a rise where you gain a view into the Furggtälli, with Furggalp just ahead.

To explore the **Furggtälli** keep to the upper path where it forks by the alp buildings. An extension is described below as Route 19.

Passing the two alp buildings of **Furggalp** (a house and a cattle byre), come to another path junction, where you descend to the Furggbach stream, cross a footbridge and turn right. ◀

Now on the south side of the stream the path goes through meadows and into more larchwoods, where you descend, steeply in places, in zigzags to emerge onto the Saastal road at Zer Meiggeru (1740m). Walk down the road to return to Saas Almagell.

ROUTE 19

Saas Almagell (1670m) –
Furggtälli (Bitzinen) (2302m) – Saas Almagell

Grade:	2–3
Distance:	12km
Height gain:	632m
Height loss:	632m
Time:	4–4½hrs
Location:	Southeast of Saas Almagell

This extension to Route 18 explores more of the Furggtälli valley, but without going as far as the Antrona pass (which is visited on Route 20). The walk offers greater variety than the previous route, with a contrast between the pastoral lower valley and the less tamed aspect of its middle section.

Follow directions for Route 18 as far as the alp buildings of **Furggalp** (2075m: 1hr 20mins), where the path forks. Instead of taking the lower path to the stream, continue up-valley on the north bank. The route initially passes through meadows, but as you progress so the valley turns more wild and stony. The path rises at a steady gradient, and about 1¼hrs from Furggalp brings you over a stony rise into a rough level of pasture, from where the Antrona pass and dying Furggen glacier can be seen.

Cross a bridge to the south side of the stream at 2302m (**Bitzinen**) and follow the path back down-valley. It will take about 45mins to reach the footbridge below Furggalp, where you either take Route 18 back to Saas Almagell or retrace the outward path via Furggstalden.

The delightful Furggtälli above Saas Almagell

ROUTE 20
Mattmark (2197m) – Jazzilücke (3081m) – Antrona Pass (2838m) – Saas Almagell (1670m)

Grade:	3
Distance:	18km
Height gain:	884m
Height loss:	1408m
Time:	7–8hrs
Location:	South and southeast of Saas Almagell

The two tributary valleys, Ofental and Furggtälli, that drain the east side of the Saastal above Saas Almagell are blocked by the high mountain ridge that carries the Swiss/Italian border. At the head of the Ofental the 2837m Ofental pass (Passo di Antigine) offers a way for trekkers to reach the Valle d'Antrona, while the Antrona pass (Passo di Saas), just 1m higher than its neighbour, is an older crossing that leads into the same Italian valley. The following route does not cross into that Italian valley, however, but links the two Swiss glens by way of a third pass, the rocky 3081m Jazzilücke, tight against the Jazzihorn. It's a long, scenically varied, and at times exposed walk that should only be attempted by experienced mountain trekkers and in good settled conditions.

Take the postbus as far as Restaurant Mattmark (2197m: *refreshments*), walk up the final stretch of road to the western end of the dam and cross to the eastern side, where a broad lakeside path heads south. About 15mins along this path you will come to a junction where you turn left and go up into the mouth of the lovely Ofental, a delight of rough pastures that become more lush in the central part of the glen. Pause for a moment to enjoy the westward view of glacier, snowfield and bold rock walls. The path remains on the north (left) side of the stream, and beyond the pastures it rises over increasingly stony terrain to reach a fork at about 2700m. The Ofental pass route continues ahead, but you veer left for the Jazzilücke.

It's a rocky ascent, and here and there cairns and waymarks are useful aids to route-finding as the way twists up to the frontier ridge at the **Jazzilücke** (3081m: 3–3½hrs). The Italian side plunges abruptly, while the rocks that form the ridge seem almost to overhang.

The continuing route to the Antrona pass takes about 45mins from here. It veers left (northwest) under the Jazzihorn and is very exposed for a while – plenty of fixed cable – then heads northeast down a broader ridge (possible snow patches), where it's necessary to keep alert for waymarks and cairns. When the ridge narrows, the route alternates from one side to the other, with occasional ledges on the Italian side. Just before coming to the pass, you'll find a roofless walled shelter. The **Antrona pass** (2838m: 3¾–4¼hrs) is a wild and uncompromising place marked by large cairns.

Breaking away from the pass, aim northwest across rocky terrain (snow patches and pools of snowmelt) on a line of cairns and waymarks without losing much height at first, before the way begins to sweep down (no real path as yet), with more waymarks and cairns guiding through a barren, sterile landscape. Remnants of the Furggen glacier are seen to the left.

The Furggtälli descends in a series of natural steps with very little vegetation until you're almost halfway down the glen. Then, as you progress through, it becomes more pastoral, green and welcoming. After passing through the first belt of larches, come to a path junction (2075m) with the two alp buildings of **Furggalp** just ahead. This junction is reached about 2¼–2½hrs from the Antrona pass. Both path options lead to Saas Almagell. The shorter and more direct route goes straight ahead via Furggstalden, while the alternative goes down the left bank of the stream and is described under Route 19.

The Furggstalden trail passes the alp buildings and curves away from the Furggtälli proper, and shortly comes onto a track. Briefly walk along this, then cut left through meadows to reach **Furggstalden** (1893m: *refreshments*), with its two restaurants and a chairlift for an optional descent to Saas Almagell. Take the footpath left of Restaurant Alpina, and go through the hamlet of dark-timber buildings to a service road, which you cross straight ahead. A twisting path now descends through larchwoods and brings you to Saas Almagell.

ROUTE 21
Mattmark (2197m) – Tälliboden (2492m) –
Ofental (2525m) – Mattmark

Grade:	2
Distance:	12km
Height gain:	383m
Height loss:	383m
Time:	4½hrs
Location:	South of Saas Almagell

On this circuit of the Mattmark reservoir, the peaceful Ofental is visited. It's a mostly easy walk, with one potentially tricky stream crossing to contend with.

The walk begins at Restaurant Mattmark, the southern terminus for the postbus. Walk up to the western end of the dam and take the service road along the right-hand (western) side of the reservoir. In 6mins come to two tunnels and enter the one on the left. On emerging from it continue ahead on a track that goes all the way to the end of the lake, but forks about 15mins from the start. The upper track goes to Schwarzbergalp, but you bear left and shortly enter a second tunnel. Out of this the track contours along the valley, and at the far end of the lake it forks again below the hut of Innere Bodmen. Keep left, cross the main stream draining the valley's upper reaches, and turn right on the Monte Moro footpath (2225m).

The way now rises through the narrowing valley with a view southwest to the Seewjinen glacier plastered against the frontier mountains. About 20mins from the start of the path, cross the stream by a footbridge (2325m), then climb a little more steeply to gain an open basin of pastureland and a path junction. This is known as **Tälliboden** (2489m: 1¾hrs).

Turn left, recross the stream on slab stepping stones and veer left. The path is a narrow one, and it slants up the hillside heading north on a steady rising traverse. The grass slopes are cluttered now and then with rocks and boulders, and on topping a high point of 2560m, marked by a distinctive cairn, a good view is gained over the Mattmarksee. The way now eases across an open hillside with ribs of rock jutting through the turf. The path rises a little more to gain the highest part of the walk at 2580m – a fine vantage point with a panorama that includes not only the frontier peaks behind, but the Strahlhorn to the west, the Allalin glacier, the Britannia Hut on its saddle with the red-brown walls of the Egginer beyond that, and the Mischabelhörner too. Also visible, of course, are the Mattmark reservoir below and

the hazy-blue mountains of the Bernese Alps on the far side of the unseen Rhône valley to the north.

The Ofental is a quiet, secluded glen near the head of the Saastal

Rounding a shoulder of the Galmenhorn you look down to the entrance of the Ofental. A minor path descends left, but you continue ahead. Almost immediately the visible path disappears into a clutter of rocks, but waymarks lead through and you soon come onto a proper path once more, easing into the shallow **Ofental**. Descending to the bed of the valley, the way cuts left to join a faint streamside trail. The stream has dug its way through rocks and has to be crossed. During research there was no bridge and the crossing place was not clearly marked, other than by a small cairn on the south side which indicated a narrow step from the rocky bank onto the north side – not as difficult as it might first appear. Once over, go up the grass bank to another path, then turn left. Soon after come to a junction and continue ahead, with splendid views across the Saastal.

Maintain direction at the next junction, then descend a slope of rocks, alpenrose, juniper and scrub alder to the lakeside path and bear right. At the end of the dam either take the continuing path all the way to

Saas Almagell (add 1½hrs to the walk) or cross the dam to its western side and descend to Restaurant Mattmark for the postbus down-valley.

ROUTE 22
Mattmark (2197m) –
Monte Moro Pass (2868m) – Mattmark

Grade:	3
Distance:	13km
Height gain:	671m
Height loss:	671m
Time:	5½hrs
Location:	South of Saas Almagell

The walk to the Monte Moro pass is one of the best known in the Saastal. The pass is an historic one, having been in use since at least the 13th century, for in 1250 Italian migrants crossed over the mountains to settle in the Saastal, and twelve years later German-speaking Valaisians were recorded at Macugnaga on the Italian side of the pass. One of the prime reasons for visiting the pass today is to catch a view of the great east face of Monte Rosa (the so-called 'mirror wall') which looms nearby, but be warned that clouds often boil up on the Italian side on fine summer days to obscure that view during the morning. An early start is advised.

Follow directions for Route 21 as far as **Tälliboden** (2492m: 1¾hrs), and take the continuing path which slants up and over a slope of rocks and slabs. In places the trail is clear and well made, but there are also sections where waymarks and small cairns guide the route. There's also one section of fixed rope, and although it's not a difficult route, it is quite demanding. As height is gained, the route works up a long stairway of stone slabs, remnants of an ancient paved mule-track (curiously this is less evident on the ascent as on the way down). Just below the pass a small snowfield is usually ascended, above which the path veers right for a final scramble

over rocks and boulders to gain the **Monte Moro pass** (2868m: 3hrs), on which stands a tall statue of the Madonna of the Snows. Just below on the Italian side lies the small, often-frozen Lago Smeraldo, the upper lift station of a cablecar from Macugnaga (a chain handrail guides the path down to it), and the **Rifugio Città di Malnate** – also known as Rif. Gaspare Oberto (2810m: *accommodation, refreshments,* 40 places, ☎ [0039] 0324 6 55 44). The view of Monte Rosa's east face can be magical from the pass, while those on the Swiss side are also very fine.

Standing in a prominent position at the Monte Moro pass, a gilded Madonna gazes into Italy

Notes
- The return to the Mattmark dam by the same route used on the ascent will take about 2½hrs, or 2¾hrs by the track on the east side of the reservoir.
- To descend to Macugnaga in Italy (passport necessary) allow 2½hrs.

ROUTE 23
Saas Grund (1559m) –
Saas Fee (1809m) (via the Kapellenweg)

Grade:	1
Distance:	3km
Height gain:	250m
Time:	1hr 15mins
Location:	Southwest of Saas Grund

The Kapellenweg provides an easy yet interesting walk from Saas Grund to Saas Fee

In several valleys included in this guide, pathways link a series of religious shrines illustrating the various Stations of the Cross. None is more prominent than that which makes a stairway from the outskirts of Saas Grund to Saas Fee. This is an ancient pathway, with 15 small stone shrines built in 1709 and an opulently decorated pilgrimage chapel of St Mary of the High Steps (Maria zur Hohen Stiege – built 1687, with Italianate portico added in 1747) at which a festival is held each year on 8 September.

From the centre of Grund cross the bridge over the Saaser Vispa river (on the road to Saas Fee) and immediately turn left on a riverside footpath that soon leads alongside a campsite. Just beyond this take a signed path on the right by a rock slab. Climbing the hillside, this takes you past all the white-painted shrines and the larger attractive chapel, after which you ascend a flight of stone steps, pass below Saas Fee's parking house, come to a final shrine and enter **Saas Fee** by the post office.

ROUTE 24

Saas Grund (1559m) –
Sengg (1798m) – Saas Fee (1809m)

Grade:	2
Distance:	4km
Height gain:	250m
Time:	1½hrs
Location:	Northwest and southwest of Saas Grund

A devious route between two Saas villages, it wanders through woodlands and along a stretch of pastureland with views across the valley to the Weissmies. Halfway along the walk, the little hamlet of Sengg affords a striking contrast to the sophistication of Saas Fee.

Leaving the centre of Grund take the road towards Saas Fee, and immediately after crossing the bridge over the river turn right on a path. Almost at once leave it and bear left on another footpath between gardens, then up a slope towards woods. When it forks on the edge of these woods bear right and go uphill among trees until reaching the road at a hairpin bend. A few paces later another path (a very narrow one) heads away from the road, climbing steeply to a track where you again turn right.

After walking along this for about 800m, come to a second track heading sharply left, signed to Saas Fee. Follow this to **Sengg**, a collection of *mazots* and old timber chalets, where a footpath goes between the buildings and on towards larchwoods. Remain on the path for about 15mins until you come to **Restaurant Fleschhorn** (1800m: *refreshments*) and a track which you now follow directly to Saas Fee.

ROUTE 25
Saas Fee (1809m) –
Saas Almagell (1670m) – Saas Fee

Grade:	1
Distance:	7.5km
Height gain:	139m
Height loss:	139m
Time:	2–2½hrs
Location:	Southeast of Saas Fee

This undemanding circular walk is offered as a family stroll or as means of filling half a day when perhaps the weather dictates keeping off the high routes.

Begin at the entrance to Saas Fee in the square near the PTT and tourist office. Take the road towards Zurbriggen Aparthotel and Restaurant, then veer left by some *mazots* on the service road leading to the Alpin Express. After crossing a bridge over a deep gorge bear left on another service road easing round the hillside to gain views through the length of the Saastal to the conical

Bietschhorn. About 15mins from the start reach **Waldhüs Bodmen** (*refreshments*). Just beyond the restaurant leave the road for a footpath descending left, dropping in zigzags through forest signed to Biel and Saas Almagell. When it forks take the right branch, angling down to a broad path near the solitary house of **Biel** (1650m). Turn right for Saas Almagell, and left for Unter den Bodmen and Saas Grund (see Route 17).

To reach Saas Almagell simply follow the path up-valley, soon joining a riverside footpath among meadows. Coming to a bridge spanning the Saaser Vispa cross into **Saas Almagell** (1673m: 45mins: *refreshments*). After spending time there, retrace the path to Biel and continue for another 15mins to reach **Unter den Bodmen** (1593m: *refreshments*). Continue down-valley, cross a side stream and shortly after walking alongside a campsite, take the path left which climbs to Saas Fee on the Kapellenweg (see Route 23 above).

ROUTE 26

Saas Fee (1809m) –
Gletschergrotte (1904m) – Spielboden (2447m)

Grade:	2–3
Distance:	4km (one way)
Height gain:	638m
Time:	2¼hrs
Location:	South of Saas Fee

Gazing up at the snow peaks that tower over Saas Fee, one is struck by the great curtain of glaciers hanging there. It is that glacier curtain, more than anything, which gives the resort its character – a dazzling cascade of ice above green meadows. But there is one prominent break in this curtain, a long tongue of rock and moraine, a strip of brown and grey amidst a turmoil of snow and ice. This is the Längflue, accessed by a two-stage cableway, from which one has a grandstand view of the Fee glacier's icefall on one side and across the glacier's buckled surface on the other, while below, sprawling in its meadows, lies Saas Fee. The lower half of the Längflue rib is grass covered and riddled with marmot burrows, and it is this marmot region that is the focus for this walk.

Wander through Saas Fee heading south, and about 2mins after passing the church take a broad tarmac path alongside the Saaser Hof hotel which soon leads through meadows. When the path forks take the left branch, and after crossing a stream take a narrow path on the right in the direction of the Gletschersee. Coming to a three-way junction take the middle option to skirt larchwoods before twisting up among the trees, then angle down beneath the Spielboden gondola to a bridge spanning the glacial torrent where a partial lake has been created. This is known as the **Gletschersee** (1904m: 30mins).

Over the bridge you soon cross a track and climb beneath the gondola line as far as a second track by a pylon. Bear right, still climbing on a path which brings you to yet another junction. Both ways lead to Spielboden and rejoin a little higher: that which goes

The meadows below Spielboden are riddled with marmot burrows

ahead is the easier option, while the right-hand path vis-its **Café Gletschergrotte** (2000m: 50mins: *refreshments*).

Immediately before reaching the café another path breaks away left and climbs steeply to join the first option, then twists up the grassy Längflue rib with close views of the Fee glacier. After passing a solitary build-ing (Gletscheralp: 2130m) keep alert for marmots, whose shrill whistling cry will no doubt be heard. There are colonies of marmots all the way up this rib, and those just below the Spielboden gondola station are invariably crowded with visitors. The lower Gletscheralp can be just as rewarding.

The path to **Spielboden** continues up the slope to reach the gondola station in a little over 2hrs from Saas Fee.

Notes
- To descend, either take the gondola down to Saas Fee, or use the same route of ascent – this will take about 1½hrs. From the Gletschergrotte, however, there are several signed options to vary the return.
- For the continued walk up the rib to Längflue proper (2869m) – an additional 400m climb – allow an extra 1–1¼hrs. The way is straightforward, but steep, and glacier views consistently fine. Alternatively, Längflue and Spielboden are linked by cableway.

ROUTE 27

Saas Fee (Hannig: 2340m) –
Schonegg (2448m) – Mischabel Hut (3340m)

Grade:	3
Distance:	3.5km (one way)
Height gain:	1029m
Time:	3–3½hrs
Location:	West of Saas Fee

The two Mischabel Huts have been built more than 1500m above Saas Fee near the base of the east-northeast arête of the Lenzspitze, below the Schwarzhorn. It's a truly airy situation with tremendous high mountain views. The approach route is notoriously steep, and although previous editions of this guide described the walk beginning in Saas Fee, this version 'cheats' and avoids the initial 300m climb by riding the gondola to Hannig.

With a climb of more than 1000m above Hannig, the path to the Mischabel Huts is both long and steep

Turn left out of the Hannig gondola station and wander down a broad path to reach a junction after about 2mins. Continuing straight ahead the path narrows, turns a spur and angles downhill into a combe below the Hohbalm glacier, whose snout can be seen high above. A footbridge carries the path across a stream issuing from the glacier, after which you come to another junction (Spissen: 2313m). Maintain direction, cross a second stream and take the path ahead when it forks, now rising across an old moraine before slanting up the hillside to yet another junction about 40mins from Hannig. This is **Schonegg** (2448m).

Continue uphill on an unrelentingly steep path that grows more and more rocky as you progress. Waymarks are blue and white, and as you gain height there are many fixed cable sections that can be more useful in descent than on the ascent. Views to the south are dominated by Allalinhorn and Alphubel above the cascading Fee glacier, then the summit fin of the Rimpfischhorn appears to rise above the Feejoch. After 3hrs or so you should arrive at the first **Mischabel Hut**, with the second (main) hut standing a little higher. ▶

ROUTE 28

Saas Fee (Hannig: 2340m) – Schonegg (2448m) – Gletschersee (1904m) – Saas Fee

Grade:	1–2
Distance:	6km
Height gain:	148m
Height loss:	688m
Time:	2¼–2½hrs
Location:	West of Saas Fee

This fairly short walk, with its consistently fine glacier views, has its strenuous moments, but the scenic quality is such that these are of little consequence, and the route should suit walkers of most abilities. Paths are good and the gradient is mostly undemanding. The route forms the western section of the Gemsweg (see Route 31), one of the classic walks of the area.

Take the Hannig gondola lift from Saas Fee, and on leaving the upper station turn left and follow directions as at the beginning of Route 27 as far as the **Schonegg** junction (40mins). ▶

Owned by the Academic Alpine Club of Zürich, the **huts** have dormitory places for 120. Meals, snacks and drinks are available when the guardian is in occupation. This is usually from July to the end of September (☎ 027 957 13 17). The hut is used by climbers tackling a number of different peaks, including the Dom, Lenzspitze, Nadelhorn, Ulrichshorn and Dürrenhorn. Allow 3hrs for the descent to Saas Fee, taking special care on the upper rocky sections to avoid knocking stones onto anyone below.

Note: If you divert from the route for another 5–6mins, by taking the Mischabel Hut path you will gain a grassy shoulder which makes a splendid picnic site with stunning views of Allalinhorn, Alphubel and the Fee glacier.

Note: An alternative descent to Saas Fee leaves from the Trift junction and is described below as Route 28a.

The route to the Gletschersee and Saas Fee descends for 2mins to another splendid viewpoint, then continues twisting down for about 20mins to the **Trift** junction (2213m: 1hr). On the way you gain an airy view of a waterfall some way below. ◀

The path descends in more zigzags below Trift to another junction, and this time you make a contour to the right. This path cuts across the mountainside, crosses the stream coming from the waterfall seen earlier, and leads directly to the moraine wall that encloses a drab basin at the foot of the Fee glacier.

Wander down the moraine crest among larches, ignoring the path that angles into the basin, and remain on the crest until you've passed beneath the Längflue gondola line. On gaining a final path junction near a bridge over the coffee-coloured glacial torrent (with the small suggestion of a lake – the **Gletschersee** – nearby), bear left on a meandering path through larchwoods. This slopes down to valley meadows where a service road leads into Saas Fee.

ROUTE 28A
Trift (2213m) – Hannig Alp – Saas Fee (1809m)

Grade:	1–2
Distance:	3.5km
Height gain:	45m
Height loss:	385m
Time:	1½hrs
Location:	West of Saas Fee (alternative descent from Route 28)

As a variation of Route 28, this makes a pleasant alternative return to Saas Fee. It crosses the combe-like scoop of hillside below the Hohbalm glacier, rises round the mountain spur and crosses pastureland to Hannig Alp, where the descent to Saas Fee goes via two restaurants on winding footpaths and tracks.

Follow directions for Route 28 to Schonegg, then steeply down to the **Trift** junction, which you gain about 1hr from the Hannig gondola station. Now take the lower, minor path in the direction of Alpenblick and Hannig. Slanting gently across the hillside, cross a footbridge over a stream, then descend a little to a second footbridge. Over this the way forks. Take the upper trail that now rises to turn a spur of mountainside – the last approach to this is quite steep, but once the spur has been turned the path eases to contour through pastures to reach the lone building of **Hannig Alp** (c.2140m: *refreshments*).

Here you join a broader path which you follow downhill, and 10mins later come to **Café Alpenblick** (2037m: *refreshments*). At the junction here bear left to wander down through the Üssere Wald larchwoods and come to yet another junction in an open area. Turn right, and in another minute slant left on a narrow path which shortly comes to a crossing path. Turn right along this to **Hotel-Restaurant Hohnegg** (1900m: *refreshments*) and continue down the track towards Saas Fee. After passing beneath the Hannig gondola lift, cut left down a footpath which brings you to the gondola's valley station and on into the heart of Saas Fee.

ROUTE 29

Saas Fee (Felskinn: 2991m) –
Britannia Hut (3030m)

Grade:	1–2
Distance:	2km (one way)
Height gain:	39m
Time:	45mins
Location:	South of Saas Fee

By taking advantage of the various cableways strung above the village, a greater selection of routes become available to the less-experienced walker who might otherwise be daunted by either the distance or height gain required to tackle them. This is one such – a short glacier crossing on a marked route (no special equipment required) leading to a very popular hut. A more demanding approach to the hut is described below as Route 30.

Note: Every effort is made to keep a path open across the Chessjen glacier during the summer, but before setting out it would be wise to check conditions on the glacier, especially after snowfall. Enquire either at the tourist office or at the Felskinn cablecar station.

The valley station for the cablecar to Felskinn is located in the meadows at the southern edge of Saas Fee. From the upper station (*refreshments*), which is also the terminus for the Metro-Alpin (an underground funicular that leads to the Mittelallalin for an elevated view of the glacier world), bear left to find the start of the marked path across the glacier – the track-like route is usually made by snowcat. DO NOT STRAY FROM THE MARKED ROUTE. Although a pathway is clearly made, the glacier remains potentially dangerous. There may well be a few narrow crevasses to step across, or they may be bridged with snow and, at certain times of the day, water from snow-melt will almost certainly be running over the ice surface, so be properly shod and take warm clothing with you.

The way rises at a gentle angle to gain the usually bare saddle of the **Egginerjoch**, with the red-brown rock tower of Egginer (3366m) rising to the left, and the billowing icefields on the right that form the lower slopes of the Hinter Allalin. It then continues across the right-hand slope of the glacier and takes only about 40–45mins in total to reach the **Britannia Hut**.

Owned by the Geneva section of the SAC, and in part financed by members of the ABMSAC (Association of British Members of the Swiss Alpine Club), the Britannia Hut is a large and sturdy building with places for more than 130 in its dormitories. Popular as a base for ski-touring in the spring and mountaineering in the summer, it is staffed from late February until the end of

September (☎ 027 957 22 88). Refreshments are on sale throughout the day.

Notes

From the Britannia Hut a view opens across the Hohlaub and Allalin glaciers, but it's worth scrambling up the easy rocks of the Klein Allalin (3069m), just 10mins to the east of the hut, where a superb panorama reveals the Allalinhorn (4027m), Rimpfischhorn (4199m) and Strahlhorn (4190m) rising to the south and southwest. Between them the great glacier passes of the Adler and Allalin are also clearly seen – their crossing played an integral part in the region's exploration by the 19th-century pioneers, especially Curé Imseng, whose statue adorns the village square in Saas Fee.

The return to Felskinn will take about 40mins, but good walkers could make a longer day out by reversing Route 30 below, which gives a descent to Saas Fee by way of a splendid balcony path that leads to the Plattjen gondola lift.

The Strahlhorn (left) and Rimpsfischhorn and their glaciers can be studied from the terrace at the Britannia Hut

ROUTE 30

Saas Fee (Plattjen: 2570m) –
Britannia Hut (3030m)

Grade:	2–3
Distance:	4.5km (one way)
Height gain:	545m
Height loss:	125m
Time:	2hrs
Location:	Southeast of Saas Fee

The standard 40–45min approach to the Britannia Hut from the Felskinn lift is described as Route 29. The following approach is a longer and more demanding alternative along an airy belvedere (not recommended for anyone with vertigo problems) that ends with a short ascent of the lower Chessjen glacier. Keep alert for a possible sighting of ibex along the balcony trail.

Take the Plattjen gondola lift from Saas Fee, and on leaving the upper station (*refreshments*) take the path which rises behind the building to a rocky saddle. From here the path swings to the right through a rough boulder tip where waymarks guide the route. The Mattmark reservoir and Monte Moro pass can both be seen as you progress beyond the boulders on a traverse of the east flank of the Mittaghorn and Egginer. The path is narrow and exposed in places, but there are a few fixed cables to give reassurance, while the toy-like buildings of Saas Almagell can be seen almost 1000m below.

After about 20mins a narrow trail diverts from the main route to make the ascent of the Mittaghorn, but we continue ahead with views growing in extent. Cutting round the stony Meiggertal, cross another clutter of rocks and boulders to gain the **Heidenfriedhof** saddle (2764m), a scenic place dotted with cairns from which the Britannia Hut is first sighted.

The path now skirts to the right beneath the Egginer cliffs and works a way towards screes and moraines of the Chessjen glacier. About 8mins after leaving Heidenfriedhof an unmarked path breaks away to the left to descend to Zer Meiggeru and Saas Fee – there's another (this one signed) shortly after in the middle of the screes. Zigzags climb onto the long moraine rib, over which you enter a basin supporting several small glacial tarns, and come to the edge of the Chessjen glacier. Red marks have been painted on rocks, and these lead the way up the ice slope to the **Britannia Hut**. (Please refer to notes at the end of Route 29 above.) Allow at least 1½hrs for a return by the same route, or reverse Route 29 for a 40min walk to the Felskinn cableway.

The Mattmark reservoir is clearly seen from the high path leading from Plattjen to the Britannia Hut

ROUTE 31
Saas Fee (Plattjen: 2570m) – Hannig (2340m) (The Gemsweg)

Grade:	2
Distance:	9km
Height gain:	415m
Height loss:	645m
Time:	3–3½hrs
Location:	Southeast of Saas Fee, making a clockwise arc

The Gemsweg (Chamois path) is a local classic that makes a sweep round the accessible slopes of the amphitheatre above Saas Fee. Scenically exciting and with plenty of variety along the way, the path crosses open mountainside, goes through regions of shrubbery and light woodland, wanders moraine walls and the shores of a glacial lake, crosses streams draining the glaciers, and edges below those same icefields. There are wild flowers in early summer, while in the latter part of the season the shrubs take on autumn textures and the Gemsweg blazes with colour. And all the time the lofty Mischabelhörner forms a dramatic backdrop. Gondola lifts are used to reach the start of the walk and to make the final descent to Saas Fee.

Take the gondola lift to Plattjen (*refreshments*) and descend the zigzag path signed to **Berghaus Plattjen** (2418m: *refreshments*), which is reached in about 20mins. Continue below the *berghaus* to a path junction, where you go ahead to the foot of a ski-lift and another junction at 2325m. The Gemsweg goes straight ahead (westward) on a contouring path with yellow and black waymarks, from which the true stature of the surrounding mountains (which is lost by foreshortening from Saas Fee) becomes apparent.

Crossing the steep slopes of the Mittaghorn among alpenrose, alder scrub and the first larches, the way then begins to lose height among carpets of bilberry. About 45mins from Plattjen you come to another junction where a path breaks away to climb to Felskinn, but the Gemsweg maintains direction, now descending in zigzags with several fixed rope sections before passing through a belt of larchwoods. Ignore an unmarked descending path and continue ahead to cross a footbridge (2010m) spanning a torrent draining the eastern Fee glacier. Over this the path contours round to a second glacial torrent, also crossed by footbridge. When the path forks take the lower branch, but a few paces later at a second fork choose the upper trail leading to **Café Gletschergrotte** (2000m: 1¼hrs: *refreshments*).

Pass in front of the restaurant and soon after descend into a dreary trough below the Fee glacier. Meandering through the moraine debris of rocks and boulders, cross the stream near a small glacial tarn, then go up onto the lateral moraine wall and walk along the crest to its far end. The path now veers right to make a rising traverse across the lower slopes of the Mischabel wall, with a lovely view east to the Almagellertal topped by the Portjengrat.

At 2065m (reached in about 2hrs 10mins) another path cuts down to Saas Fee, while the Gemsweg begins a long zigzag climb to the Trift junction (2213m – see Route 28a for an alternative return to Saas Fee). Take the path ahead, signed to Hannig, which rises at a more leisurely gradient into a combe-like scoop topped by a hanging glacier. Cross a stream draining this glacier, climb up to another junction

then contour once more to a second stream crossing, after which you climb again to turn a spur. The final short section of the walk is along an easy path that brings you directly to **Hannig** (2340m: *refreshments*) for the gondola descent to Saas Fee.

The huge Mischabel wall looms over the Gemsweg

Other routes from Saas Fee

• **The Balfrin Höhenweg** (or Höhenweg Grächen) is a splendid balcony path running along the west flank of the Saastal, and linking Saas Fee with Grächen, above St Niklaus in the Mattertal, by a walk of about 6½hrs. It forms part of both the extensive Grand Tour of Monte Rosa (see two-volume guidebook of the same name published by Cicerone Press) and the shorter eight-stage Tour Monte-Rosa publicised locally. The *höhenweg* is described from Grächen to Saas Fee under the Mattertal chapter of this guide (Route 36), and it is in this direction that it is most often tackled by walkers staying in the Saastal. The PTT runs an early morning postbus during the summer from Saas Fee to Grächen especially to enable walkers to tackle this route. Check times at the PTT and buy your ticket there in advance.

• By linking five of the routes described in the above section, a scenic and worthwhile three-day **Tour of the Saastal** can be created. Begin at the northern end of the valley at Gspon, and head south along the Gspon Höhenweg to Kreuzboden (Route 12). From here take the Höhenweg Almagelleralp (Route 15), followed by a section of Route 17 to the Kapellenweg, which you then ascend to Saas Fee (Route 23). The final section of the tour adopts the Balfrin Höhenweg (Route 36 – in reverse) along the west flank of the valley to Grächen.

• Combining three other described routes, a 5½–6hr walk makes a splendid **Saas Fee high route** to bask in the best high scenery of the Saas Fee amphitheatre. First take the cablecar to Felskinn and walk along the easy Chessjen glacier to the Britannia Hut (Route 29), then reverse Route 30 along the balcony path to Plattjen. Once there, join the Gemsweg (Route 31) and follow this to Hannig.

• For the experienced mountain walker, equipped and knowledgeable with regard to moving on crevassed glaciers, the high country beyond the Allalinhorn ridge is a true wonderland to be explored. There are the great glacier passes of **Alphubeljoch** (3773m) and **Allalinpass** (3564m) that give access to Täsch in the Mattertal, as well as the **Adlerpass** (3789m), whose crossing leads to Zermatt. Each of these reveal some of the most spectacular high mountain landscapes in all the Alps.

THE MATTERTAL

With the Matterhorn its primary attraction, the Mattertal is unquestionably one of the best-known valleys in Europe. At least, the head of the valley above Zermatt is known (by reputation, if not through experience) by hundreds of thousands of walkers, climbers and general tourists, thanks to the great collection of 4000m peaks that contain it and all the publicity that proclaims its splendour. But the beauty of the rest of the valley is less well known – the villages below Zermatt, the tributary valleys that drain down to the Mattervispa, the unspoilt high alps, huts, passes and scenic trails – in fact, the wealth of magnificent panoramas that rival those calender and chocolate-box views of the Matterhorn. Away from Zermatt and the valley head there are walks to enjoy in solitude – a wonderland worth spending time to discover.

ACCESS AND INFORMATION

Location:	South of Visp, immediately west of the Saastal.
Maps:	LS 274T *Visp*, 284T *Mischabel* & 283T *Arolla* at 1:50,000 Also available, and of use to walkers staying in Zermatt, is the tourist authority's *Wanderkarte Zermatt* at 1:25,000.
Bases:	Grächen (1618m), Randa (1408m), Täsch (1450m), Zermatt (1620m)
Information:	Verkehrsbüro, CH-3924 St Niklaus (☎ 027 956 36 63, website: www.st-niklaus.ch)
	Tourismusbüro Grächen, CH-3925 Grächen (☎ 027 955 60 60, e-mail: info@graechen.ch)
	Verkehrsbüro Randa, CH-3928 Randa (☎ 027 967 16 77)
	Verkehrsbüro Täsch, CH-3929 Täsch (☎ 027 967 16 89, e-mail: info@taesch.ch website: www.taesch.ch)
	Zermatt Tourism, Bahnhofplatz, PO Box 247, CH-3920 Zermatt (☎ 027 966 81 00, e-mail: zermatt@wallis.ch, website: www.zermatt.ch)
Access:	By train from Visp to Zermatt and most villages in the Mattertal. Note that private motor vehicles are not allowed beyond Täsch.

Approach to the Mattertal from the Rhône valley, whether by road or rail, gives little indication of the valley's true splendour. The journey up to Stalden at the confluence of the Saaser Vispa and Mattervispa rivers is pleasant enough, and Stalden itself has a picturesque site, but turning to the southwest the Mattertal is entered via a gorge – in sunshine dramatic, in rain dark and gloomy – and it's only when St Niklaus is reached that the steep walls lean back, so to speak, to let the light in.

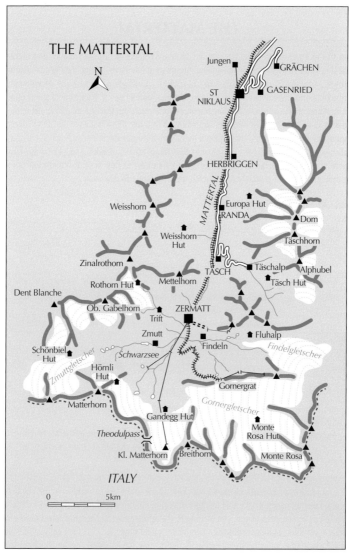

THE MATTERTAL

N

Jungen

GRÄCHEN

ST NIKLAUS

GASENRIED

HERBRIGGEN

MATTERTAL

Weisshorn

Europa Hut

RANDA

Dom

Weisshorn Hut

Täschhorn

Zinalrothorn

TÄSCH

Täschalp

Alphubel

Mettelhorn

Rothorn Hut

Täsch Hut

Dent Blanche

Ob. Gabelhorn

ZERMATT

Trift

Zmutt

Fluhalp

Schönbiel Hut

Findeln

Findelgletscher

Zmuttgletscher

Schwarzsee

Hörnli Hut

Matterhorn

Gornergrat

Gornergletscher

Gandegg Hut

Theodulpass

Monte Rosa Hut

Kl. Matterhorn

Breithorn

Monte Rosa

ITALY

0   5km

St Niklaus is the one-time capital of the Mattertal, an old workaday village that was home to three of the great guiding families, the Knubels, Lochmatters and Pollingers, whose exploits enriched the history of alpinism and who now lie in the local churchyard. St Niklaus has suffered in the past from both avalanche and earthquake, but it survives and thrives today without even the pretence of a resort, despite the daily grind of traffic aiming blindly for Täsch and Zermatt and the BVZ trains that call here on the regular shuttle between Zermatt and Visp.

At the entrance to the village a side-road breaks away and twists up the eastern hillside to a sunny terrace where Grächen and Gasenried enjoy privileged views unguessed from below. On the opposite side of the valley, perched precariously on a tilt of pasture 800m above St Niklaus, the tiny alp hamlet of Jungen (or Jungu) is one of the loveliest in all the Alps – a little white chapel, a chalet-restaurant, a clutch of hay barns and dark-timbered houses, and a vista of such beauty to take your breath away.

As you continue up-valley out of St Niklaus, the huddled settlements of Mattsand and Herbriggen are barely noticed in the rush for Zermatt, and the steepness of the walling mountains that pass by allows only a hint of glacier and snowfield to be caught. Shortly before Randa is reached, where the valley is more open, a chaos of rocks and boulders and what looks like a quarry on the east side of the river are potent reminders of a major rockfall that occurred here in April 1991, cutting the railway and blocking the river, and isolating the upper valley for several days.

Randa is a straggling community of typical Valaisian chalets and hay barns and more modern houses built in the traditional style. It lies up the slope a little away

Alp huts near Zmutt, with the Täschhorn seen in the background

from the river, and the valley road conveniently keeps its distance. With Weisshorn to the west and Dom towering above to the east, the village is trapped between two giants. On its edge, beyond the pastures and small garden plots, woodland clothes the lower slopes, and streams dash down from barely perceived glens with icefields at their head and rocky peaks crowding over all.

To some Täsch appears to be little more than a huge parking lot at the roadhead and a railway station to ferry the crowds to a Matterhorn view. But that is unfair, for of all Mattertal villages Täsch is one of the least altered by tourism. Standing back in a huddle below the entrance to the Täschalp valley, the narrow streets and old buildings have a charm all their own, while those who have the energy and inclination to fight their way up into the tributary valley that lies half-hidden in secrecy to the east will discover an alp hamlet snug among big mountains and some fine paths to wander in peace. One of these is the final section (for those heading south) of the Europaweg, a tremendous route created along the mid-height slopes of the Mattertal's east wall between Grächen (or more precisely Gasenried) and Zermatt. This is by far the finest way to approach Zermatt from the north – not by road or by rail, but on foot, through an avenue of lofty mountains to the Alps' greatest collection of 4000m summits spread in a huge arc of snow, ice and rock round the head of the Mattertal, and with Zermatt in full admiration below, the crooked pyramid of the Matterhorn casting its benediction on every wide-eyed pilgrim.

Zermatt is very much a place of pilgrimage. Everyone wants to go there: mountaineers, walkers, skiers, tourists of every persuasion. Everyone knows the Matterhorn, that symbol of mountain grandeur, national symbol of Switzerland. Everyone knows its unmistakable profile and wants to see it for themselves. And why not? It is, after all, one of the world's most beautiful mountains, and one that may be viewed from the comfort of a chair at a table with a drink before you, without the necessity of walking for several hours over wild terrain with a rucksack on your back. But if that is your preferred way of getting to know a mountain, you won't need this book.

Yet there is more to Zermatt and the head of the Mattertal than just the Matterhorn – though to be truthful, that in itself would be sufficient to ensure the resort's popularity. The Matterhorn is not even one of the highest in that great arc of peaks lost to view from the village streets, but make some effort and all will be revealed. From steeply winding footpaths mountains appear one by one. Mountains that are not only memorable from their height or breadth, but by their character, shape, substance, history and charm.

There's Monte Rosa, for example, a great iced gateau of a mountain crowned by many individual summits above a cascade of glaciers. There's Liskamm, its close neighbour, ice-strewn with a billow of snow; the vast Breithorn, a complex massif of rock ribs and hanging glaciers; the shy Dent d'Hérens, that crusty fin in the Matterhorn's shadow. There's the wedge of Dent Blanche to the west, as grand from this view as it is from Bricola in Val d'Hérens; Ober Gabelhorn like a fang guarding the stiletto point of Zinalrothorn, with the graceful Weisshorn rising to the north along a great jagged wall. All these, and so many more, appear as part of the backdrop to a rich collection of walks.

MAIN BASES

ST NIKLAUS (1127m) Until 1955 St Niklaus was the only place in the Mattertal served by motor road from Visp. With access to good walking country on the walling mountainsides both east and west of the village, it could be adopted as a base for a few days. Although busy with road and rail traffic by day, it is peaceful by night, and there are at least seven hotels and pensions in which to stay. There are several shops, restaurants, a post office and bank. The tourist office is situated near the railway station.

GRÄCHEN (1618m) is a straggle of flower-adorned chalets and hotels spread over a sun-trap terrace 500m above St Niklaus on the eastern side of the valley, with which it is linked by bus. With more than 250km of marked footpaths, many of which lead to superb viewpoints, a walking holiday based there is worth considering. There are numerous hotels of all standards, as well as *matratzenlagers* and apartments. Apply to the tourist office for a full accommodation list. The village has plenty of shops and restaurants, banks, tourist office and PTT. Nearby **GASENRIED** (1659m) shares the same terrace and footpaths, with similar views, but it's much smaller and with minimal facilities. It has just one hotel, the Alpenrösli (☎ 027 956 17 81) in the village square, a shop or two, restaurants and PTT, and above it a row of old granaries with meadows reaching to forest, and the Ried glacier nosing down the mountainside as its backdrop.

RANDA (1408m) offers a quiet, low-key alternative to Zermatt. Lying far enough away to be free of the pressures suffered by its more illustrious neighbour, Randa retains the atmosphere of an alpine village concerned more with crops and cattle than with the demands of an international tourist trade. It has just a few hotels, pensions and apartments, and on the southern outskirts of the village is a campsite with good facilities. There's limited shopping, but Randa has a tourist office, PTT and a railway station on the Visp–Zermatt line.

TÄSCH (1450m) lies 4km south of Randa at the roadhead for all tourist vehicles in the Mattertal. (Only permit-holders may continue by road to the outskirts of Zermatt.) The meadows below the old village have been largely taken over by Zermatt tourist traffic, with large car- and coach-parks, an extremely busy railway station, and souvenir shops between the two. There's a campsite on the west bank of the river near the station, several three-star hotels and a large number of apartments for rent. Täschalp, in the valley southeast of the village, has a little inn with *matratzenlager* accommodation (15 places). Formerly known as Restaurant Täschalp, it has been renamed the Europaweghütte (☎ 027 967 23 01). The tourist office is situated beside the road just east of Täsch railway station near the PTT, and there's a bank in the village by the church.

ZERMATT (1620m) is one of the great Alpine resorts whose history since the 1860s has been inextricably bound with that of the Matterhorn, for it was from here that the young wood engraver Edward Whymper and his party set out on that summer's day in 1865 to make the first ascent of the mountain by the Hörnli ridge. Having successfully reached the summit on 14 July, Whymper and his six companions began their descent, but the relatively inexperienced Douglas Hadow slipped, pulling others with him, and had the rope not broken the whole party would no doubt have perished. As it was, four men fell to their deaths and news of the tragedy swept across Europe, thereby gaining both the Matterhorn and Zermatt considerable publicity. Anything added here may seem superfluous, for the amount of books, articles and pamphlets written on the tragedy would almost overtop the mountain itself. Both Zermatt and the Matterhorn are, quite simply, incomparable.

At the heart of Zermatt old Valaisian houses guard the village square

For those who require such things, the boutiques that line Zermatt's streets are filled with extravagant gifts, jewellery, fashionable clothes, and the like. But there are, of course, supermarkets and bakeries, banks, a PTT and shops selling mountain equipment, books and maps. There are over 100 hotels offering every degree of comfort, 1500 apartment beds, *matratzenlagers*, a youth hostel and a small campsite near the railway station. There are many cableways, mountain railways and atmospheric mountain inns on alps above the village and a number of climbers' huts in remote locations. In the heart of the village between the railway station and church, the mountain guides' office (Alpin Center – open June–Sept, Mon–Fri and Sun 8.30–noon and 16.00–19.00; Sat 16.00–19.00) arranges guided climbs and privately led walks (☎ 027 966 24 60, e-mail: alpin-center@zermatt.ch, website: www.zermatt.ch/alpincenter). The tourist office by the railway station is worth an early visit.

OTHER BASES

In the bed of the valley south of St Niklaus both **MATTSAND** and **HERBRIGGEN** have one hotel each, while **JUNGEN** high above St Niklaus has limited *matratzenlager* accommodation in a traditional chalet.

MOUNTAIN HUTS

EUROPA HUT (2220m) Built midway along the Europaweg on the east flank of the valley by the Randa *gemeinde*, this timber-built refuge has 42 places in dormitories and rooms of 4–6 beds, and is manned between mid-June and mid-October (☎ 027 967 82 47).

WEISSHORN HUT (2932m) Reached by a walk of about 4½hrs from Randa, this hut looks across the valley to the Dom and Täschhorn. It has places for 36 and is manned during July and August (☎ 027 967 12 62).

TÄSCH HUT (2701m) Situated at the foot of the Rotgrat, about 1¼hrs from Täschalp, the Täsch Hut is owned by the SAC, has 60 places and is staffed at Easter, and from the end of June to the end of September (☎ 027 967 39 13). It is a useful base for climbers tackling the Alphubel, Täschhorn and Rimpfischhorn.

ROTHORN HUT (3198m) Owned by the Oberaargau section of the SAC and built on the southeast arête of the Zinalrothorn at the head of the Trift gorge, this hut has 100 places in its dormitories, and is manned from the beginning of July to the end of September (☎ 027 967 20 43). It is reached by a very steep path in 4–4½hrs from Zermatt.

SCHÖNBIEL HUT (2694m) Providing one of the nicest approach walks of all from Zermatt, the Schönbiel Hut stands on the lateral moraine of the Zmutt glacier below Pointe de Zinal and looks across the glacier to the Dent d'Hérens and Matterhorn. With 80 dormitory places, the hut is staffed for ski-tourers from Easter until mid-May, and from the end of June until mid-September (☎ 027 967 13 54).

HÖRNLI HUT (3260m) Also known as Berghaus Matterhorn, this hut is perched at the foot of the Matterhorn's Hörnli ridge and is the base for climbers tackling the normal route on the mountain. Reached in about 2hrs by an interesting path from Schwarzsee, it has places for 170, tremendous views across the glaciers to Monte Rosa, and is manned from the beginning of July to the end of September (☎ 027 967 22 64).

GANDEGG HUT (3029m) Easily reached by the Zermatt–Trockener Steg cablecar between the Oberer and Unterer Théodule glaciers, it can sleep 30 in its dormitory, and is staffed from the end of June to the end of September (☎ 079 607 88 68).

MONTE ROSA HUT (2795m) This large SAC-owned hut, which has a wonderful location at the foot of Monte Rosa with a direct view along the Gorner glacier, has 150 places and is open in April and May, and from July to mid-September (☎ 027 967 21 15). The hut is reached by a walk of about 2½hrs from Rotenboden station below Gornergrat and involves a glacier crossing.

The terrace outside the Hörnli Hut on the slopes of the Matterhorn

ROUTE 32

St Niklaus (Jungen: 1955m) – St Niklaus (1127m)

Grade:	1
Distance:	3.5km
Height loss:	828m
Time:	1½–2hrs
Location:	North of St Niklaus

High above St Niklaus the tiny alp hamlet of Jungen (Jungu on the LS maps) is an attractive huddle of hay barns, dark-timber chalets and a small white chapel perched on steeply sloping meadows. On the opposite side of the valley, to which the hamlet has a direct view, a long, gently angled crest of snow and ice rises to the pinnacles of Nadelhorn, Lenzspitze and Dom, with the long, trunk-like Ried glacier trailing from them towards the Mattertal. It's a glorious view, but it's just one portion of a larger panorama that stretches to the distant head of the valley and includes the Brunegghorn and Weisshorn on the west flank.

A small cablecar enables visitors to reach Jungen from St Niklaus without effort, while the twisting footpath alternative will take about 2½hrs to ascend. The plan here is to ride the cablecar to the alp, spend time enjoying the views (refreshments are available at the splendid Jungerstübli restaurant), then walk back down to St Niklaus.

The cablecar building is found near the railway station in St Niklaus, and the lift operates from mid-June to mid-September. On arrival at Jungen there are several paths you could take to vary the views. Just above the hamlet there's a junction. The left branch gives an opportunity either to explore the lonely Jungtal that digs into the mountains to the west or to climb to the 2894m Augstbordpass (in 3¼hrs). The right branch leads to Embd and Moosalp, the latter being at the end of a 3½–4hr *höhenweg* route, perhaps best walked in the opposite direction. ▶

After spending time in Jungen return to St Niklaus by the path which begins its descent alongside the chapel, at first steeply beyond the lowest buildings, then twisting in

The **Moosalp–Jungen Höhenweg** is a visually delightful walk, about 9km long, that remains above the 2000m contour most of the way. Moosalp, where it begins, is a saddle on a ridge spur above Torbel, and may be reached by postbus from Stalden.

The charming hamlet of Jungen, high above St Niklaus

forest – a series of small white shrines have been placed beside the path on the way down to the valley, most having been dedicated by local families. About 35mins from Jungen come to a path junction and continue ahead, the alternative path cutting sharply back to the left.

The way leads into a rocky cleft drained by the Jungbach, which is crossed by footbridge, after which the gradient eases, with the path winding round the hillside in long loops before leaving tree cover and crossing through parcels of meadowland to reach St Niklaus railway station.

ROUTE 33

St Niklaus (1127m) – Randa (1408m) – Täsch (1450m) – Zermatt (1620m)

Grade:	1–2
Distance:	18km
Height gain:	493m
Time:	4½hrs
Location:	South of St Niklaus

There are two walker's routes to Zermatt from St Niklaus. The longer and more challenging of the two is the epic two-day Europaweg (see Route 38), which hugs the mid-height slopes of the Mattertal's east wall, while the route described here remains in the bed of the valley throughout, and visits each of the villages and hamlets on the way to Zermatt.

From the village square below the railway station make your way through a narrow street to the old main road and turn right. After about 400m bear right on a minor road beside Restaurant zum Frävler, and follow this upvalley. In 20mins pass through **Zum Schwidernu**, and continue for a further 20mins to **Mattsand** (1227m), where there's accommodation at Hotel Mattsand (☎ 027 956 12 00).

Still on the old road recross both the railway line and river to skirt a large settlement reservoir, then continue along a track. Go through a brief woodland and across open meadows where the track forks by a bridge. One way leads across to **Herbriggen** (1262m), but we continue on the right-hand side of the Mattervispa river. Ignore another bridge spanning the river, but maintain direction, soon rising among trees. When the path forks keep ahead over a footbridge, then twist uphill through mixed woodland. Now descend to the river, cross by footbridge and turn right on a track signed to Randa which leads to a service road by a bridge.

Walk up the road and continue ahead when it forks. On reaching some haybarns take a track cutting ahead to the right. Ten minutes later (2hrs) come to a road by a bridge on the outskirts of **Randa**. Cross the bridge and turn left on a riverside footpath leading to a junction 5mins later. Remain on the riverside path, but at its next fork cross the river to another service road, recross the river once more and continue on a footpath which shortly brings you to the Matterhorn Golf Course.

Skirting the golf course's right-hand side, eventually reach a group of buildings and a track. The track winds round a large building, continues upvalley a short distance, then kinks left to cross a side stream. Turn left on the continuing track which soon curves right and goes alongside a man-made lake, at the far end of which there's a large car- and coach-park.

Cross the car park to an access road then resume alongside the river. In 3hrs come to Camping Alphubel opposite **Täsch** (1430m). Remain on the west bank of the river, and 20mins later reach a group of barns where the way divides. Take a path on the right which climbs among larchwoods and eventually brings you into **Zermatt** by the railway station.

ROUTE 34
St Niklaus (1127m) – Grächen (1618m)

Grade:	1–2
Distance:	4km
Height gain:	491m
Time:	2hrs
Location:	Northeast of St Niklaus

This short and easy walk is used as a linking route, an alternative to riding the bus.

The walk begins in the village square below St Niklaus railway station, where you go down an alley to the main road and cross directly ahead into Eyeweg. This leads to a bridge over the Mattervispa river, across which you turn left and, after passing several houses, you come to the St Niklaus–Grächen road. Over this continue along a minor road rising among more houses and curving right to a staggered crossroads. Once more cross over and continue ahead, and when you come to the edge of woodland keep ahead on a footpath. Over a stream the way then rises among trees. Out of the woods make a rising traverse of a steep hillside overlooking the northern outskirts of St Niklaus.

About 20mins from the start, come to a collection of old timber chalets. This is **Wichul** (1195m), where you bear right onto a narrow road for about 50m.

When it makes a right-hand bend, take a footpath on the left rising among pinewoods. The St Niklaus–Grächen road is crossed once more, and you continue to climb the hillside at a steady gradient; keep above an old farm and, soon after passing a wooden crucifix, cross the road yet again. The broad path leads to **Bodme** (1280m), where a narrow road is crossed, and immediately after passing a house on the left bear left at a path junction by another crucifix.

The path now rises steeply between meadows with views towards the head of the Mattertal. Soon after crossing a stream pass alongside a white-walled chapel and come to a road at Rittinen (1455m). Walk ahead, and a few minutes later enter Nieder-Grächen (1478m). Turn right by another white chapel and climb among houses and hay barns to a crucifix where the path forks. Both options lead to Grächen – the left branch (in effect the continuing path) goes between more meadows, farms and small granaries built upon staddle stones.

ROUTE 35
St Niklaus (1127m) – Gasenried (1659m)

Grade:	2
Distance:	4km
Height gain:	532m
Time:	1½–2hrs
Location:	East of St Niklaus

As with Route 34, this short walk makes a useful link between the valley bed and an attractive, typically Valaisian village built among meadows high above St Niklaus. Gasenried lies at the start of the Europaweg and has accommodation in just one hotel (see details above).

The first 20mins or so of this walk are the same as that for Grächen, described above as Route 34. At the old timber chalets of **Wichul** (1195m) bear right onto a narrow

Gasenried, with the Ried glacier behind, at the start of the Europaweg

road, then take a path on the left which climbs along the edge of a meadow and comes onto the St Niklaus–Grächen road. Turn left and almost immediately take a continuing footpath on the right to climb among woods of larch and pine. This leads onto the road once more. Bear right and turn a hairpin bend with a fine view up-valley. About 100m after the hairpin a track rises among trees above the road. When it forks shortly after passing a timber building, take the upper option, which winds uphill and brings you to a four-way path junction about 1hr from St Niklaus.

Maintain direction, and at the next junction beside a shrine and a crucifix bear right for the final climb to Gasenried. This path takes you beside vegetable plots, and leads to the lower village to gain a view of the Bernese Alps to the north. Follow a narrow road steeply uphill to the main part of **Gasenried** (*accommodation, refreshments*), with the Ried glacier seen at the head of a hanging valley behind it.

ROUTE 36

Grächen (1618m) – Hannigalp (2121m) – Saas Fee (1809) (the Balfrin Höhenweg)

Grade:	3
Distance:	19km
Height gain:	984m
Height loss:	796m
Time:	7–7½hrs
Location:	Northeast of Grächen, then heading south

This classic walk, also known as the Höhenweg Grächen or Höhenweg Saas Fee, was opened in 1954 after a great deal of work had been undertaken to connect old shepherds' paths, in places by blasting tunnels through intruding rock walls. The trail winds above the Saastal at an average altitude of about 2000m, much of it along the slopes of the Balfrin – hence its name. It's an energetic route, with some fairly exposed sections that make it unsuitable for anyone suffering vertigo. Between Hannigalp and Saas Fee there's no opportunity for refreshment or shelter, but it's a tremendous walk, and it forms part of the locally publicised 'Swiss Tour Monte Rosa'. The höhenweg proper begins at Hannigalp, which is reached by cableway from Grächen, although the walk described here goes all the way from Grächen. If you choose to take the cableway, the time taken for the walk will be reduced by about 1½hrs.

East of the village church in Grächen a signpost directs the start of the walk to Hannigalp with a footpath between buildings – Chalet Wiedersehen on the right. Passing several chalets, the way goes alongside Hotel Alpina then passes beneath the cables of the Seetalhornbahn. A gravel track now takes you ahead into larchwoods, rising easily to a small tarn with Hotel Zum See on its shore.

Just beyond the tarn come to crosstracks. Maintain direction rising ahead on an obvious track that leads all the way to **Hannigalp** (2121m: 1½hrs: *accommodation, refreshments*), where there's a restaurant with *matratzenlager* and a panorama of big mountains. This panorama

125

includes the distant Matterhorn in one direction and the Bietschhorn across the Rhône valley in another. A signpost shows the route of the Höhenweg Saas Fee, which soon reaches an attractive modern chapel on the edge of pinewoods. The path curves to the right and begins to skirt the northern spur of mountains that separate the Mattertal and Saastal.

Turning now to the south the trail makes a steady rising traverse of the steep slope, the path narrow and exposed, but protected in the worst places. As the trail cuts in and out of rocky combes, views are shuffled and reordered. In one place it goes through a short tunnel, and about 1hr from Hannigalp you come to the high point of the route at a promontory shown on the map as **Stock** (2370m).

The path continues its undulating course high above the Saastal and is joined by a path descending from the Seetalhorn (the Höhenweg Seetalhorn). Shortly after, turn the shoulder of Rote Biel (with a view of the Balfrin glacier to the south) and cut into the combe beneath the glacier. Here the path slopes down among trees and shrubs, then crosses the Schweibbach stream and rises again on the other side. Rounding a corner to leave the combe, the trail then makes a traverse of hillside, again rather exposed in places, before crossing a rock and boulder tip with waymarks as a guide. Beyond this, high above Saas Balen, the path has been cut into the rock face, with more fixed cables as a safeguard.

Along a stretch with slabs and boulders interspersed with shrubs and a few dwarf trees, Saas Grund and the outskirts of Saas Fee come into view ahead. You then slope down across the grass hillside of **Stafelalp** (2084m: 5½hrs). Ten minutes later cross a glacial torrent by footbridge below the hanging Bider glacier, and soon after enter the Biderwald forest. Through this come to **Senggboden** (2150m) and another trail junction. The Saas Fee path continues ahead to another junction where both options lead to Saas Fee. Take the continuing path, for the alternative goes via Hannig and is a longer route. Descend to a solitary chalet and a crossing track.

Go straight over on a narrow footpath, and thereafter all path junctions are clearly marked, and you arrive in the heart of Saas Fee about 7–7½hrs after leaving Grächen (see the previous Saastal chapter for details).

ROUTE 37

Grächen (1618m) – Gasenried (1659m)

Grade:	1
Distance:	2.5km
Height gain:	41m
Time:	30mins
Location:	South of Grächen

This very short and easy walk is included here as a lead-in to the two-day Europaweg which goes all the way to Zermatt. Although this splendid high route is publicised from Grächen, in truth it is probably better to begin the walk from Gasenried, a lovely small village lying at the foot of the Ried glacier.

From the village square in Grächen near the tourist office, walk along the left-hand side of the church, where a Europaweg sign gives a generous 45mins to Gasenried. The way passes through Grächen alongside old buildings and those of more recent construction, nearly all of which are festooned with flowers and share a fine view up-valley. At junctions where any confusion might otherwise occur, the Europaweg is marked.

After 15mins pass a tiny chapel on the outskirts of the village, and shortly after enter an area of woodland. Almost immediately branch left ahead on a gravel path rising among trees. Out of the woods pass a few chalets, then take the left branch at the Chäschermatte fork (1636m). The way now goes along the edge of more woodland and comes onto a road at the entrance to **Gasenried** *(accommodation, refreshments)*. ▶

The village of **Gasenried** is built on two levels and consists of a number of Valaisian chalets and granaries. There are several restaurants, a shop, post office and a single hotel in the village square. Just above it footpaths wander through steep pastures and forests to extend the views.

ROUTE 38

Gasenried (1659m) – Europa Hut (2220m) –
Zermatt (1620m) (The Europaweg)

Grade:	3
Distance:	31km
Height gain:	1379m
Height loss:	1432m
Time:	11–12hrs (2 days)
Location:	South of Gasenried

Perhaps the most dramatic and spectacular high-level route in the Valais is this two-day epic which, with its succession of tremendous viewpoints, is a visual extravaganza virtually from start to finish. Officially opened in a blaze of publicity in July 1997, it soon became apparent that the overall distance was too great for most walkers to complete in a single day, so two years later the Randa gemeinde built the Europa Hut almost exactly halfway along the trail. The Europaweg climbs high above the Mattertal, as much as 1400m above it in some places, but it traverses such hostile terrain that its precise course varies from year to year. If official waymarks vary from the route described here, follow the waymarks which should indicate the current route. Heavy rains, snowmelt and frost attack several sections where rockslides bombard the trail or threaten to sweep it into the valley, and notices warn trekkers not to linger when crossing the most vulnerable places. These hazards probably amount to a total of 20–30mins throughout the whole walk, so it's necessary to put them in perspective, but it is important to be aware that this is a serious and demanding trek. Note, too, that on the second stage (Europa Hut to Zermatt) the route goes through a curving rock tunnel about 100m long, and a headtorch could be useful. You're also advised to telephone the Europa Hut (☎ 027 967 82 47) to book bedspace before setting out.

Leaving Gasenried walk along the road past the church and curve left into the Riedbach valley. When the road forks by a small chapel take the lower option, which turns a corner and crosses a bridge over the Riedbach, the river which drains the Ried glacier, then take a signed path uphill through woods to a signed junction (15–20mins from Gasenried). Remaining on the upper route,

the trail becomes steeper and (50mins from the start) forks once more. The left branch goes to the Bordier Hut, but you veer right and continue to climb, with occasional views of the Bietschhorn glimpsed through the trees. In a little over 1½hrs gain the vantage point of **Grat** (2300m) – with the first of many fine panoramas on show. Just above this a large cross extends the view.

On the early stage of the Europaweg above Gasenried

The path curves through a rocky gap to win a view of Weisshorn and Barrhorn, and 5mins later reaches another viewpoint from where the Matterhorn can be seen up-valley. Bear left and work a way higher up the ridge to a broad open shoulder with a statue of St Bernard (patron saint of mountain travellers) nearby. The Ried glacier is seen to good effect from here, with the Bordier Hut on its east bank.

Continuing to rise, cross a rocky area to another path junction and keep ahead, and about 2½hrs from Gasenried come to the first major area exposed to stonefall, where you cross the **Grosse Graben** combe. A combination of caution and speed is advised as you cross this section. On the south side of the combe there are several sections of fixed rope, then rounding a spur at about

Open from mid-June to mid-October, the **Europa Hut** is owned by the Randa gemeinde. It has 42 places and full meals service (☎ 027 967 82 47).

2690m you gain the highest part of the Europaweg, with more great views of the Weisshorn across the valley.

The way continues, and after a while it contours along a wooden walkway followed by more fixed ropes and views that now include the Breithorn at the head of the valley. In a combe below the hanging Hohbarg glacier (beware falling ice) a suspension bridge takes the path across a stream, beyond which you round another spur then slope down among larches to reach the **Europa Hut** (2220m: 5½–6hrs: *accommodation, refreshments*). ◀

In 2002 a section of path just beyond the hut was destroyed by rockfall, resulting in a diversion from the high route which necessitated descent on the Randa path to a low point of about 1600m, followed by a 600m ascent to rejoin the original route just before the Wildikin combe. Check with the hut guardian for the current situation, but in any case follow waymarks and Europaweg signs.

Turning a spur into the **Wildikin** combe enter a tunnel 100m long which curves inside the rockface and, in so doing, limits the amount of light that can penetrate. A headtorch is recommended. Out of the tunnel a steel footbridge crosses the Wildibach torrent and then curves round the south side of the combe to gain a view of the Matterhorn. The path then makes a winding descent below the Leiterspitzen and goes under an avalanche defence system whose projecting lip is designed to deflect falling stones. This is followed by a series of short corrugated tunnels, then up to more larchwoods. Signs to follow are for Ottovan (Täschalp) and Zermatt, and the path rises among slopes of alpenrose and juniper before cutting into the Täschbach valley guarded at its head by the Rimpfischhorn.

Eventually come onto to a minor road just below **Täschalp** (2214m: 3¼hrs from the Europa Hut) and walk up the road to pass the **Europaweg Hut** (formerly known as Restaurant Täschalp: *accommodation, refreshments – 15 dorm places open June–Sept,* ☎ 027 967 23 01). As the road curves left go ahead on a track, then cross the Täschbach stream by footbridge and turn right on a contouring path heading northwest with a direct view to the Schalihorn and Weisshorn. Ignore alternative paths and curve round a hillside spur among larch-woods, eventually coming to a track at a hairpin bend. Follow this uphill to a path junction and bear right on the continuing Europaweg.

The way progresses high above the Mattertal, with Zermatt coming into view and the Matterhorn growing more dominant ahead. About 1½–1¾hrs after leaving Täschalp come to a track at the alp hamlet of **Tufteren** (2215m: *refreshments*), where there's a choice of routes to Zermatt. Any one will do, but the preferred (longest) option remains on the track rising gently to **Sunnegga** (2288m: *refreshments*) in 15mins. Here you take the con-tinuing track and subsequent footpath sloping down to **Findeln** (2051m: *refreshments*), the archetypal alp hamlet with its little white chapel and classic Matterhorn view.

Beyond this hamlet follow the Winkelmatten path through larchwoods, descending in long loops, cross-ing the Gornergrat railway line and finally entering **Winkelmatten** (1672m: *accommodation, refresh-ments*), a suburb of Zermatt. Turn right by the church and wander down to **Zermatt** (1620m:) about 6½–7hrs after leaving the Europa Hut.

ROUTE 39
Randa (1408m) – Schaliberg (1968m) – Randa

Grade:	2
Distance:	7km
Height gain:	560m
Height loss:	560m
Time:	3½hrs
Location:	Southwest of Randa

Built upon a shoulder of hillside steeply above the Mattertal, with the Schalikin gorge immediately to the south and the Weisshorn above, stands the collection of alp huts of Schaliberg. They occupy a delightful site, with trees below, rocks above and views across the valley to the Mischabel peaks. On a summer's day Schaliberg is a peaceful place to lie in the sun and take in the atmosphere. But the walk to it can seem a mite severe in its steepness.

Out of Randa walk up-valley beside the road until a few paces before reaching the campsite entrance (seen to the left), where you cross the road and go over a bridge to the west bank of the river. Turn right along the riverside path for a short distance, then at a junction take the left-hand option, virtually turning back on yourself. This leads to a farm and another path junction. Bear right and rise steeply on the northern edge of the Schalikin gorge, with fine views to its head where the Hohlicht glacier spills down from the Zinalrothorn. Ignoring alternative trails to right and left, the way climbs in tight zigzags and longer windings past several old hay barns until at last you emerge onto the hillside shelf of **Schaliberg** (2¼–2½hrs). ◀

Note: Shortly before reaching Schaliberg there's a path junction where the left-hand option offers a way to the Weisshorn Hut in another 2½–3hrs.

Return by the same path as far as the second junction. Turn left on a path which descends to a rocky section protected by chains, then into forest where you come to a line of 15 wayside shrines, the last of which is found a few paces from the river at another path junction. Bear left alongside the river, then across a bridge to Randa.

ROUTE 40
Täsch (1450m) – Täschalp (2214m)

Grade:	3
Distance:	4km (one way)
Height gain:	764m
Time:	2½hrs
Location:	East of Täsch

Täschalp (Ottavan on the LS map) comprises a scattered collection of chalets, cowsheds, a tiny chapel and a dairy farm at the confluence of the Rotbach and Mellichbach streams. There's dormitory accommodation to be had there (in the Europaweg Hut) and pleasant mountain scenery to gaze at. The Europaweg passes through, and the Täsch Hut is easily accessible from it. From Täsch a service road climbs into the Täschalp valley, and it's possible to hire a taxi to carry you there. However, the approach described here for walkers is a very steep one that makes a direct ascent of the hillside above the village on the north side of the Täschbach stream. A slightly less strenuous path goes up the south side of the stream, but this is decribed in descent as Route 42.

From the railway station go to the main road and turn right, then first left just beyond the PTT on the approach to Täsch village, alongside the Täschbach stream. When the road makes a left-hand bend continue ahead where a footpath sign directs you up the slope by some old houses to the left of the little Täschbach gorge. (An alternative route to Täschalp crosses the stream.) The grass slope steepens, and the narrow path tacks uphill before emerging onto the minor road by a group of houses and a little chapel at **Täschberg** (1696m). Turn right and walk round the hairpin bend, and almost immediately leave the road for a continuing narrow path that resumes the steep ascent of more grass slopes. If the grass is long this path may be rather indistinct, in which case you'll need to concentrate to stay on the correct route. After climbing a little way above the road, it then angles across the slope to the right to a few barns, then makes a more direct ascent to reach the road once more by a hay barn.

Turn right for a very short distance, then go left onto a track which you follow to some dilapidated *mazots* and a few small timber chalets at **Eggenstadel** (1950m). The gradient has eased considerably by the time you get here. A footpath continues now among larches along the left-hand side of the Täschbach and brings you onto the road again at **Stafelti** (2075m). Wander up the road (there are footpath shortcuts to avoid the bends) to **Täschalp** (2214m: *accommodation, refreshments*). ▶

Beyond the alp hamlet a path continues through pastures towards the head of the valley where the Rimpfischhorn dominates. Another path crosses the stream below the alp and leads to Zermatt in 3hrs along a section of the Europaweg – see Route 38.

ROUTE 41
Täschalp (2214m) – Täsch Hut (2701m)

Grade:	1–2
Distance:	3km (one way)
Height gain:	487m
Time:	1¼–1½hrs
Location:	Southeast of Täschalp

Sitting high above the Täschalp valley at the foot of the Rotgrat, the Täsch Hut has a splendid outlook to the Weisshorn and Zinalrothorn. The walk to it is straightforward and undemanding.

Note: The left-hand option leads in 1½hrs to the Weingartensee, a small lake below the Alphubel.

Above the Europaweg Hut (Restaurant Täschalp) the road continues up-valley, then curves towards a long cowshed with a chapel on the left. Pass to the left of the cowshed, where the paved road becomes a track which you follow on a long slant up the hillside. It makes a few bends and divides about 40mins from Täschalp. ◀

The Täsch Hut

Curve right and remain on the track which rises at a regular gradient and makes a few more twists before reaching the Täsch Hut (2701m: *accommodation, refreshments*). Owned by the Uto section of the SAC, the hut can sleep 60 in its dormitories, and is staffed from the end of June to the end of September (☎ 027 967 39 13). Allow about 45mins for a return to Täschalp. ▶

ROUTE 42
Täschalp (2214m) – Täsch (1450m)

Grade:	1
Distance:	5.5km
Height loss:	764m
Time:	2hrs
Location:	West of Täschalp

Note: From the Täsch Hut a path climbs northwest into the basin below the Alphubel and visits the Weingartensee (see note above). From there you descend in a curve to rejoin the track above Täschalp. By this route it's possible to return to Täschalp in 2¼hrs.

This descent to Täsch is somewhat less severe than the path described in ascent (Route 40), but even so there are some steep sections to contend with.

Walk up the road beyond the Europaweg Hut (Restaurant Täschalp) and then take the track which projects from it heading up-valley. This leads to a footbridge over the stream to the right. Cross the bridge and turn right on a fine path which contours along the hillside among alpenrose, juniper and bilberry, and with the Weisshorn seen ahead. The way rises a little, then eases among larch trees and across a rock tip.

About 30mins from Täschalp leave the main path at a junction (2140m), descend to the right on a delightful twisting path through larchwoods and come onto a road at about 2035m. Bear left for a few paces, then resume the descent on a continuing path through more larchwoods. Once again this brings you onto the road which you cross directly ahead, to the left of a solitary chalet and *mazot,* and descend beside a fence. Eventually you come onto a broader path which leads to a major crossing at **Blasiboden** (c1880m: 1hr 20mins), where there's a picnic table and water supply.

Turn right, and about 8mins later turn right again to descend a more narrow trail (signed to Täsch). This woodland path gets wider as it twists downhill. Cross a narrow road twice, descend behind some houses and come to the edge of **Täsch**, where the Täschbach sprays from its narrow gorge.

ROUTE 43

Zermatt (Sunnegga: 2288m) – Tufteren (2215m) – Täschalp (2214m) – Täsch (1450m)

Grade:	2
Distance:	11.5km
Height gain:	50m
Height loss:	973m
Time:	4½hrs
Location:	Northeast of Zermatt

This walk reverses a section of the Europaweg (Route 38), but is described here to encourage walkers based in Zermatt, who may not have tackled that epic route, to enjoy this fine high balcony path as far as Täschalp. It's a well-made path with many splendid viewpoints along it, and it makes a good day out.

Begin by riding the Alpen Metro, or Sunnegga Express, underground funicular. This is invariably very busy, but once you leave the upper station the path to Täschalp will no doubt be peaceful. At Sunnegga, with its magnificent views and access to several recommended walks, descend a fenced path to crosstracks and continue across these to descend another 50m, where you then turn right on a broad path/track. This contours along the hillside and in 30mins brings you to **Tufteren** (2215m:

refreshments), an attractive huddle of alp buildings with a restaurant below on the left.

Tufteren, a neat alp hamlet above Zermatt

Leave the track here in favour of a path which strikes across the hillside rising easily. When the path forks 4mins later (right to Blauherd) continue ahead, still rising. About 10 mins later it forks again (right for an ascent of the Rothorn), but once more you continue ahead. The way rises a little further then eases along a balcony with the spiky ridge of the Leiterspitzen seen ahead. About 1hr from Sunnegga the path divides at 2335m. Both routes lead to Täschalp and are described. The high route which crosses Ober Sattla (2686m) is described below *after* the lower (main) route has reached Täschalp.

The main route swings left then right, soon reaches its high point of 2350m, then begins to slope downhill very gently across the steep hillside, with Täsch seen in the valley below. On coming to a junction go downhill a few paces, then turn right. The path narrows a little and has a cable handrail for security over a short rocky section, and soon after turns a spur to enter the Täschalp valley among larches. ▶

Note the minor path descending to Täsch at a junction about 2hrs from Sunnegga. For a quick descent take this path (see Route 42 for details).

For Täschalp continue ahead, rising slightly. After alternating between stands of larch and brief rock tips, cross
an open hillside, with Täschalp seen below and the
Täschhorn rising behind it. Eventually come to a footbridge (the high path option via Ober Sattla descends to
this point), cross and turn left. Shortly after come to
Täschalp (2214m: 2½hrs: *accommodation, refreshments*).

Ober Sattla high-route option
From the path divide at 2335m, 1hr from Sunnegga,
walk ahead through a little grassy trough, then over rock
patches before resuming the ascent in a steady rise
across high pastures. The Weisshorn is impressive across
the valley, while the conical Bietschhorn is seen in the
distance on the far side of the Rhône valley. The path
climbs on, sometimes quite steeply, and is joined by
another at 2563m. Beyond this junction the gradient
steepens and the path is exposed in places (one fixed
cable section). So gain the high point of **Ober Sattla** (or
Ober Sattlen, 2686m: 2hrs 20mins), a grassy shoulder
guarding the entrance to the Täschalp valley. The
panorama includes Breithorn, Klein Matterhorn,
Matterhorn, Zinalrothorn, Weisshorn, Bietschhorn, two
Mischabel peaks, Alphubel, Allalinhorn and the
Rimpfischhorn at the head of the Täschalp valley. The
descent to **Täschalp** is by a steeply twisting path down
grass slopes, and you reach the hamlet in another
50mins – about 2hrs 10mins from the path divide.

To descend to Täsch (for the train back to Zermatt) walk
down the road below the Europaweg Hut for a short distance, then use footpath shortcuts as far as the barns of
Stafelti, where the road crosses a bridge. Stay on the right
bank of the stream on a footpath descending among
larch trees to reach **Eggenstadel** (1950m), a collection of
small chalets and old granaries, where you join a track
that continues as far as the road. Bear right, then just
below a chalet named Zer Resti cut left on another footpath by a barn. Descending steeply through meadows,
pass more barns before coming to **Täschberg**, where you

join the road again near a white-painted chapel. The final descent goes down by the chapel, alongside some chalets and more hay barns, then steeply over grass slopes to enter **Täsch** (1450m: *accommodation, refreshments*) by a few old houses near the Täschbach gorge. Walk ahead to the main road, then turn right and left to the railway station.

ROUTE 44

Zermatt (Sunnegga: 2288m) –
Fluhalp (2607m) – Grünsee (2296m) –
Findeln (2051m) – Zermatt (1620m)

Grade:	2
Distance:	13km
Height gain:	416m
Height loss:	996m
Time:	4½–5hrs
Location:	East and southeast of Zermatt

Standing on a crown of land in the ablation valley near the Findelgletscher, Berghütte Fluhalp looks west across the Stellisee to the Ober Gabelhorn and Zinalrothorn, and southwest to the Matterhorn. Thanks to the Sunnegga underground funicular, the walk to it is fairly short and easy. By taking the Blauherd cableway from Sunnegga the approach is even shorter, but that is not on this agenda. On the walk described here, you not only visit Fluhalp, but make a tour of four small lakes, including the Stellisee, walk along a moraine ridge and return to Zermatt by way of Findeln, one of the most attractive hamlets in the neighbourhood.

Start the day by riding the Alpen Metro to Sunnegga, where you confront a panorama that encompasses a large number of 4000m peaks and their glaciers. Not surprisingly this is nearly always crowded, and the sound of camera shutters matches the babble of a dozen different languages. Escape by descending a path just left of the restaurant, then turn left at a junction by a wooden cross. The

The Stellisee below Fluhalp captures the Matterhorn to perfection

The **Berghütte Fluhalp** is a tall timber inn often used as a base for climbers attempting the Rimpfischhorn. Open from the end of June to the middle of October, it has 8 bedrooms and 45 dormitory places (☎ 027 967 25 97).

path slopes down to the little **Leisee** (2232m) in 5mins. Bear left along its shoreline, beyond which you come to another path junction after another 5mins. Keep left for Grindjisee, Stellisee and Fluhalp, and rise easily along the hillside to a third junction where the path forks (2335m: 40mins). Take the left branch (the right-hand option slopes down to the Grindjisee which you visit later), but at the next fork keep ahead (the right branch) contouring the hillside above the Grindjisee heading towards a mass of moraines and glaciers crowned by the Strahlhorn. After a while the path rises to a four-way junction, about an hour from Sunnegga.

Turn left and walk up a track which cuts back in a long uphill slant, and at the next junction turn right and 5mins later come to the **Stellisee** (2537m). There are paths along both sides of the tarn which unite at the far end (wonderful reflected views of the Matterhorn), then continue over rough grass slopes to the red-shuttered **Berghütte Fluhalp** (2616m: 1½hrs: *accommodation, refreshments*). ◀

A path continues beyond the inn, descending a little into the grassy ablation valley contained on the right by a wall of moraine. Pass a semi-derelict building – predecessor to the Fluhalp *berghütte* – and keep ahead as far as a couple of small pools. The path forks. One branch goes ahead, climbing to a rough pass at over 3100m (experienced high mountain trekkers only) which leads into the head of the Täschalp valley, but you take the right-hand option and go up onto the crest of the moraine wall overlooking the

From the Grünsee a line of high peaks can be seen, including Ober Gabelhorn (left), Zinalrothorn and Weisshorn

Findel glacier, then walk along it heading west. The path is narrow, and in places it's necessary to step away from the actual crest where it is crumbling. But with care the walk is fine, and has splendid views to enjoy over a vast area.

Towards the end of the moraine wall descend to the track below and follow this downhill. This takes you a little to the left of the **Grindjisee** (2334m) – one of the nicest of the neighbourhood tarns; its southern shore is lined with trees, and a neat grass slope at its eastern end is sliced by a tumbling feeder stream.

Beyond the Grindjisee the track makes a long curve left round the head of a basin which falls below the Findel glacier's moraines; the track then passes below and to the right of the **Grünsee** (2300m). Several minor paths strike up across a vegetated slope to the lake, which is invariably busy with visitors on bright summer days. About 3mins beyond the lake, come to a four-way junction. If coming from the lake itself, cross directly ahead, but if you approach along the track bear right (sign for Riffelalp, Findeln and Zermatt). Shortly after come to **Bärghüs Grünsee** (2296m: *accommodation, refreshments*). ▶

More easily reached by a 1hr walk along a contouring path from Riffelalp station on the Gornergrat line, **Bärghüs Grünsee** has 10 beds and 28 dormitory places. Open in winter and from mid-June to mid-October (☎ 027 967 25 53).

Just beyond the Bärghüs the way forks. Continue ahead for just a few more paces and turn right on a footpath which descends through larchwoods to a bridge spanning the Findelbach stream. Then go up the continuing path to **Findeln** (2051m: *refreshments*), a charming little hamlet of dark-timber chalets and granaries, restaurants and a tiny 18th-century chapel.

Turn left in the hamlet and 3mins later, when the path forks, take the left branch (for a longer return to Zermatt see below), soon entering larchwoods, where you zigzag down to the Gornergrat railway line. Cross the line and soon after come to **Winkelmatten** (1672m: *accommodation, refreshments*), a 'suburb' of Zermatt with another attractive chapel (built 1607), a few shops and many fine *mazots*. You could also ride the battery-powered bus back to Zermatt from here, while the walker's route takes a tarmac path and subsequent service road – about 20mins from Winkelmatten to **Zermatt** (1620m).

Alternative return to Zermatt from Findeln

When the path forks 3mins from Findeln keep ahead. On coming to a four-way junction take the path ahead signed to Tufteren and Ried. This makes a long contour high above Zermatt, mostly across a wooded hillside but with fine views between the trees. For some of the way the path accompanies a pipeline, but eventually comes to a track which leads to Tufteren. Immediately before reaching this track, however, take a descending path on the left. When it forks, with both options signed to Zermatt, choose whichever suits – the left-hand trail descends to the upper end of the village, the right-hand option brings you to the lower end.

ROUTE 45
Zermatt (1620m) –
Findeln (2051m) – Eggen (2177m)

Grade:	2
Distance:	3.5km (one way)
Height gain:	557m
Time:	1½hrs
Location:	Southeast of Zermatt

The previous route visited Findeln as part of a circular walk, but this is a more direct route to it. The hamlet must be one Switzerland's most photogenic – a steep slope of meadow, a huddle of timeless hay barns and chalets, and a tiny white chapel make the perfect foreground to a study of the Matterhorn. It will rarely be visited in solitude, but that hardly matters. The scene is one of near-perfection, while the neighbouring hamlet of Eggen a little further up the slope overlooks that scene.

From the church square walk up-valley along Zermatt's main street to the southern outskirts and cross the river towards the cablecar station for destinations including Schwarzsee. Bear right, then curve left beneath the cableway towards the Findelbach gorge, and on the edge of Winkelmatten cross a bridge over the Findelbach and turn left on a footpath climbing through woods. Go over the Gornergrat railway line and continue up the south side of the gorge. Eventually come out of the trees where the path divides. Take the left branch, recross the Findelbach and go up a slope to **Findeln** (2051m: 1¼hrs: *refreshments*). Turn right through the hamlet, pass the chapel on the outskirts and continue ahead to the next hamlet, which is **Eggen** (2177m: 1½hrs: *refreshments*). From here, or shortly before reaching Eggen, a backward glance shows the picture-postcard view of Findeln.

Note

There are several options for continuing the walk.

* return to Zermatt by the same path
* take the alternative high path suggested at the end of Route 44
* go up the slope above Eggen to Sunnegga and ride the Alpen Metro down
* continue up-valley to the east of Eggen on a path that leads to the Grindjisee
* take the right-hand path at the junction just below Eggen to pass the Mosjisee after which you climb the southern slope in long loops to reach Bärghüs Grünsee (see Route 44).

ROUTE 46

Zermatt (Riffelberg: 2582m) – Riffelsee (2757m) – Riffelalp (2222m) – Zermatt (1620m)

Grade:	1–2
Distance:	9km
Height gain:	180m
Height loss:	1137m
Time:	3–3½hrs
Location:	South of Zermatt

A ride on the Gornergrat railway is one of the most popular of all Zermatt excursions, and the views from Gornergrat itself among the most celebrated in Switzerland. The walk described here is a rather convoluted descent from one of the highest stations on the Gornergrat line. It visits several scenically spectacular sites and could easily make a full-day's outing. Refreshments are available at Riffelberg, Riffelalp and various places on the way down to Zermatt.

Note: Before descending to the lake it would be worth crossing to a dip in the ridge to the south, where a wonderful view is obtained across the Gorner glacier to Monte Rosa, Liskamm, Castor, Pollux and Breithorn.

Begin by taking the Gornergrat railway as far as Riffelberg station – try to get a seat on the right-hand side of the carriage for the best views. On leaving the train walk up the slope on a footpath parallel with the railway line, and 1min later veer left. For about 35–40mins the path crosses gentle rolling pastures (always to the right of the railway), then comes to an unmarked crossing path close to the railway line. Bear right, and shortly after come to a signed junction above the **Riffelsee**, a much photographed tarn with its mirror image of the Matterhorn that appears on countless postcards, calendars and chocolate boxes. ◀

Wander down to the lake and along its right-hand shoreline to a second, much smaller tarn. This is also passed along its right-hand side, and when the path forks soon after continue down the slope to a second junction. Ignore the right fork and keep ahead to a region known as **Gagenhaupt**, where there's yet another path junction at 2564m. Here you turn right.

Notes

Again, it might be worth delaying the continuing route for a few minutes. If you slant left ahead you'll come to another viewpoint at the western end of the Riffelhorn. From here there's a dramatic view of the north face of the Breithorn directly ahead soaring above the Gorner glacier.

The little rock peak of the Riffelhorn has some complex routes on the face overlooking the Gorner glacier. Although short, a number of technically difficult test-climbs make it a useful training ground, and Zermatt guides often test new clients there before making attempts on higher summits.

The right-hand path at Gagenhaupt curves round and across more pastures and returns to **Riffelberg** (accommodation, refreshments) by a small chapel. From a path junction just below Hotel Riffelberg (60 beds, open mid-June to mid-October, ☎ 027 966 65 00) walk ahead on a descending path which makes a number of switch-backs down the Riffelbord into a scoop of pastureland with a small stream running through it. The path swings left to a crossways at **Obere Riffelalp** (2222m: accommodation, refreshments). Berghotel Riffelalp is just off to the right (40 beds, open mid-June to end September, ☎ 027 966 46 46).

At the crossways keep ahead, descending through larchwoods to **Untere Riffelalp** (2114m: refreshments), passing a restaurant and coming to a path junction where you bear right. Almost all the way now to Winkelmatten is through larchwoods. There are several signed junctions, and at each one you follow the direction of Winkelmatten and Zermatt. About 15mins from Untere Riffelalp pass Chalet Ritty, another restaurant with fine views, and beyond this continue down to a narrow service road. Cross straight ahead, through woods still, then across meadows to rejoin the road once more. This is now followed as far as **Winkelmatten**, then along a tarmac road to Zermatt.

ROUTE 47

Zermatt (Rotenboden: 2815m) –
Monte Rosa Hut (2795m)

Grade:	3
Distance:	6km (one way)
Height gain:	278m
Height loss:	298m
Time:	2½hrs
Location:	South of Zermatt

The Monte Rosa Hut enjoys a privileged position on the rocky Unter Plattje at the northwest foot of the Monte Rosa massif, with direct views along the Gorner glacier to the Matterhorn and a cascade of ice coming from Liskamm to the south. It's a stunning location. Whilst catering mainly for climbers using it as a base for a variety of routes on neighbouring peaks, the hut is often visited on a day-trip, but since the way to it crosses a crevassed glacier it is not a route to take lightly, and inexperienced walkers are advised against tackling it. Should you lack the experience to attempt this route, it would be worth going part of the way to the glacier to appreciate the magnificent panorama that is gained from its lateral moraine.

Note: This is as far as inexperienced walkers should go. There's a neat little grassy terrace just below the path which serves as a good picnic site with first-rate panoramic views.

From Rotenboden station (although little more than a halt it is the penultimate stop on the Gornergrat railway) descend towards the Riffelsee, then veer left on a path which makes for the low walling ridge to the south. Here a good path swings left and angles across the south flank of the Gornergrat, with the Gorner glacier below, Monte Rosa ahead, and across the glacier a long line of snow-peaks whose summit ridge carries the Italian border. The monolithic Matterhorn rises in the west.

The path makes a contouring belvedere, rises a little, then angles downhill in a long slant. In the past this path continued to a broad bluff of grass and rock immediately above the glacier, but during research in 2002 the path to the hut had been directed away from the original route about 5mins before the bluff (45–50mins from Rotenboden). It now cuts down the moraine wall in steep zigzags. ◀

As you near the foot of the moraine it becomes less stable, and caution is needed where the path is both steep and narrow. Take extra care if others are below, for it's easy to dislodge stones. Eventually arrive at the glacier's edge where marker poles direct the way across the rubble-strewn icefield. It is important to **keep to the marked route**. There will inevitably be narrow crevasses and surface streams to cross, as well as a narrow band of central moraine. Allow at least 1½hrs to get from the edge of the glacier to the hut.

The route makes for the moraine below and to the left of the hut, which can be seen from the glacier (although it's partly camouflaged among rocks). Once you leave the glacier the ascent path to the hut is marked with paint flashes and cairns. It begins messily, then goes up a long ramp-like, grit-covered ledge with some wood-braced steps before making a few zigzags onto a moraine, then up ladders to gain the Monte Rosa Hut. The panorama from the hut terrace is spectacular. Allow about 2hrs for the return walk to Rotenboden. ▶

Owned by the SAC, the **Monte Rosa Hut** has places for 150; it is staffed during April and May, and from July to mid-September (☎ 027 967 21 15). Monte Rosa itself is unrecognisable from here, but Liskamm is impressive with its big cascade of ice, then come Castor and Pollux and the great mass of the Breithorn. The Matterhorn, of course, is splendid, but so too are the distant Dent Blanche, Ober Gabelhorn and Zinalrothorn.

A short walk from Rotenboden gives arctic views of Monte Rosa and the Gorner glacier

The Monte Rosa Hut enjoys a privileged view along the Gorner glacier to the distant Matterhorn

ROUTE 48

Zermatt (Schwarzsee: 2583m) – Hörnli Hut (3260m)

Grade:	2–3
Distance:	6km (one way)
Height gain:	677m
Time:	2hrs
Location:	Southwest of Zermatt

The Hörnli Hut is situated at the foot of the steep Hörnli ridge by which the Matterhorn was first climbed, and is used each year by hundreds of climbers prior to tackling the standard ascent route. This hut approach, steep and strenuous in part, is extremely popular not only with climbers but with walkers who wish to get as close to the mountain as possible in order to experience its unique atmosphere. However, though it may be heresy to admit it, the closer one gets to the Matterhorn the less appealing it looks, and on close inspection the truth is revealed that the mountain is in fact a great pile of disintegrating rubble! Where this walk scores is in the broader view: the side-long vision of Monte Rosa across banded rivers of ice; the view north to the Dent Blanche, Ober Gabelhorn, Wellenkuppe, Zinalrothorn and Weisshorn; and off to the northeast where the Mischabel wall fades into shadow. And from a little way above the hut there is a clear view onto the Matterhorn's forbidding north face.

The cable lift to Schwarzsee saves a steep 2½–3hr walk from Zermatt. From the upper station near the Hotel Schwarzsee (14 beds, open mid-June to mid-October, ☎ 027 967 22 63) a famed panorama includes most of the 4000m peaks that arc around the head of the Mattertal. From here take a broad path sloping downhill towards the Schwarzsee lake, but at a signed junction take the left-hand path which leads above and to the left of the lake. It is so well defined and busy that detailed descriptions are unnecessary. It climbs, very steeply in places, a series of steps in the mountain's lower ridge. At first grassy hillsides, the terrain then

From the Hörnli Hut path above the Schwarzsee the Matterhorn rises as an abrupt pyramid

The **Hörnli Hut/ Berghotel Matterhorn** has room for 170 in its dormitories, and is staffed from the beginning of July to the end of September (☎ 027 967 22 64). The SAC hut was opened in 1966 next to what was then known as the Belvedere Hotel, which belongs to the Zermatt commune. It's a bustling place on a bright summer's day with a waitress service dispensing refreshments to visitors crowded on the terrace overlooking a jumble of glaciers and high mountains.

becomes more barren and rocky as you approach a metal ladder and a catwalk built away from the rockface. Above this the path winds among rocks, then eases along a gently angled slope of shale high above the Zmutt valley. At the end of this section the path narrows and in places is protected with fixed ropes before leading onto the east side of the ridge and climbing directly to the hut. Allow 1½–2 hrs to descend by the same path to the Schwarzsee hotel. ◀

ROUTE 49

Zermatt (Schwarzsee: 2583m) – Stafelalp (2200m) – Kalbermatten (2105m) – Zmutt (1936m) – Zermatt (1620m)

Grade:	2
Distance:	10km
Height gain:	35m
Height loss:	998m
Time:	2¾–3hrs
Location:	Southwest of Zermatt

By taking this easy but varied descent through the Zmutt valley from the Schwarzsee to Zermatt, a very fine walk is achieved without too much effort. Views are consistently fine, and there are several possible refreshment stops along the way. It's especially recommended as a return route for anyone who has been to the Hörnli Hut (Route 48).

Descend from the Schwarzsee lift station on a broad path/track passing to the right of the Schwarzsee lake which, with its little chapel of Maria zum Schnee on its north shore, is another of those much-photographed sites above Zermatt. The path/track continues to wind downhill between rough pastures, and soon passes a second, much smaller tarn. About 30mins from the start come to a path junction (2392m) with a bench-seat immediately ahead.

Leave the track here and follow the path, which descends beyond the seat into a rock-pitted area carpeted with low-growing shrubs of alpenrose, juniper and bilberry. It skirts a boggy area with a fence round it, and shortly after this another path breaks left to climb to the Hörnli Hut on the Matterhorn. Ignoring this, continue downhill, now alongside a stream, and soon come to **Restaurant Stafelalp** (2200m: *refreshments*) at a junction of ways. There are at least two options here. The first, main route, is longer and takes a devious course to another restaurant, Kalbermatten, while the second is rather more direct and is described below. First the longer option.

At the foot of the Matterhorn the little Schwarzsee is one of the best-known features of the Zermatt area

Bear left along a farm track, and 4mins later at a four-way junction go ahead on the lower of two forward routes. About 1min after this take a path on the right which descends a short distance to cross two footbridges below an electricity building. A stony path then rises among a few larches to gain a crossing path, where you go right and descend to another footbridge. The way now cuts round a steep slope among trees, then by a rock-tip before rising to another path. Turn right and follow this to **Restaurant Kalbermatten** (2105m: *refreshments*). Continue along the path for another 30mins to reach **Zmutt** (1936m: *refreshments*), where the alternative route from Stafelalp is joined.

Alternative (more direct) route from Stafelalp

Pass in front of Restaurant Stafelalp, then fork left on a minor path that descends among trees to a group of farm buildings. Turning left, slope down to a service road and follow this down-valley, soon coming to the alp hamlet of Stafelalp (Biel on the LS map). Shortly after this the road divides. Keep to the main, lower route, and on reaching the end of a reservoir, cross the dam to the north side where a path angles up to join the Kalbermatten route. Turn right and soon come to Zmutt.

On the edge of Zmutt the path forks. One option leads into this attractive hamlet, the other continues ahead on the way to Zermatt. The Zermatt route needs no description, takes 30–40mins from Zmutt, and is downhill virtually all the way.

ROUTE 50

Zermatt (1620m) – Zmutt (1936m) – Zum See (1766m) – Blatten (1738m) – Zermatt

Grade:	1
Distance:	6.5km
Height gain:	364m
Height loss:	364m
Time:	2hrs
Location:	Southwest of Zermatt

A short stroll beyond Zermatt leads to a group of attractive hamlets, each one consisting of little more than a handful of Valaisian timber chalets and hay barns and a tiny chapel. Refreshments are available at all three, and linking paths enable a pleasant, if undemanding, half-day's walk to be created.

From the village square by Zermatt's church walk up-valley towards the Matterhorn, keeping on the right-hand side of the river. On the outskirts of Zermatt, about 50m beyond the bridge leading to the cablecar station, fork right at a signpost, and 6mins later when the path forks again, take the right branch once more. The path rises between meadows and after a few minutes comes to another junction.

Although the left branch is signed to Zum See, ignore this and remain on the upper path, now wandering through larchwoods. On emerging from the woods the path winds uphill between more sloping meadows, passes a few *mazots* and about an hour from Zermatt reaches **Zmutt** (1936m: *refreshments*). Huddled above the north bank of the Zmuttbach, this is one of the prettiest hamlets in the Valais. It has two restaurants, and if the sun is shining you may expect both to be busy.

In Zmutt veer left by the chapel and, walking through the hamlet, descend to the Zmuttbach gorge, which you cross on a footbridge. Rising on the south side to a service road, turn left. About 15mins down this road come to a path junction marked as Bielti. Descend to the left through larchwoods, and soon you'll see a path cutting left to **Zum See** (1766m: *refreshments*), another huddled group of buildings set in the midst of meadows.

About 8mins beyond the Zum See feeder path stands **Blatten** (1738m: *refreshments*), with a cablecar swinging overhead. Pass in front of the chapel and descend to a bridge over the Gornera Bach (the river which drains the Gorner glacier and lower down becomes known as the Mattervispa). Cross to the right bank, wander downstream to another bridge which takes you back to the left bank, and continue into Zermatt.

ROUTE 51

Zermatt (1620m) – Herbrigg (1755m) –
Hubel (1946m) – Zmutt (1936m)

Grade:	2
Distance:	3.5km (one way)
Height gain:	326m
Height loss:	10m
Time:	2hrs
Location:	Southwest of Zermatt

Route 50 described the conventional walk to Zmutt from Zermatt. Although a very pleasant outing, the views were somewhat limited. This walk, however, whilst having the same destination, rewards with fine views and is less busy, but is much more strenuous. It also visits two other alp hamlets, neither of which provides refreshment.

Beginning in Zermatt's church square walk up-valley along the main street for just 1min. You will then find a signpost on the right, at the entrance to Schälpmattgasse, showing the way to Herbrigg, Hubel, Edelweiss and Trift. Walk up the steep cobbled path between houses, *mazots*, apartments and gardens. Above the last houses turn left at a junction signed to Herbrigg, Hubel and Zmutt.

The path now angles at a more comfortable gradient across the steep hillside, and soon reaches the timber chalet and collection of hay barns that comprise the hamlet of **Herbrigg** (1755m: 25mins), with a fine view onto the rooftops of Zermatt. The path forks. (The lower option is the Panoramaweg, which takes a lower route to Zmutt in 45mins.) Take the upper path which zigzags up the slope to gain successive levels of stone-built barns.

Passing to the left of these the way continues to climb, veers left and turns a corner to reach the larger alp of **Hubel** (1946m: 1hr 10mins). Most of the old *mazots* here stand in a huddle below the path, although some line the continuing way as you wander southwest with the Matterhorn soaring ahead. Just beyond the alp buildings another path breaks off to the right. Ignore this and continue ahead, now rising gently, crossing a stream and soon coming to yet another path junction. Both routes lead into the Zmutt valley – the upper path goes to Kalbermatten and the Schönbiel Hut, while the lower trail is the direct route to Zmutt. Take this lower path which undulates across the hillside, then descends a little, turns a rocky spur and comes to two more junctions in quick succession. (At the first junction the left-hand path is the Panoramaweg coming from Herbrigg.) Follow obvious signs to **Zmutt** (1936m: *refreshments*), which you enter beside its small chapel.

Note

There are several options for a return to Zermatt:

- via Zum See and Blatten as described in Route 50
- take the main path down-valley to reach Zermatt in 30-40mins
- return via the Panoramaweg mentioned above.

ROUTE 52

Zermatt (1620m) – Zmutt (1936m) –
Schönbiel Hut (2694m)

Grade:	3
Distance:	11km (one way)
Height gain:	1074m
Time:	4hrs
Location:	Southwest of Zermatt

Of the two main routes to the Schönbiel Hut this is the easier and more straightforward. Both are wonderful walks – and rank among the very best outings from Zermatt. They are long routes, to be sure, and when planning to tackle either remember that you will need about 3hrs for the return to Zermatt, so make a point of setting out early. (The second of these hut walks is described below as Route 56.)

The Schönbiel Hut itself is located on the left-hand lateral moraine bordering the Zmutt glacier, with a direct view across the glacier to the Tête de Valpelline, Dent d'Hérens, and the Matterhorn, which looks rather different and more complex from the hut than it does from Zermatt. Behind rise the Dent Blanche and Pointe de Zinal. Down-valley, a far-off wall of snow mountains spreads out from the cornerstone of Monte Rosa, while nearby three glaciers come together around the rocky island of the Stockji in a billow of ice that dazzles in the sunshine.

The walk starts by following Route 50 as far as **Zmutt** (1936m: 50mins: *refreshments*). Leaving the hamlet on your left continue up-valley on the clear and obvious path with views across the valley to the Matterhorn's north face. Passing above a dam that forms part of the Grande Dixence hydro-electric scheme the valley bed

*The Schönbiel Hut,
with the Matterhorn
across the valley*

takes on a sombre appearance, but views begin to
improve as the path steadily rises to the little restaurant
of **Kalbermatten** (2105m: *refreshments*), reached about
an hour from Zmutt.

A short distance beyond Kalbermatten, rockfall has
changed the route. The path now descends to the bed of
the valley where it snakes through a growth of young
larches, then among a charming area of wild 'rock gardens' before working up the slope to rejoin the original
path near a spectacular waterfall. Climb a series of
zigzags beside the waterfall and soon after come to the
mouth of the Arben tributary valley and a path junction.
(The right-hand path leads to Höhbalmen, and is used on
Routes 55 and 56.) Continue ahead across the tributary
valley, where you have a choice of routes.

The main footpath goes ahead along the right-hand
side of a stream, while an alternative track follows on the
left. Should you take the former route, and water levels
have risen through the ablation valley alongside the
moraine wall ahead, it's usually quite easy to leap the
various stream braidings. If the water is particularly
deep, however, you may be forced to wade through, in
which case caution is advised.

Beyond the Arben the path climbs onto the moraine wall and, becoming more narrow as you progress, follows along its crest, then finally zigzags up a grassy slope on which sits the **Schönbiel Hut**. ▶

ROUTE 53
Zermatt (1620m) – Trift (2337m)

Grade:	2
Distance:	3km (one way)
Height gain:	717m
Time:	2hrs
Location:	West of Zermatt

Owned by the Monte Rosa Section of the SAC, the **Schönbiel Hut** has places for 80 in its dormitories, and is staffed from Easter until mid-May and from the end of June until mid-September (☎ 027 967 13 54).

At the head of the Trift gorge, Hotel du Trift is a characteristic Victorian building that for many years stood abandoned and semi-derelict, but since being renovated as a berghotel it now provides both dormitory accommodation and private rooms, as well as refreshments for passing walkers and climbers. Nestling in a cirque of mountains at the foot of Zinalrothorn, Unter Gabelhorn and Mettelhorn, and with a number of paths splaying from it, Hotel du Trift (with the character of a mountain hut) suggests a peaceful and alternative base for a few days of a walking holiday. The walk to it is strenuous but rewarding.

Leave the church square in Zermatt and walk up the main street towards the Matterhorn for just 1min, then turn right into Schälpmattgasse, a steeply climbing cobbled path between houses (this is the same start as for Route 51). A signpost here points the way to Herbrigg, Hubel, Zmutt, Edelweiss and Trift. Rising between houses, *mazots* and gardens, take the right branch when the path forks and continue climbing above the last houses. When the Herbrigg path breaks left, take the right-hand option which leads between meadows to join another path coming from Zermatt. The way rises towards the Trift gorge, soon among larches, then skirts below some crags (several bolt-protected climbs here) to zigzag up to the Alterhaupt

Hotel du Trift is privately owned and open from the end of June to the end of September. It can sleep 10 in bedrooms and 20 in dormitory accommodation (☎ 079 408 70 20).

To descend to Zermatt by the same path allow 1–1½hrs, but for a choice of recommended circular walks see Routes 54 and 55 below. Continuing walks from Hotel du Trift include a visit to the Rothorn Hut (Route 57) and the ascent of the Mettelhorn (Route 58).

viewpoint and **Restaurant Edelweiss** (1961m: 45mins: *refreshments*). From the terrace outside the restaurant you gain a bird's-eye view of Zermatt. Just past the building an alternative path cuts off to the left to Höhbalmen.

Ignoring the Höhbalmen path, walk on along a brief contouring section before rising steeply again and crossing to the right-hand side of the Triftbach. The way then pushes through the gorge with a steady ascent along its north flank, and as you make progress, so the first of the high mountains comes into view ahead. The hotel itself is not seen until shortly before you reach it, but about 1hr 15mins after leaving the Edelweiss restaurant you emerge from the gorge to a rough meadowland at the base of the cirque where you'll find the pink-walled **Hotel du Trift** on the right. ◀

ROUTE 54
Zermatt (1620m) – Trift (2337m) – Höhbalmen (2665m) – Hubel (1946m) – Zermatt

Grade:	3
Distance:	8.5km
Height gain:	1045m
Height loss:	1045m
Time:	5hrs
Location:	West of Zermatt

Making a very fine circular walk via the Trift gorge, this is a strenuous route with wonderful high mountain views, some steep uphill sections and a very steep descent.

Follow directions in Route 53 as far as **Hotel du Trift** (2hrs: *refreshments*), and a few paces beyond the hotel you will come to a junction of paths. Take the left branch which curves behind some boulders and crosses a footbridge, then begins to ascend the southern hillside. The ascent is straightforward as it tacks back and forth in long twists, with good views of Zinalrothorn at the head of the Trift cirque, and of Rimpfischhorn and Strahlhorn to the east. After crossing a grassy shoulder you turn southwest onto the splendid high pastureland of Höhbalmenstafel, from which an astonishing panorama of big snow mountains is revealed. The Matterhorn rises directly ahead, a massive and wonderfully formed pyramid of rock. It is one of the finest aspects of this captivating mountain.

The path meanders across this pastureland and comes to the **Höhbalmen** junction (2665m), complete with bench seat from which to study the view. This is reached about an hour from Trift.

Turn left and descend in countless zigzags down the very steep grass-covered hillside – take this descent gently or your knees will suffer! After about 50mins of descent you come to another path junction at about 2150m. Bear right (the alternative path goes to Restaurant Edelweiss), still descending steeply for another 20mins to reach the alp huts of **Hubel** (1946m) and a crossing path. Turn left here and continue down to the close huddle of *mazots* at **Herbrigg** – an attractive spot with direct views onto Zermatt's rooftops. Follow the obvious path which soon brings you down to Zermatt along the Schälpmattgasse, where the walk began.

ROUTE 55

Zermatt (1620m) – Trift (2337m) –
Höhbalmen (2665m) – Arben (2327m) –
Zmutt (1936m) – Zermatt

Grade:	3
Distance:	16km
Height gain:	1121m
Height loss:	1121m
Time:	6½–7hrs
Location:	West of Zermatt

The second recommended circular walk via Hotel du Trift is much longer than the first, but for strong walkers it makes a magnificent outing. Although refreshments are available in both the early and later stages of the walk, it's advisable to carry a packed lunch and plenty of liquid to enable you to enjoy a picnic on the remote Höhbalmen pastures.

The way is the same as for Route 54 as far as the **Höhbalmen** junction (2665m: 3hrs). Instead of turning left here continue ahead, soon curving to the right with the Matterhorn constantly in view. The path becomes a long but tremendous belvedere across sloping pastures high above the Zmutt valley, much of it along an easy contour, but exposed in places. Views to the head of the Zmutt valley are excellent, especially to the Dent d'Hérens and a convergence of glaciers.

Eventually the way begins to descend into the Arben tributary valley, using long loops and a few tighter zigzags. On reaching the mouth of this tributary glen turn left on the Zermatt–Schönbiel path (4½hrs). The way is now straightforward. It descends in steep zigzags

Hotel du Trift stands at the head of the Trift gorge in challenging walking country

beside an impressive waterfall, and soon after goes down to the bed of the Zmutt valley through an area of wild natural rock gardens, then among young larch trees before returning up the slope to the original path east of a major rockfall. Shortly after this come to the isolated **Restaurant Kalbermatten** (2105m: *refreshments*). Continue along the path and in another 30mins you reach **Zmutt** (1936m: *refreshments*). From here to Zermatt will take 30–40mins, and the way is clearly signed and obvious at all junctions.

ROUTE 56

Zermatt (1620m) – Trift (2337m) – Höhbalmen (2665m) – Schönbiel Hut (2694m)

Grade:	3
Distance:	12km (one way)
Height gain:	1535m
Height loss:	461m
Time:	6hrs
Location:	West and southwest of Zermatt

Route 52 described the standard approach to the Schönbiel Hut from Zermatt. The following walk is a variation of that, a high route in every sense, which makes a tremendous day out. Since it takes another 3hrs or so to return to Zermatt by the shortest route, it would be worth considering spending a night at the hut itself.

Each section of this approach has already been described as part of other walks, so begin by heading up the Trift gorge to **Hotel du Trift** (2337m: 2hrs: Route 53), then crossing to the south side of the cirque and climbing round the hillside to **Höhbalmen** (2665m: 3hrs: Route 54), with its magnificent panoramic views that include most of the 4000m peaks of the region. From here take the balcony path running westward high above the Zmutt valley, then descend into the **Arben** tributary glen (2327m: 4½hrs: Route 55) that spills into the Zmutt valley halfway between Zmutt and the Schönbiel Hut. On reaching the mouth of this valley, turn right on the continuing path which soon climbs onto the crest of the Zmutt glacier's lateral moraine and leads directly to the **Schönbiel Hut** (2694m: 6hrs) as described in Route 52.

ROUTE 57
Zermatt (1620m) –
Trift (2337m) – Rothorn Hut (3210m)

Grade:	3
Distance:	6km (one way)
Height gain:	1590m
Time:	4½–5hrs
Location:	Northwest of Zermatt

Perched among steep crags at the base of the Zinalrothorn's southeast ridge, the Rothorn Hut makes a challenging objective for a day's walk. Reached by way of a long cone of moraine above Hotel du Trift the path is uncompromisingly steep, but visual rewards more than make up for the effort required to reach the hut.

The first stage of this walk leads through the Trift gorge to **Hotel du Trift** (2337m: 2hrs) as described in Route 53. From here walk ahead into the folds of a vegetated glacial basin, ignoring the path heading left to Höhbalmen, and 3mins from the hotel the path forks. (The right-hand path returns to Zermatt via Schweifinen in 2hrs.) Continue straight ahead, twisting up into an inner basin, where in 15mins from Trift the Mettelhorn path (see Route 58) breaks off to the right. A great arc of mountains forms an amphitheatre around you: Unter Gabelhorn, Ober Gabelhorn, Wellenkuppe, Trifthorn, Pointe du Mountet, Zinalrothorn, Unter Äschhorn,

Platthorn and Mettelhorn. The basin here is rimmed with glaciers, and the path edges along its right-hand side above a rock tip, then enters a little flat-bottomed plain below the Trift glacier. Cross a stream flowing from the right, then go straight up the obvious moraine cone edging the glacier. It's a steep ascent, but the moraine is speckled with plants, and when you pause for breath the views are gradually expanding. From about the 3000m mark the hut becomes visible another 200m above to tease you on. So reach the **Rothorn Hut** about 2½hrs after leaving Hotel du Trift. ▶

ROUTE 58
Zermatt (1620m) –
Trift (2337m) – Mettelhorn (3406m)

Grade:	3
Distance:	7km (one way)
Height gain:	1786m
Time:	5–6hrs
Location:	North of Zermatt

The ascent of the Mettelhorn, though long and strenuous ('interesting but toilsome' is how it was described in early Baedeker guides), is justified by its superlative 360° summit panorama. Standing at the eastern end of a crest of mountains extending from the Zinalrothorn almost 1100m above Hotel du Trift, it forms an unparalleled vantage point from which to survey the whole of the Mattertal and its walling peaks. The first recorded ascent was made in 1851, and for many years it was seen as one of the two classic training climbs of the region, the other being the Unter Gabelhorn on the opposite side of the Trift amphitheatre. As Robin Collomb pointed out in his 1969 guide to Zermatt and district, the vertical distance between Zermatt and the summit is as much as experienced on

Set amid wild glacial scenery, the **Rothorn Hut** belongs to the Oberaargau Section of the SAC, has places for 100 in its dormitories and is manned from the beginning of July to the end of September (☎ 027 967 20 43). The LS map quotes its height as 3198m, but a sign at the hut gives 3210m. Views are magnificent, and include not only the topmost triangle of the Matterhorn seen across an intermediate ridge, but the Mont Rosa group to the southeast, and the Dom and Täschhorn in the northeast. The hut is used almost exclusively by climbers as a base for routes on such peaks as Zinalrothorn, Trifthorn, Wellenkuppe and Ober Gabelhorn. Allow 2½hrs for the descent to Zermatt.

most mountaineering routes between a hut and the crown of a 4000m peak. But the Mettelhorn is the province of the 'tourist' as opposed to the climber, for there are no technical difficulties, no rock climbing pitches, and the small patch of névé crossed just below the summit is crevasse-free.

That being said, the ascent of a peak over 3000m should be taken seriously. If there's been recent snowfall (rain in the valley will doubtless fall as snow at 3000m) then the attempt should be delayed for a few days. Fine, settled weather is needed, and good visibility is a prerequisite, as is an early start – at least 6.00am if making the ascent from Zermatt. Considering the amount of height to be climbed (and allowing 3½–4hrs for a return to Zermatt), it would be worth spending a night at Hotel du Trift and starting from there. In any case, check current conditions – either at the guides' office (Alpin Center) in Zermatt or at Hotel du Trift – before setting out.

The **summit panorama** from the Mettelhorn includes all the main peaks of the district: the Weisshorn nearby, the Bernese Alps at the northern end of the Mattertal, the complete Mischabel chain across the valley dominated by the sharply pointed 'twins' of Dom and Täschhorn. There's the Monte Rosa group in the southeast leading the eye round to the Matterhorn, then the Ober Gabelhorn and Zinalrothorn making a ragged line to the west. A memorable landscape indeed.

From Zermatt take Route 52 to **Hotel du Trift** (2337m: 2hrs), and from there continue ahead into the rough folds of the lower glacial basin, ignoring the first path branching right (to Zermatt via Schweifinan), and twist up to an upper basin where, 15mins from the hotel, a sign marks the turning point for the Mettelhorn path. (The sign suggests 2hrs 45mins to the summit.) The way now climbs a steep grass slope to the left of a stream draining the Triftkumme (Triftchumme) into which the path leads. The gradient eases and the view opens out to extend far beyond the immediate cirque of mountains. At the end of an easy meadow stretch the way begins to climb again and evidence of the path fades. There are cairns, however, to keep you on course as you ascend the narrow combe (the Triftkumme) towards a little saddle to the NNE. On the right the rock crest rises to the Platthorn, a summit easily mistaken for the Mettelhorn, which cannot be seen from here.

On the approach to the saddle, the way traverses left to turn a rock barrier, then swings right and gains the saddle (little more than a notch in the skyline) to find the snowfield (névé) ahead and the summit cone of the Mettelhorn to the right. There will usually be a track across the snowfield, and over this you climb the final cone of the mountain in a series of zigzags – cairns guide the way. ◀

ROUTE 59

A Tour of the Upper Mattertal

Grade:	2–3
Distance:	60km
Time:	7 days
Start:	Zermatt
Finish:	Täsch
Location:	Around the head of the Mattertal

The Zermatt tourist authority publishes a leaflet entitled 'Hike Around Zermatt' (Höhenweg rund um Zermatt), which suggests a number of ways of making a tour of the high country above the resort, with details of mountain huts and berghotels that provide accommodation. The following seven-day tour is loosely based upon possibilities illustrated by this leaflet, and adopts several routes already described above.

Day 1: A short (2hr) stage begins the tour by walking out of Zermatt and up to **Hotel du Trift** (2337m) as described in Route 52. The hotel has both dormitory accommodation and private rooms (☎ 079 408 70 20).

Day 2: This is one of the most scenically spectacular stages, for it crosses the high Höhbalmen pastures on the way to the **Schönbiel Hut** (2694m: 4hrs), as described in Route 56. The hut can sleep 80 in its dormitories (☎ 027 967 13 54).

Day 3: From the Schönbiel Hut the way backtracks down the moraine wall to the mouth of the Arben tributary and continues down towards Zermatt a short way before crossing the Zmutt valley to Restaurant Stafelap (2200m), then reversing Route 49 to **Hotel Schwarzsee** (2583m) at the foot of the Matterhorn. The hotel has wonderful views, four-bedded dormitories and private rooms (☎ 027 967 22 63).

Ober Gabelhorn and Zinalrothorn, seen from the path below the Hörnli Hut

Day 4: With a steep descent to Furi, followed by a long climb via Riffelalp, Gagenhaupt and the Riffelsee to Gornergrat, this is quite a demanding stage, but the panorama from **Hotel Kulm Gornergrat** (3130m) makes the effort worthwhile. Claiming to be the highest hotel in the Alps, the two-star Hotel Kulm has 43 beds and is open throughout the year (☎ 027 966 64 00, e-mail:gornergrat.kulm@zermatt.ch).

Day 5: There are two ways of linking Gornergrat with the Fluhalp inn. One follows the railway down to Riffelalp, then curves round the hillside to Grünsee and reverses part of Route 44, while the other, more direct, route descends roughly north from Gornergrat and joins the Riffelalp path near the Grünsee. Whichever route is chosen, the stage ends at **Berghütte Fluhalp** (2616m) overlooking the Stellisee and a very fine sweep of high mountains. The inn has eight bedrooms and 45 dormitory places (☎ 027 967 25 97).

Day 6: Much of the 5hr stage to the Täsch Hut has been described in Routes 43 and 41. The day begins by taking a path to Sunnegga, then follows a splendid high-level route via Tuftern to Täschalp (Route 43). On arrival at Täschalp an easy track leads in a little over 1¼hrs to the nicely situated **Täsch Hut** (2701m), which has dormitory places for 60 (☎ 027 967 39 13).

Day 7: A short valley walk which is, nonetheless, very steep in places, ends the tour as you descend to Täschalp, then follow directions in Route 43 all the way down to **Täsch**, which has frequent railway links with Visp and mainline routes through Switzerland for the journey home.

THE TURTMANNTAL

A complete contrast to its neighbour the Mattertal, the Turtmanntal is a throwback to another age, with just one small village and limited tourist infrastructure, but more than a suggestion of the atmosphere that would have been familiar to the pioneers of Alpinism a century and more ago. The valley is distinctly pastoral. Cattle graze meadows on either side of the stream, and flocks of sheep spend the summer months on alps high above forests of larch and stone pine. There are clusters of farm buildings on both flanks and in secluded tributary glens that drain the walling mountains. At its head the impeccable Weisshorn shines its snowfields and glaciers, and casts its personality over the whole valley.

ACCESS AND INFORMATION

Location:	On the south side of the Rhône valley, between the Mattertal and Val d'Anniviers.
Maps:	LS 274T *Visp*, 273T *Montana* at 1:50,000. The majority of the valley is also contained on sheet 5006 *Matterhorn Mischabel* at 1:50,000.
Base:	Gruben-Meiden (1822m)
Information:	Verkehrsverein, CH-3948 Oberems
Access:	A tortuous minor road climbs into the Turtmanntal from Turtmann in the Rhône valley via Unterems and Oberems. For public transport access take a cablecar from Turtmann to Oberems, from where a minibus service goes to Gruben-Meiden.

The Turtmanntal is one of the shortest of the Pennine valleys south of the Rhône. It's also the most westerly of the German-speaking valleys, and one with very few permanent settlements. The only village within the main body of the valley is little more than an amalgam of two small hamlets, Gruben and Meiden, which for the visiting tourist boasts just one hotel, a restaurant with *matratzenlager* accommodation, and a small store with limited opening hours. In addition there's an attractive chapel dating from 1708, and a few timber chalets and granaries.

The road into the Turtmanntal leaves the Rhône valley at the village of Turtmann, roughly halfway between Visp and Sierre and served by railway. From here the road swings up the hillside in long loops, and passes through Unterems and Oberems before entering the valley proper. It's an interesting journey, for to all

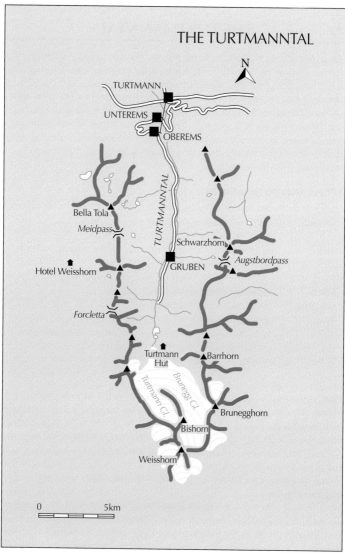

THE TURTMANNTAL

N

TURTMANN

UNTEREMS

OBEREMS

TURTMANNTAL

Bella Tola

Meidpass

Schwarzhorn

GRUBEN

Augstbordpass

Hotel Weisshorn

Forcletta

Turtmann
Hut

Barrhorn

Turtmann Gl.

Brunegg Gl.

Brunegghorn

Bishorn

Weisshorn

0   5km

Gruben, base for walks in the Turtmanntal

intents and purposes the Turtmanntal appears to belong to the age of the mule, rather than the automobile. Nowhere has it been developed for tourism. There are no ski tows nor funiculars, no bustling shops nor bright lights, no obvious reasons for diverting there except to enjoy the peace, some fine walking, and memorable views near the head of the valley, where the Weisshorn, Bishorn, Brunegghorn, Tête de Milon and Les Diablons rise above a chaos of glacier and snowfield.

Wandering upstream from Gruben those views grow in splendour, but are perhaps seen at their best from one of several vantage points on shelves of hillside on the west side of the valley. From one of these the Victorian pioneer Leslie Stephen was moved by what he saw: 'Above us rose the Weisshorn in one of the most sublime aspects of that almost faultless mountain,' he wrote in *The Playground of Europe*. 'The Turtmann glacier, broad and white with deep regular crevasses, formed a noble approach, like the staircase of some superb palace. Above this rose the huge mass of the mountain, firm and solid as though its architect had wished to eclipse the Pyramids. And, higher still, its lofty crest, jagged and apparently swaying from side to side, seemed to be tossed into the blue atmosphere far above the reach of mortal man. Nowhere have I seen a more delicate combination of mountain massiveness, with soaring and delicately carved pinnacles pushed to the verge of extravagance. Yet few people know of this side of a peak, which every one has admired from the Riffel.'

North of the Weisshorn and its neighbours the mountains are mostly snowfree in summer, and to east and west of Gruben the high ridges are cleft by

169

walkers' passes that lead over the mountains to St Niklaus in the Mattertal in one direction and to St Luc, Vissoie, Ayer or Zinal in Val d'Anniviers in the other. The Turtmanntal is a valley of passage, then, but one that is also worth spending a few days in to explore and to absorb its air of unfussed tranquility. None who love mountain scenery on a grand scale, but who are drawn as much by the little-known as by landscapes of familiarity, will be disappointed by venturing into the Turtmanntal.

MAIN BASE

GRUBEN-MEIDEN (1822m) is severely limited in its tourist infrastructure, but that is part of its charm. The single hotel, the Schwarzhorn (☎ 027 932 14 14), is open from June to October, and has excellent *matratzenlager* accommodation as well as rooms. Just 5mins down-valley, Restaurant Waldesruh also has a *matratzenlager* and is open from mid-June to mid-September (☎ 027 932 13 97).

MOUNTAIN HUT

TURTMANN HUT (2519m) This is the valley's only SAC hut, but it's ideally placed for climbs on the Brunegghorn, Barrhorn, Stellihorn, Bishorn, Weisshorn and Les Diablons. Reached in 2½–3hrs from Gruben, or in just one hour from the roadhead near a small dammed lake, it stands below the Barrhorn, is owned by the Prévôtoise Section of the SAC and has places for 74. The hut is fully staffed from mid-March to mid-May, and mid-June to end of September (☎ 027 932 14 55, website: www.turtmannhuette.ch).

ROUTE 60
Gruben (1822m) – Chalte Berg (2488m)

Grade:	2
Distance:	4.5km (one way)
Height gain:	666m
Time:	2½hrs
Location:	Southwest of Gruben

The quotation from Leslie Stephen in the introduction to this chapter could very well have emanated from his visit to one of a number of points along the path to the alp of Chalte Berg, for as you progress towards it, so the big snow mountains grow in stature ahead. And at Chalte Berg itself the view of the Weisshorn is extravagantly beautiful. Chalte Berg (or Kaltenbergalp) is a collection of alp buildings – huts, cattle byres and cheese-makers' lodgings – set upon a broad shelf of pasture at the northeastern end of the Blüomatttälli, at whose head is the Forcletta, a fine walker's pass leading to the Val d'Anniviers, a crossing of which is described in the opposite direction as Route 67. In early summer the pastures are rich in alpine flowers, but it is the magnificent panorama of high mountains that will hold your attention in all seasons.

From Gruben walk up-valley for a little over 1km, either along the road or by a faint footpath on the western side of the Turtmänna stream, until you come to the farm buildings of Blüomatt on the true left bank of the stream. Waymarks here lead from the south side of the buildings over a meadow and into forest, where the path, clear but sometimes crowded with undergrowth, winds up the hillside, fairly steeply at first, then easing as you gain height. On coming to a dirt road cross straight ahead and continue, still rising, and rejoin the road by an alp hut. Bear left and walk along it for a few paces to the buildings of **Massstafel** (2235m). Go round the hairpin bend, and a few metres beyond this slant up the hillside once more on a continuing path. Views are consistently fine, and get even better as height is achieved.

Soon the path parallels the still-climbing farm road and eventually rejoins it again. Fortunately you don't

Above Chalte Berg, on the way to the Forcletta, a cluster of peaks near the head of the Turtmanntal comes into view

need to walk very far along it, for as it curves round the hillside look for a line of waymarks heading up to the right through sloping pastures. Follow these to the alp of **Chalte Berg** and enjoy the setting of this collection of rustic farm buildings amid so much glorious mountain scenery (allow 1–1½hrs for the return to Gruben by the same path).

Note

An alternative return to Gruben (3½hrs), making a circular walk via the dammed lake at the roadhead, can be achieved by returning roughly halfway down the farm road towards Massstafel, then breaking off on a path which descends below the road and cuts back to the right to more alp buildings of Bitzu Oberstafel (2268m). Continue beyond these, cross a stream and then along an easy contour heading almost due south to the lake (1hr from Chalte Berg). Then wander down-valley for 2½hrs to Gruben.

ROUTE 61

Gruben (1822m) – Meidpass (2790m) –
Hotel Weisshorn (2337m)

Grade:	2
Distance:	9km (one way)
Height gain:	1104m
Height loss:	589m
Time:	4½hrs
Location:	West of Gruben

The Meidpass is the lower and easier of the two main routes by which the Val d'Anniviers may be reached from the Turtmanntal (the Forcletta is the other). With Gruben situated midway between it and the Augstbordpass, it clearly forms a strategic crossing point, and is one that has been adopted by the Walker's Haute Route. The way to it visits alp farms and a small tarn, while Hotel Weisshorn at the end of the walk is a somewhat eccentric Victorian establishment perched way above the Val d'Anniviers. A night spent there is recommended – for reservations see details below.

A footbridge spans the Turtmänna stream just below Gruben, and from it a signed path climbs into pinewoods, steeply in places, making a way up the western hillside. Above the trees reach the alp buildings of **Mittel Stafel** and a farm road above them. Either cross the road and continue up the slope or wind uphill along the road to the larger alp of **Ober Stafel** (2334m).

From here a path rises easily into the hanging valley of Meidtälli, where the little Meidsee tarn (2661m) brightens an otherwise rather drab scene. The head of the valley is rimmed with a number of eroded rock towers (the Meidzänd). From the lake's southwest shoreline the trail rises, then curves leftwards over scree and with a few twists comes to the **Meidpass** (2790m: 2½hrs) to gain a view that includes Mont Blanc de Cheilon four valleys to the southwest, the Grand Combin beyond that, and, far off, the snow dome of Mont Blanc itself may be seen on a clear day.

Open June to October, and December to April, the **Hotel Weisshorn** has private rooms and *dortoir* accommodation, plus restaurant service (☎ 027 475 11 06), Hotel Weisshorn, CH-3961 St-Luc. From here a splendid balcony path leads to Zinal in 2½hrs, while a pleasant descent path goes down through a complex of forest and meadowland to Ayer in the bed of the valley in about 2hrs. Allow 4hrs to return to Gruben by the same route.

The path now descends in zigzags and is quite obvious in its southwesterly route through a rough bowl of pastureland. Reaching an isolated alp hut in a walled enclosure (La Roja: 2308m), pass round the right-hand side and continue down, soon coming to a collection of farm buildings and a track. Bear left and wander down the track as it winds below the rocky peak of Le Touno, then follow signs to **Hotel Weisshorn**. ◀

ROUTE 62
Gruben (1822m) – Augstbordpass (2894m)

Grade:	3
Distance:	6.5km (one way)
Height gain:	1072m
Time:	3–3½hrs
Location:	East of Gruben

Linking the Turtmanntal with the Mattertal, the Augstbordpass has been in use as a trading route since the Middle Ages. Today it forms one of the loveliest of crossings on the classic Walker's Haute Route between Chamonix and Zermatt, and whilst the full route to St Niklaus makes a magnificent day's outing, the walk to and from the pass itself provides plenty of interest and fine views. Although steep in places, the path mostly chooses a generous line, breaking the severity of the slope with long loops and, for the first half of the approach, allows distant views of the Bernese Alps between stately pines.

On the south side of Hotel Schwarzhorn a grass path rises through an open meadow towards sparse woods of larch and pine. Within the woods you embark on an easy winding course, gaining height without too much effort, and in a little under an hour reach a four-way path junction which the signpost names as Grüobalp

(2151m). (The right-hand trail here is one of several routes to the Turtmann Hut.)

Continue directly uphill, emerge from the pinewoods to pass above a solitary hut, and 15mins from the Grüobalp junction come onto a dirt road. Turn right along it, and 2mins later take a footpath on the left which climbs the slope and winds up to an open shelf of pastureland with the two alp buildings of **Ober Grüobu Stafel** (2369m) facing across the valley to the Meidpass, which is clearly seen to the west (see Route 61). To the north the Bietschhorn rises above the Rhône valley, while to the southwest Les Diablons dazzles its modest glacier.

Passing just to the right of the huts the path continues upwards through the little glen of Grüobtälli, then reaches a more stony inner region, with screes lining the southerly mountain wall. Hummocks of grass and rock make this a rough, contorted area. Cross a bluff with a small tarn below it, then go over a clutter of rocks and boulders before making the final climb (more steeply now) to the pass itself.

The **Augstbordpass** enjoys a wild view to the east over a wilderness of grey rock and scree. The glacier-draped Fletschhorn and outliers of the Mischabel wall, which divides the Saastal from the Mattertal, dominate the view, while back in the west the long ridge forcing northward from Les Diablons displays its two main passes, the Forcletta and the Meidpass. Allow 1½–2hrs for the return to Gruben.

For an even more impressive view scramble up the ridge to the north in order to reach the summit of the easy **Schwarzhorn** (1hr from the pass), where the extensive panorama is, according to one Victorian visitor, 'one of surpassing magnificence'. Judged by Baedeker to be even finer than that from the Bella Tola, the panorama includes the line of the Bernese Alps from the Finsteraarhorn to the Doldenhorn, the Alps of Ticino, Weissmies and Mischabel, Monte Rosa and Weisshorn.

Other routes from Gruben

The three routes described above represent mere scratchings on the surface of possibilities. Exploring the Turtmanntal in detail would keep the walker happy for many days, and the following ideas are all worth pursuing.

- **The Turtmann Hut** below the tongue of the Brunegg glacier can be reached in about 2½hrs by the most direct route along the valley road/track as far as the dammed lake, followed by a signed path. Another possibility is to take the Augstbordpass route as far as the Grüobalp junction, then turn right along a hillside path – signed at all junctions.

- A three-hour walk down-valley on paths and tracks leads to **Turtmann** in the Rhône valley, while there are more mid-height paths that could be adopted to reach the same destination.

- The crossing of the 2874m **Forcletta**, either to **Zinal** or **Hotel Weisshorn**, would provide a superb day's walking and, returning via the **Meidpass** (see Route 61), would create a memorable two-day circuit with an overnight spent at Hotel Weisshorn. To reach the Forcletta, follow directions for Route 60 as far as Chalte Berg, then continue up into the seemingly remote Blüomatttälli, where the path climbs directly to the pass.

- There's a route which climbs through the Bortertälli to the 2897m **Pas de Boeuf** in the ridge north of the Meidpass, and from there continues easily along the ridge to the much-lauded summit of **Bella Tola**.

VAL D'ANNIVIERS

The Val d'Anniviers has been hailed as the grandest or greatest of all the Swiss valleys of the Pennine Alps – and who would dispute that claim? Some 16km from Sierre it divides into two distinct branches. The main branch continues slightly east of south as the Val de Zinal, while the southwest stem becomes the Val de Moiry. Both valleys are headed by magnificent snow mountains and a turmoil of glaciers, and on the approach to these the great potential for the mountain walker and lover of fine scenery becomes evident. As the walker penetrates deeper and approaches the head of these valleys, so the landscape grandeur intensifies, and the trails grow more demanding, yet immensely rewarding for those who accept their challenge.

ACCESS AND INFORMATION

Location:	South of Sierre in the Rhône valley, west of the Turtmanntal.
Maps:	LS 273T *Montana* & 283T *Arolla* 1:50,000
Bases:	Zinal (1675m), Grimentz (1572m)
Information:	Office du Tourisme, CH-3961 Zinal (☎ 027 475 13 70, e-mail: zinal@vsinfo.ch, website: www.zinal.ch)
	Office du Tourisme, CH-3961 Grimentz (☎ 027 475 14 93, e-mail: grimentz@vsinfo.ch, website: www.grimentz.ch)
	Office du Tourisme, CH-3961 Chandolin (☎ 027 475 18 38, e-mail: chandolin@vsinfo.ch, website: www.chandolin.ch)
	Office du Tourisme, CH-3961 St-Luc (☎ 027 475 14 12, e-mail: saint-luc@vsinfo.ch, website: www.saint-luc.ch)
	Sierre Anniviers Tourisme, Case Postale 59, CH-3960 Sierre (☎ 0848 848 027, e-mail: info@sierre-anniviers.ch, website: www.sierre-anniviers.ch)
Access:	By postbus from Sierre through the length of Val d'Anniviers to Zinal, Grimentz and Lac de Moiry.

Val d'Anniviers is a magical district. As you enter from the broad, vine-clad Rhône, swinging in tight hairpins to gain sufficient height in order to get onto the eastern shelf above its protective gorge, there's more than a hint of grandeur about the long groove of a valley stretching ahead. At first it is green, with the hillsides dense with forest and shrub, and the river scouring a deep bed below. Summer warmth draws a seething of insects from the lush vegetation, but a gleam of ice and snow in the south promises even better things, and as you draw closer,

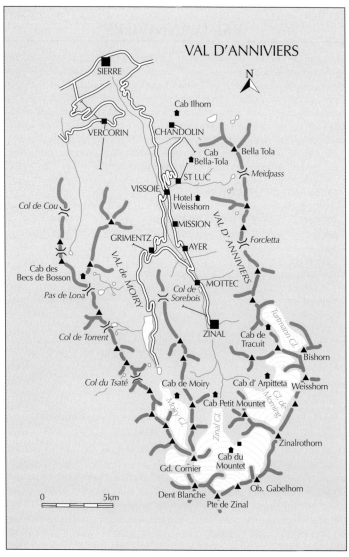

VAL D'ANNIVIERS

N

SIERRE

Cab Ilhorn

VERCORIN

CHANDOLIN

Bella Tola

Cab
Bella-Tola

Meidpass

ST LUC

VISSOIE

Col de Cou

Hotel
Weisshorn

VAL D'ANNIVIERS

MISSION

Forcletta

GRIMENTZ

AYER

Cab des
Becs de Bosson

VAL de MOIRY

MOTTEC

*Col de
Sorebois*

Pas de Lona

Col de Torrent

ZINAL

Cab de
Tracuit

Turtmann Gl.

Bishorn

Col du Tsaté

Cab de Moiry

Cab d' Arpitteta

Col de Morning

Weisshorn

Moiry Gl.

Cab Petit Mountet

Zinal Gl.

Zinalrothorn

Gd. Cornier

Cab du
Mountet

Ob. Gabelhorn

Dent Blanche

0   5km

Pte de Zinal

From the path between Sorebois and the Petit Mountet, a walker contemplates the Weisshorn

so that promise becomes a reality. Up there, at the very head of the valley, is some of the loveliest mountain scenery imaginable.

A little south of Vissoie Val d'Anniviers divides. Ignoring for a moment the southwest branch, continue ahead into the upper reaches known as Val de Zinal, where a towering rock peak assumes a stature that outstrips its true position in the scale of things. Lo Besso is a pretender. Admittedly it stands 3668m high, but that's modest by comparison with some of its neighbours, and its apparent domination of the upper valley is only devalued when Zinal itself has been left behind. Zinal is the last and highest of the villages, and when the road runs out a short way beyond it and you take to the footpaths, Lo Besso is put into perspective, for it is only then that the great ice-caked peaks show their worth: Weisshorn, Schalihorn, Pointe Sud de Moming, Blanc de Moming, Zinalrothorn. Beyond these a fabulous cirque of mountains blocks the southern end of the valley and swings round to the west of its deep glaciated trench: Ober Gabelhorn, Mont Durand, Pointe de Zinal, Dent Blanche, Grand Cornier, the airy ridge of the Bouquetins and Pigne de la Lé. Several of these peaks are more than 4000m high, the remainder pushing close to that elevated point. Glaciers hang suspended from walls of rock, one peak laced to its neighbour by waves of glistening cornice, while below the ice-sheets sweep together in an arctic, crevasse-sliced, and often rubble-strewn river.

But while the snow- and ice-peaks hold your attention, there are green shelves and terraces high above the valley with alp huts scattered here and there with narrow paths meandering between them. These paths provide access to that special wonderland – the middle mountain kingdom. It is this region that affords some of the very best of all mountain views. It is from here that the mountains begin to reveal their secrets. They certainly do above the Val de Zinal: the alps of Combautanna and Ar Pitetta on either side of the Roc de la Vache on the eastern slopes are the very substance of dreams, while almost opposite these on the western hillside La Lé is a green bowl of splendour with an incredible view of that most noble of mountains, the Weisshorn.

As for the Val de Moiry stem of Val d'Anniviers, this too leads into realms of enchantment. But here one must go deeper, for the dam at the northern end of Lac de Moiry projects its presence over part of that valley. However, on the western side of the lake rolling pastures lead to a farm or two and a splendid tarn under Col de Torrent, while at the southern end there's another ice-bound district with glaciers pouring from the heights in one of the most dramatic and turbulent icefalls to be seen anywhere in the Alps. The approach to the Moiry Hut provides a close view of this icefall, and a privileged introduction to the inner sanctuary of high mountains.

MAIN BASES

ZINAL (1675m) is an unpretentious village and long-time mountaineering centre near the head of the valley, with an impressive range of walks on its doorstep. Many of its buildings are of traditional Valaisian style, but the village has its share of modern apartment blocks too. There are several one-, two- and three-star hotels, and dormitory accommodation is available at Auberge Alpina (☎ 027 475 12 24). There's a campsite at the southern end of the village: Camping Les Rousses, open June to end September (☎ 027 475 20 22, e-mail: info@camping-zinal.ch). Zinal has a few shops, restaurants, bank, PTT and tourist office, and a cablecar to Sorebois on the west flank of the valley. Next to the tourist office is the local Bureau des Guides, open July and August 16.00–18.00 (☎ 027 475 12 00, e-mail: guides.anniviers@bluewin.ch, website: www.anniviers-montagne.ch).

GRIMENTZ (1572m) must rank among the most attractive of Valaisian villages. Set at the mouth of Val de Moiry on a steeply sloping hillside, dark-timbered chalets and barns stand in tiers one above another, their windows adorned with boxes of geraniums and petunias, their alleyways narrow and filled with shadow. It has several hotels, two- and three-star rated, and dormitory accommodation in the Chalet Ecole (☎ 027 475 26 26, e-mail: alamarenda@vtx.ch, website: www.alamarenda.ch). There are cafés and restaurants, a few shops, PTT and tourist information. Free camping is also available; enquire at the tourist office for details.

OTHER BASES

As well as Zinal and Grimentz, several other villages have accommodation available. Towards the northern end of the valley, and set upon the eastern hillside, **CHANDOLIN** has two two-star hotels and a number of apartments. **ST-LUC** also stands high above the valley, 400m above Vissoie, and has four hotels, while **VISSOIE** has the two-star Manoir de la Poste and three-star Hotel Anniviers. Licensed campsites are located in St-Luc, Vissoie and Mission. Each of these villages is served by postbus.

MOUNTAIN HUTS

CABANE DE L'ILLHORN (2145m) is located about 30mins above Chandolin with a very fine view of the distant snowpeaks that head the valley. Owned by the Monte Rosa section of the SAC, the *cabane* is open from mid-June to mid-September, at weekends in October, and from mid-December to mid-April. The refuge has 32 dormitory places (☎ 027 475 11 78).

CABANE BELLA TOLA (2346m) is, as its name suggests, built on the slopes of the prominent Bella Tola, and is reached in a 30min walk from the St-Luc/Tignousa funicular. With 92 places, the *cabane* is manned from mid-June to the end of September, and from mid-December to mid-April (☎ 027 475 15 37, website: www.funiluc.ch).

CABANE DE TRACUIT (3256m) is perched high on the col of the same name between Diablon des Dames and Tête de Milon, and enjoys a fabulous outlook

Walkers on the path below Cabane d'Ar Pitetta

across the Turtmann glacier to the Bishorn. Owned by the Chausses section of the SAC, it has 130 places and is manned from mid-June to mid-September (☎ 027 475 15 00). It is reached by a steeply climbing path in 4–4½hrs from Zinal.

CABANE D'AR PITETTA, also spelt Arpittetaz (2786m), is located within a dazzling arc of mountains below the Weisshorn, about 4–4½hrs walk from Zinal. A small, stone-built hut with 30 dormitory places, it is owned by the La Dôle (Nyon) section of the SAC and is manned from the end of June to the end of September (☎ 027 475 40 28).

CABANE DU GRAND MOUNTET (2886m) has a stunning location at the head of the Val de Zinal directly opposite the north face of the Ober Gabelhorn. Reached in 4–4½hrs from Zinal the hut belongs to the Les Diablerets section of the SAC and has 120 places. It is staffed from the end of June to the end of September (☎ 027 475 14 31).

CABANE DU PETIT MOUNTET (2142m) was rebuilt following a fire in 2001, and stands on the left-hand lateral moraine of the Zinal glacier. It can now sleep 40 in its dormitories, and is open from mid-June to mid-October (☎ 027 475 13 80). It is reached by a popular walk from Zinal in a little under 2hrs.

CABANE DE MOIRY (2825m) enjoys a lofty position at the head of the Val de Moiry, with the icefall of the Moiry glacier nearby and a horseshoe of shapely peaks above it. Owned by the Montreux section of the SAC, it is reached in a little under 2hrs from the roadhead south of Lac de Moiry. The hut has 96 dormitory places and is manned from the end of June to the end of September (☎ 027 475 45 34, e-mail: info@cabane-de-moiry.ch, website: www.cabane-de-moiry.ch).

CABANE DES BECS DE BOSSON (2985m) Situated near the Pas de Lona on the south side of Becs des Bosson high above Grimentz, this cabane has 50 places and is manned from the end of June to October (☎ 027 281 39 40, e-mail: info@nature-evasion.ch, website: www.nature-evasion.ch).

OTHER ACCOMMODATION

Val d'Anniviers has several other remote and semi-remote lodgings of value to walkers. Some are traditional mountain inns, others are *gîtes d'étape*, *cabanes* or chalets. The following list offers a selection.

Visited by Route 61 from Gruben in the Turtmanntal, the large Victorian **HOTEL WEISSHORN** (2337m) enjoys an elevated position on the east flank of the valley.

Built in 1884, it suffered serious fire damage in 1913 and was then rebuilt. In 1990 the hotel lost its roof in a storm, and was later refurbished without compromising its somewhat eccentric charm. It has private rooms and dormitory accommodation, and is open from June to October and December to April (☎ 027 475 11 06).

At the Sorebois cablecar station above Zinal, **CABANE DE SOREBOIS** (2440m) has 35 dormitory places and is open from mid-June to the end of September, and from Christmas to mid-April (☎ 027 475 13 78, e-mail: pascal@poudreuse.ch, website: www.zinal.net).

Standing just above the dam at the northern end of Lac de Moiry, the **CHALET DU BARRAGE DE MOIRY** (2300m) has 26 dormitory places and is open from mid-June to mid-September (☎ 027 475 15 48, e-mail: clems@bluewin.ch).

On the left bank of the valley north of the Val de Moiry stem, the village of St-Jean has a *gîte* with 26 dormitory places. The **GÎTE DE ST-JEAN** (1400m) is owned by the local commune and is open from May to the end of October (☎ 027 475 22 60, e-mail: legîte@bluewin.ch, website: www.anniviers.ch/gîtedest-jean).

Included within the restaurant building at the Crêt du Midi cableway station above Vercorin at the northern end of the valley, the **GÎTE DE CHANTOVENT** (2332m) has 22 places in four rooms. It is open from June to October, and mid-December to mid-April (☎ 027 452 29 00, e-mail: televercorin@netplus.ch, website: www.vercorin.net).

The Victorian Hotel Weisshorn is almost a Swiss institution

ROUTE 63
*Chandolin (1920m) – Cabane de l'Illhorn
(2145m) – Illhorn (2716m)*

Grade:	2
Distance:	4km (one way)
Height gain:	796m
Time:	2½hrs
Location:	Northeast of Chandolin

An impressive panoramic view greets your arrival on the summit. Directly across the Rhône valley the Wildstrubel spreads its long ridge, with the Bietschhorn to the northeast, Les Diablerets to the northwest. To the south the long trench of the Val d'Anniviers leads the eye to its ice-crusted end, while the shattered cliffs of the Illhorn's northern side plunge into the Illgraben. Three small tarns lie below the mountain's southeast flank. Return to Chandolin by the same path in about 1½hrs.

The modest Illhorn is the northernmost summit along the Val d'Anniviers' walling east ridge. Standing above slopes scarred by ski pistes and avalanche barriers it is, nonetheless, an exceptionally fine viewpoint.

The walk begins in the centre of Chandolin, where there's a two-tier car park, behind which you follow a track rising into woods past the end of a ski tow. Follow signs to **Cabane de l'Illhorn** (2145m: 30mins: *accommodation, refreshments*). Above the hut a signed path leads uphill across meadows and ski pistes, and bears right round the upper slopes of the Illhorn towards the grassy **Pas de l'Illsee** (2544m) and a junction of paths. Turn left here and ascend the summit cone of the mountain, mostly on grass but with curious rock formations near the summit itself, which is marked by a cross. ◀

Other routes from Chandolin
Reached by a winding road that snakes up the hillside from Vissoie, first visiting St-Luc, Chandolin enjoys a splendid location. Several short and reasonably undemanding walks are available from the village, as briefly outlined here.

• The ascent of the **Schwarzhorn** (2790m), which stands southeast of the Illhorn above the little Lac Noir, is feasible in about 2½hrs by well-signed paths.

- North of Chandolin a pleasant 3hr circular walk along tracks and footpaths leads to the **Plaine Madeleine**, overlooking the Illgraben precipices.

- An easy and very popular 1hr walk takes a belvedere path along the hillside heading south to the **Tignousa** funicular, as part of the classic Sierre– Zinal route (see Route 66).

ROUTE 64
St-Luc (Tignousa: 2169m) – Cabane Bella Tola (2346m) – Bella Tola (3025m)

Grade:	2–3
Distance:	5km (one way)
Height gain:	856m
Time:	3–3½hrs
Location:	Northeast of St-Luc

The Bella Tola is one of the most famous viewpoints in the Valais accessible to walkers. A great favourite with Victorian visitors to the region, its ascent remains a popular excursion more than a hundred years later.

The Tignousa funicular quickly lifts walkers above St-Luc, saving 500m of ascent. From Tignousa (*refreshments*) walk directly up the slope ahead, and after about 20mins you'll come to the **Cabane Bella Tola** (2346m: *accommodation, refreshments*) and a junction of paths. Continue straight ahead, still rising, and soon the path curves east then northeast, often guided by blue painted letters 'BT' for Bella Tola. The way cuts across a dirt road several times, and about 1hr from Cabane Bella Tola comes to another junction (2520m), where a path breaks off to the right for the Meidpass. Ignore this and follow a gravel path to yet another junction – once again the right-hand option goes to the Meidpass.

'An admirable and favourite viewpoint,' said Baedeker in his 1901 guide to Switzerland. 'The view embraces the whole of the Bernese and Valaisian Alps; opposite, to the N., the whole gorge of the Dala is visible, up to the Gemmi. The mountains to the S., from Monte Leone to Mont Blanc, are particularly grand.'

Continue to climb in zigzags towards the ridge linking the Schwarzhorn, Rothorn and Bella Tola, and when the path forks again at 2900m take the right branch (the left-hand path ascends the 2998m Rothorn) along the rather exposed ridge. Although not difficult under normal summer conditions, the exposure suggests you exercise caution. After passing two rock pillars at about 2910m take the left-hand path which climbs the summit cone. ◀

ROUTE 65
St-Luc (Tignousa: 2169m) –
Meidpass (2790m) – Gruben (1822m)

Grade:	2–3
Distance:	11km
Height gain:	621m
Height loss:	968m
Time:	4½–5hrs
Location:	East of St-Luc

Of the three walkers' passes across the ridge east of St-Luc, linking Val d'Anniviers with the Turtmanntal, the Meidpass is the easiest. (The others are Pas du Boeuf and the Forcletta – see Route 67.) There are several approach routes to the Meidpass, and two of these are included below. The main route begins, as Route 64, by taking the funicular from St-Luc to Tignousa, while the alternative makes a more direct ascent from Hotel Weisshorn – see 'Route from Hotel Weisshorn' below.

Out of the funicular station (*refreshments*) turn right along a track heading for Hotel Weisshorn. On reaching the farm of Chalet Blanc (2179m) fork left at a junction to climb roughly eastward (sign for Lac de l'Armina and Meidpass), looping up the hillside without too much effort, passing the ruined Armina chalets, then curving left to gain the **Lac de l'Armina** at 2562m. Above the lake to the north rises Bella Tola, and in the ridge running between that summit and the Corne du Boeuf/Meidspitz lies the alternative crossing of the Pas du Boeuf, while the Meidpass lies almost due east of Lac de l'Armina.

Leaving the lake to your left, the path continues round towards the pass and joins the route from Hotel Weisshorn. A few zigzags now lead onto the **Meidpass** (2790m).

Route from Hotel Weisshorn

Go onto the track above and behind the hotel and bear right. The way leads round in a curve and comes to a signed junction. Continue to a second signpost overlooking a strangely contorted basin below the 'island peak' of Le Touno. The way to the Meidpass is directed along a farm road that curves leftward below Le Touno and, about 30mins from the hotel, brings you to a collection of white alp buildings. A few paces beyond these turn right on a path signed to the Meidpass. Ten minutes later pass round the left-hand side of an isolated hut set in a walled enclosure, and at another signpost continue up-valley over pastureland. Veering slightly left, the path comes to a stream which it follows to the junction with the main route from Tignousa. Zigzag up to the pass, which is reached in a little under 2½hrs from Hotel Weisshorn.

Views from the pass are very fine in both directions. On the eastern side the path descends in zigzags into the Meidtälli, then slants leftward to the edge of the Meidsee tarn (2661m). Breaking away from this you now descend through a modest pastureland, eventually reaching the alp buildings of **Ober Stafel** (2334m). Beyond these descend steeply over a lip of hillside to **Mittel Stafel**, a smaller alp, then down through forest on a clear path which leads directly to **Gruben-Meiden** in the bed of the valley. (See the Turtmanntal section for further details, including availability of accommodation and onward routes.)

ROUTE 66

St-Luc (Tignousa: 2169m) –
Hotel Weisshorn (2337m) – Zinal (1675m)

Grade:	2
Distance:	16km
Height gain:	231m
Height loss:	725m
Time:	4hrs
Location:	Northeast of St-Luc, heading south

This walk follows a section of the route adopted by the annual Sierre–Zinal mountain marathon, which usually takes place in early September. It is a highly scenic walk along a series of tracks and footpaths keeping high above the valley and making towards the amphitheatre of ice-peaks that block the valley in the south. The first part of the walk, from the Tignousa funicular station to Hotel Weisshorn, goes along the Sentier Planétaire ('path of the planets'), beside which a number of sculptures have been placed depicting the Sun, Mercury, Venus, Earth, Mars, Jupiter, Saturn, Uranus, Neptune and Pluto.

From St-Luc ride the funicular to Tignousa and there turn right on a clearly marked track which runs along the hillside to the farm of Chalet Blanc (2179m) and continues easily to **Hotel Weisshorn** (2337m: *accommodation, refreshments*), with its great view across the Rhône valley. From the track junction behind the hotel a signpost directs the route along a path which is frequently blazed by a yellow letter 'Z'. The over-exuberance of this waymarking, thought to have been done for the benefit of marathon competitors, is to be regretted, for it smacks of graffiti.

The way makes a traverse below the Pointes de Nava, and about 40mins from Hotel Weisshorn you come to the highest part of the route (2424m), where avalanche protection work has reshaped the hillside with extensive dykes and stone-buttressed walls. Here you briefly follow a rising track, then break away to the right on the continuing path round the spur of Montagne de

Nava. Signs keep you on the correct course at all junctions, and views come and go as you round the hillside then dip into various grooves and bays. At one junction near a small hut a path climbs left to the Forcletta to make a crossing into the Turtmanntal, but for Zinal you continue ahead, cross a stream then curve round the Crête de Barneuza to reach the simple buildings of **Barneuza Alpage** (2211m).

Beyond this alp the path crosses another stream in a tight little combe, turns another spur and continues along its delightful scenic belvedere before entering larchwoods and, after a while, descending through avalanche defences to the northern end of **Zinal**.

Other routes from St-Luc

Between them St-Luc and Chandolin have around 300km of footpaths, so a walking holiday based in either of these villages will produce enough routes for a week or so. The following offers a brief summary of possibilities.

- A very full day's walking (7hrs) leads to **Sierre via Chandolin** and the Plaine Madeleine which overlooks the Illgraben cirque. The descent from Plaine Madeleine to Sierre in the Rhône valley is both long and steep, with a difference in altitude of almost 1500m.

- A valley walk, suitable for a day when the weather dictates keeping off the high places, leads in about 3hrs to **Zinal**. It begins by crossing the Torrent des Moulins, then cuts through forest, some of the way alongside a *bisse*, or irrigation canal, before coming into the bed of the valley at Ayer. From there to Zinal short stretches of road walking are broken by footpaths and tracks.

- The ascent of the island peak of **Le Touno** (3018m), which rises east of Hotel Weisshorn, makes for an exhilarating 5–6hr round trip from Tignousa. Le Touno is a dramatic little peak with an intimidating north face seen from St-Luc. Whilst this face is beyond the reach of walkers, the south side above the bowl of Tsa de Touno has weaker defences with a path to the top.

- A **circuit of the Pointes de Nava** is also worth considering. The Pointes de Nava constitute a spiky ridge which dominates the skyline above the villages of Ayer and Mission. From Hotel Weisshorn (reached from Tignousa) a path leads up into the little bowl-like valley of Tsa de Touno, which lies east of the ridge, between the Pointes de Touno and the Anniviers/Turtmanntal dividing ridge. At the head of Tsa de Touno cross a low 2621m col and descend to a track below alp Tsahelet. This track leads west to the St-Luc to Zinal path and an easy way back to Hotel Weisshorn for a walk of 4–5hrs.

ROUTE 67
Zinal (1675m) –
Forcletta (2874m) – Gruben (1822m)

Grade:	3
Distance:	14km
Height gain:	1199m
Height loss:	1052m
Time:	5½–6hrs
Location:	North of Zinal

For walkers based in Zinal, the Col (or Pas) de Forcletta provides the most practical route of access to the Turtmanntal. It's a splendid route, full of variety and wonderful views, and if linked with a return via the Meidpass and Hotel Weisshorn would give a very fine three-day circular walk (see Routes 61 and 66 which describe these return stages). The Forcletta itself is a windblown saddle above a wild mountain corrie, but it has an extensive panorama and, on the eastern side, leads to magical views of the Weisshorn, Bishorn and Brunegghorn. Since there are no opportunities for refreshment between Zinal and Gruben, it is important to carry food and drink with you.

Begin at the Zinal tourist office, which is found at the northern entrance to the village. Walk up the minor road which slants uphill behind it, winding round to the left, then back to the right. Immediately after passing an apartment block turn left along a service road between buildings, then left towards a parking area. Here you take a rising track on the right, up between larch trees, through a tunnel and across an avalanche defence system.

Across this the path rises in forest and, by way of a series of zigzags, soon takes you high above the valley. About 50mins from the start the gradient eases into a gently rising traverse, leaves the forest and comes onto an open shelf with fine views towards the head of the valley.

The path now makes a splendid belvedere, and 1hr 45mins from Zinal brings you to the **Barneuza Alpage** (2211m). Just past the buildings there's a path junction. Take that which is signed to Hotel Weisshorn; this is the upper path rising ahead. It eventually turns a spur and enters a deep combe, crosses a stream and comes to the solitary hut of **Alpe Nava** (2340m: 2hrs 20mins) and another signed junction.

Turn right to climb grass slopes, the path faint in places, but with red–white waymarks as a guide, and about 20mins from the Alpe Nava junction you come to the alp buildings of **Tsahelet** (2523m) and a large wooden cross. From the right-hand end of the cattle sheds the path continues over a pitted grassland to a rocky slope which you then climb in long zigzags to gain the **Forcletta** (2874m), about 3hrs 45mins from Zinal. Distant views to the southwest show the Aiguilles Rouges above Arolla, and beyond them a vast sea of peak and glacier and snowfield. The pass itself is a narrow, windswept crest between horns of rock. Ahead lies the Blüomatttälli into which the route descends.

Slant left across a slope of shale, then along the left-hand side of the shallow hanging valley where a stream drains between cushions of moss and flowering plants. Views begin to expand as you near the open end of the glen, and as the path veers left over rolling pastures, so the full sweep of high mountains and glaciers

The alp farm of Chalte Berg below the Forcletta

to the right demand photographic halts. 'I doubt whether there is a more spiky panorama to be seen in the Alps than this view across the Turtmanntal,' wrote Showell Styles in *Backpacking in the Alps and Pyrenees*. 'Every peak is a Horn – Stellihorn, Barrhorn, Brunegghorn, Bishorn, Weisshorn.'

Views are particularly fine from the alp of **Chalte Berg** (2488m), which is reached in 4–4½hrs. Go between the buildings and continue down the slope on a line of way-marks to reach a dirt road, where you bear left. After about 150m take a footpath on the right which runs below the road, then descends to more alp buildings (**Massstafel**). Rejoin the road and turn right along it as far as the last hut, where the continuing path descends the slope and comes onto the road once more. Cross ahead and wander down to forest in which the path zigzags its way, sometimes through undergrowth, finally reaching the valley bed by more farm buildings about 1km above Gruben.

Either walk down the valley road or take a faint foot-path on the left bank of the Turtmänna stream, eventually coming to a path junction near a pair of chalets. Turn right, cross the Turtmänna on a bridge and enter **Gruben-**

Meiden. For details of accommodation and facilities, please refer to the Turtmanntal section.

ROUTE 68
Zinal (1675m) –
Hotel Weisshorn (2337m) – Ayer (1476m)

Grade:	2
Distance:	16km
Height gain:	725m
Height loss:	861m
Time:	5½–6hrs
Location:	North of Zinal+.2

Already included in walks from Gruben and St-Luc, Hotel Weisshorn is something of an institution among walkers in Switzerland. This somewhat eccentric Victorian establishment perched high above the valley overlooking St-Luc and the Rhône valley has had a chequered history. It is a magical place in which to spend a night or simply to visit on a day's walk. The path leading to it enjoys a spectacular panorama, while the descent to Ayer in the bed of Val d'Anniviers is a very pleasant walk through forest and over pasture. Ayer is linked with Zinal by postbus.

Follow directions given in Route 67 as far as **Alpe Nava** (2340m: 2hrs 20mins). Ignore the right-hand path which leads to the Forcletta, and continue ahead where the sign suggests 1hr to Hotel Weisshorn. All this route is used by the Sierre–Zinal mountain marathon, and is abundantly waymarked with yellow letters. The path rises to a track, and you continue ahead on a path running parallel to it, but at a higher level. This leads to a second track among avalanche defences. Bear left for a short distance, then take another footpath rising ahead. This takes an undulating course along the hillside and soon brings you in sight of the tall square building of Hotel Weisshorn. Just above the hotel come onto a track and turn left down it to reach **Hotel Weisshorn** (2337m: 3½–4hrs). ▶

Open June to October, and December to April, **Hotel Weisshorn** has private rooms and *dortoir* accommodation (☎ 027 475 11 06).

On the south side of the hotel a path descends into forest with signs to St-Luc, Gillou and Ayer. On coming to a junction where the path to St-Luc breaks to the right, take the left-hand option and keep following signs for Ayer, heading south. The path briefly accompanies an irrigation canal, known as a *bisse*, then drops below the forest to pass through and alongside meadows, with a few hay barns and isolated chalets, before coming onto a road. Bear left, and on turning a hairpin break off along another footpath to the left. This leads directly to **Ayer** (*refreshments*), a pleasant village with attractive Valaisian houses and barns perched on staddle stones. The postbus halt for Zinal is found beside the main road.

The high path between Zinal and Hotel Weisshorn, also used by the Tour of the Val d'Anniviers, rewards with consistently fine views

ROUTE 69
Zinal (1675m) – Cabane de Tracuit (3256m)

Grade:	3
Distance:	7km (one way)
Height gain:	1581m
Time:	4–4½hrs
Location:	Southeast of Zinal

Cabane de Tracuit occupies an airy position on the high ridge that runs between Tête de Milon and Diablon des Dames. Overlooking the Bishorn across the Turtmann glacier, it's a tremendous location and a demanding one to reach. This is a steep and challenging walk – definitely not one to attempt on the first day of a holiday – but it is rewarding for all who complete it. Choose a settled day with good visibility, but beware that the upper section could be dangerous following snowfall.

At the southern end of Zinal's main street, about 150m past Hotel Les Bouquetins, turn left on a narrow service road and, in a few paces, follow a track which runs left of the road. Up a slope take a footpath on the left which rises through larchwoods, then brings you onto the road again. Turn left and pass a few chalets, beyond which the road becomes a track. When it curves left, go directly ahead on another track, and when this also curves left leave it for a footpath (sign to Tracuit) which climbs, then contours, then rises again to make a steady ascent of the hillside among trees.

About 45mins from the centre of Zinal come out of the trees to a view of a fine waterfall draining the Combautanna cirque. The path heads up towards this, then cuts left towards a group of farm buildings at 2061m. Keep to the right of these and climb in long windings towards the waterfall. As you draw near to it, so the path climbs steeply up the left-hand side, and in 1hr 45mins you come to a path junction and a signpost (2460m). The right-hand path goes to the Roc de la Vache (Route 70), while the Tracuit path continues straight ahead.

The way now rises into the pastoral Combautanna cirque and shortly passes a little alp hut (2578m). From here the Cabane de Tracuit can be seen on the headwall ridge to the northeast, and appears much closer than it really is. Climbing easily up the left-hand (northern) hillside, on a clear path for much of the way, height is gained quite comfortably. About 1hr from the Combautanna junction the path forks again at about 2960m. The right-hand path goes to the Col de Milon

Owned by Section Chaussy of the SAC, the **Tracuit Hut** is manned from mid-June to mid-September and has 130 dortoir places (☎ 027 475 15 00). The outlook is sensational.

and Cabane d'Ar Pitetta, but you continue ahead into an increasingly stony landscape. Eventually come onto the crest of the ridge at Col de Tracuit and bear right to the **Cabane de Tracuit**. ◀

ROUTE 70
Zinal (1675m) – Roc de la Vache (2581m) – Alp d'Ar Pitetta (2248m) – Zinal

Grade:	2–3
Distance:	11km
Height gain:	906m
Height loss:	906m
Time:	5hrs
Location:	Southeast of Zinal

If I were to be restricted to just one day's walking in the whole of the Valais region, this is probably the walk I would choose. It has everything: an ever-varied vegetation, dashing streams and cascades, glistening tarns, a high grassy col to cross, attractive and isolated alp huts along the route, and some of the most delectable mountain scenery one could possibly wish to gaze upon. It's a steep haul up to the Roc de la Vache and a steep descent on the southern side, but the stunning views more than compensate for the effort involved. Since there are no opportunities for refreshment along the way, take a packed lunch and a flask of drink, set out early, walk slowly and absorb the beauty around you – and be thankful for the health and strength that enable you to achieve it.

The first third of the walk is the same as that taken on the approach to the Cabane de Tracuit, so follow directions for Route 69 as far as the path junction above the waterfall in the mouth of the Combautanna cirque (2460m: 1hr 45mins). Where the Tracuit path goes ahead, turn right, cross the Torrent du Barme and rise over grass slopes to emerge onto the saddle of **Roc de la Vache**, about 15mins from the Combautanna junction (2hrs from Zinal). The view from here is glorious.

The bed of Val de Zinal is some 900m below, but the eye is drawn by glaciers snaking from a wonderful amphitheatre at the head of the valley, where shapely peaks stab at the sky, and ice walls appear like blue mirrors between perfectly formed snow slopes topped by wave-like cornices along the ridges. There's the contrast of height and depth, light and shade, white snow and brown rock, glacier and grass… Lo Besso appears to hold back the tumultuous form of the Moming glacier, with Zinalrothorn peering over, and Pointe Sud de Moming next to it just coming into view. As you descend from the saddle, so the cirque dominated by the Moming and Weisshorn glaciers spreads itself for inspection on the left.

Below Roc de la Vache, the abandoned hut of Tsijiere de la Vatse makes a foreground to the dramatic Moming glacier

The descending path is clear, if narrow, and works its way down to the south, passes a deserted and semi-dilapidated hut (Tsijiere de la Vatse: 2388m) and continues to a little lake in an idyllic setting near the alp buildings of d'Ar Pitetta (3hrs). Here the path forks. The left branch goes to Cabane d'Ar Pitetta, but for the return to Zinal take the right-hand option. This goes through a vegetated gully to another path junction with a signpost. Bear left to descend through a region of alpenrose, juniper and larch, still with splendid views ahead. Stay with this main path, ignoring an alternative (marked *difficile!*) leading to the right, and eventually you'll come to a footbridge spanning a glacial torrent. Over this turn right and follow a track down to Zinal.

ROUTE 71

Zinal (1675m) – Alp d'Ar Pitetta (2248m) –
Cabane d'Ar Pitetta (2786m)

Grade:	2–3
Distance:	9km (one way)
Height gain:	1111m
Time:	4–4½hrs
Location:	Southeast of Zinal

At Alp d'Ar Pitetta (the 'little alp') you gaze up at the giant Weisshorn and at hanging glaciers topped by Schalihorn, Pointe Sud de Moming and Zinalrothorn. Lo Besso stands guard at the southwest entrance to the amphitheatre; Pointe d'Ar Pitetta is the northern sentry. But in the heart of the cirque stands the small, stone-built climber's hut from which some of these peaks may be tackled. It is an exceptionally fine location within that dazzling arc of mountains, and its approach makes a first-class outing, if rather steep and demanding at times.

Walk south out of Zinal heading up-valley, and when the road ends cross the bridge on the right and follow a track which cuts through the flat meadows known as the Plats de la Lé. At the far end of these meadows the track rises ahead, passes a junction where a path breaks off to the right to visit an old copper mine, and later goes below a fine waterfall cascading down from Alp La Lé. The track forks just after passing a white-walled building (the right branch goes to the Petit Mountet) and you continue ahead, but shortly after, when the track forks once more, turn left to cross a footbridge over a glacial torrent.

Dent Blanche and the Grande Cornier, seen from Lac d'Ar Pitetta

Immediately over the bridge take the left-hand path which climbs through lush vegetation to another junction where the left branch is marked as *difficile!* Keep ahead, but at the next fork bear right, go through a vegetated gully and emerge beside the little **Lac d'Ar Pitetta** (2248m: 2hrs 30mins). This is a charming spot, and it's worth resting here for a while before tackling the 1½hr onward climb to the hut.

Walk along the left-hand side of the tarn and, ignoring the path forking left to Roc de la Vache, continue ahead into the cirque. The path makes a steady ascent of the left-hand hillside, occasionally climbing in steep zigzags and with magnificent views throughout – the Weisshorn ahead, and the icy cirque walls curving round to Zinalrothorn and the rocky Lo Besso. Two or three streams are crossed by footbridge before you tackle a final steep haul up a great prow of rock and grass, topped by a tall cairn, which brings you to the **Cabane d'Ar Pitetta.** This stands above the moraines of the Moming glacier and below the Glacier du Weisshorn. ▸

With just 30 places, and manned from the end of June to the end of September, **Cabane d'Ar Pitetta** is owned by the La Dôle (Nyon) section of the SAC (☎ 027 475 40 28). Allow at least 3½hrs for the return to Zinal by the same path.

ROUTE 72

Zinal (1675m) –
Cabane du Grand Mountet (2886m)

Grade:	3
Distance:	11km (one way)
Height gain:	1211m
Time:	4–4½hrs
Location:	South of Zinal

'It is worth a king's ransom to wander up into that world of towering crag and eternal snow, and lunch in the sunshine with sight regaled meanwhile by an almost unsurpassed prospect of stupendous peak, and glittering glacier.' So wrote G.D. Abraham of the amphitheatre of mountains seen from the Mountet cabane. This walk gives an opportunity to share Abraham's enthusiasm. It's an energetic route with some exposed sections, but the scenery is awe-inspiring almost every step of the way. Since it is a high route, with some dramatic situations, it should only be attempted in good, settled weather conditions.

Follow directions as for Route 71 as far as the footbridge over the glacial torrent, about 1hr from Zinal. Immediately over the footbridge the path forks. While the Ar Pitetta route takes the left branch, you take the right-hand option and gain a splendid view of the Grand Cornier at the head of the valley and the Weisshorn almost directly ahead.

Easing between trees, the way then climbs onto the crest of the lower east bank moraine of the Zinal glacier that has been carpeted here with dwarf alder scrub and juniper. Before long the path leaves the moraine and climbs steeply beside a rockface, then continues above it in zigzags to cross the flank of Lo Besso several hundred metres above the glacier. It's a well-engineered path made by the Swiss army to replace the former west bank route. At times it's narrow and a little exposed, but fixed ropes and chains have been provided in the most dramatic places, and as you progress so views of the Grand

Cornier, Dent Blanche and Pointe de Zinal become more and more impressive. Eventually turn a spur of Lo Besso, where the path then angles southwest with Ober Gabelhorn soaring ahead, and you arrive at the **Cabane du Grand Mountet**.

On the way to the Mountet Hut, the Grand Cornier assumes a Himalayan dimension

The large **Cabane du Grand Mountet**, owned by the Les Diablerets section of the SAC, can sleep 120 in its dormitories, and is manned from the end of June to the end of September (☎ 027 475 14 31). Standing above the confluence of the Durand and Mountet glaciers, it commands a stupendous panoramic view of what J. Hubert Walker (among others) reckoned to be much grander even than the head of the neighbouring Mattertal. The view is one of the finest in the Alps, the amphitheatre walled by Zinalrothorn, Trifthorn, Ober Gabelhorn, Mont Durand, Pointe de Zinal, Dent Blanche and Grand Cornier – a more glorious company no mountain lover could wish to keep. Allow at least 3hrs for the return to Zinal.

ROUTE 73
Zinal (1675m) –
Cabane du Petit Mountet (2142m)

Grade:	1–2
Distance:	5km (one way)
Height gain:	467m
Time:	1hr 45mins
Location:	South of Zinal

This short and easy stroll makes an ideal introduction to the country south of Zinal, for it gives a close-up view of the high peaks, their hanging glaciers and snow basins. There are, in fact, two routes. One, suitable for families with small children, follows a broad and well-graded track all the way, while the alternative branches away from the track about 45mins from the Petit Mountet and climbs among shrubs on a narrow path that is rather steep in places. Both options are given. The Cabane du Petit Mountet was rebuilt following a fire in 2001. It stands on the west bank moraine walling the Zinal glacier, with a collection of high peaks in full view.

The **Cabane du Petit Mountet** makes a popular destination for families, groups and individuals. Privately owned, it can accommodate 40 in its dormitories, and is open from mid-June to mid-October (☎ 027 475 13 80). Advanced booking is essential for overnight accommodation.

As with Routes 71 and 72, this walk begins by heading south out of Zinal as far as the end of the paved road, then across the bridge spanning the Navisence and along the track which cuts through the meadows of the Plats de la Lé. At the end of the meadows the track winds uphill, goes below a waterfall and forks just before reaching the white-walled building of Le Vichiesso (1862m: 1hr). The footpath route (Grade 2) leaves to the right, while the 'standard' route (Grade 1) continues on the track (see below).

Take the footpath, which rises to another junction after about 5mins. The right-hand path climbs steeply to Alp La Lé, but you continue straight ahead. The trail is bordered by shrubbery, but with good views across the valley into the Ar Pitetta cirque topped by the Weisshorn. Among shrubbery the path drops into a narrow gully, crosses the stream leaking through it, then climbs steeply onto the old moraine bank on which stands the **Cabane du Petit Mountet**. ◀

Grade 1 track route

At the fork (see above) continue on the track/dirt road as it angles along the hillside. Ignore other paths that break from it, and remain with the track, which makes a long switchback onto the moraine wall overlooking the rubble-strewn Zinal glacier. It leads directly to the hut.

The approach to the Petit Mountet Hut passes through a small vegetated valley

ROUTE 74

Zinal (Sorebois: 2438m) – Alp La Lé (2184m) –
Cabane du Petit Mountet (2142m) – Zinal

Grade:	3
Distance:	13km
Height gain:	102m
Height loss:	865m
Time:	4hrs
Location:	West of Zinal and heading south

Following a high-level path along the western hillsides, this walk is forever inter-esting. Gazing across to the east one has views of Les Diablons, the long ridge leading to Tête de Milon, then the steep-walled Weisshorn and a crowd of glaciers hanging like curtains of ice over a wild cirque. The valley lies far below for much of the walk, but ahead – and drawing ever closer – are the enticing big peaks that hem the valley in to the south.

Take the cablecar to Sorebois, and on leaving the lift sta-tion turn left to head south along a clear track signed to Petit Mountet. When this forks take the upper branch, but keep alert for a narrow path (signed) which drops to the left. The path is waymarked in yellow, and it makes a traverse of the hillside, crosses a stream on a wooden footbridge and continues on an undulating course with very fine views across the valley. In places this path is rather exposed (some fixed chains for security) and can be difficult for those a little unsteady with the effects of vertigo. Caution is advised.

About 2hrs from Sorebois, the path brings you to a grassy bluff – a wonderful viewpoint – just beyond which it descends across the pastures of **Alp La Lé**. Once again a sign indicates the way to Petit Mountet. Pass a little hut tucked against a boulder on the left of the path and wind round the hillside, with views being rearranged both ahead and across the valley to the east.

Come to a path junction where the left branch returns to Zinal by way of Le Vichiesso (the most direct route). Instead, take the right branch which contours, then descends into the little ablation valley below the moraine wall on which the **Cabane du Petit Mountet** is perched. Go up the moraine path to the hut for refreshments, then descend to Zinal by the track/dirt road used in Route 73.

Other routes from Zinal

Routes described above represent the very best walks in the Val de Zinal, but there are a few more which might be worth considering, and these are briefly outlined below.

- A pleasant 2½hr valley walk leading to the Val de Moiry stem of Val d'Anniviers heads downstream to the hamlet of Le Bouillet, then on to Pralong and Mottet, after which a woodland path (signed at junctions) skirts the long mountain spur that separates the two upper stems of the valley and leads directly to **Grimentz**. This is described in the reverse direction as Route 80.

The Weisshorn (left) and rock peak of Lo Besso (right) guard the Ar Pitetta cirque, seen across the valley from Alp La Lé

- Grimentz can also be reached by a much more demanding route which crosses the 2840m **Col de Sorebois**. If walked all the way, it will take around 6hrs Zinal–Grimentz, but by use of the Sorebois cablecar the ascent to the pass could be reduced by 2hrs and 750m. The crossing of Col de Sorebois from the Barrage de Moiry is described in the reverse direction as Route 75.

- **Alp La Lé**, visited from Sorebois on Route 74, may be approached in 3hrs by reversing part of that earlier route. From Zinal walk up-valley towards Cabane du Petit Mountet, but turn right on a steeply climbing path that leaves the track at the Vichiesso junction and breaks away from the Petit Mountet trail. Once Alp La Lé has been reached, one could spend an hour or two wandering across the pastures and into the wild cirque that backs it. Views are outstanding.

ROUTE 75

Grimentz (Barrage de Moiry: 2249m) –
Col de Sorebois (2840m) – Zinal (1675m)

Grade:	2
Distance:	8km
Height gain:	591m
Height loss:	1165m
Time:	4–4½hrs
Location:	South of Grimentz

This is another ridge crossing used by trekkers tackling the Walker's Haute Route from Chamonix to Zermatt. It's a fine crossing which consists of a fairly easy ascent during which it's sometimes possible to see chamois grazing, but the final 750m of descent into Zinal are very steep and tiring. Views are as exhilarating as may be expected when there are so many high mountains in sight, but the slopes between the col and Sorebois have been badly scarred on behalf of the ski industry. The route begins at the dam at the northern end of Lac de Moiry. There's a restaurant on the edge of the dam and a dortoir just above it. The dam is served by postbus from Grimentz.

From the eastern end of the dam an obvious track winds uphill and soon comes to the junction with the Haut Tour du Lac, which breaks off to the right. Continue uphill in long loops until, after making a right-hand hairpin, you leave the track for a narrow waymarked path rising on the left. Views down to Grimentz and back across the upper Val de Moiry are impressive as you gain height. Without being diverted from the uphill course the path leads directly onto the easy saddle of **Col de Sorebois** after about 1hr 40mins. Here another world is revealed, for a great line of peaks to the southeast is dominated by the shapely Weisshorn – it's a view that becomes even more impressive on the descent. ▶

Note: For an even more extensive view, walk along the ridge to the left as far as the Corne de Sorebois (2895m) – about 5mins from the col.

Zinalrothorn and Lo Besso are just two among an impressive collection of peaks on display from the hillside near Sorebois

207

From the col bear left towards the Corne de Sorebois, then slant down to the right on a track/ski piste that sweeps in long switchbacks to the cablecar station of **Sorebois** (2438m: 2hrs 45mins: *accommodation, refreshments*). Bear right along the track for a short distance, then take a signed track/path on the left. After crossing a sloping pasture the path zigzags downhill, passes beneath the cableway and enters forest. From here down to Zinal the gradient steepens to make a knee-jarring approach to the village. At the foot of the slope cross a footbridge over the Naviscence, and walk up into **Zinal**, which you enter in the main street a little south of the tourist office.

ROUTE 76

Grimentz (Parking du Glacier: 2409m) –
Cabane de Moiry (2825m)

Grade:	2–3
Distance:	3.5km (one way)
Height gain:	416m
Time:	1½–2hrs
Location:	South of Grimentz

This route gives an opportunity for walkers to intrude safely into the untamed heartland of the glacial mountain world. It treads along a narrow crest of moraine overlooking the chaos of an icefall, as dramatic as any likely to be found with such ease elsewhere in the Valais, while the view from the hut is one to excite the imagination. Referring to the Moiry icefall and glacier in 1864, A. W. Moore wrote (in 'The Alps' in 1864): 'Between the Pigne de l'Allée on the east, and a spur running down from the highest peak…on the west, is a tremendous ice-fall of great height and very steep. The lower part of this extends completely from one side of the glacier to the other, but higher up…is a belt of smooth ice, which we had no doubt would give access to the field of névé above the fall. Below this great cascade of séracs, the ice is as compact and level as above it is steep and dislocated. Indeed, I never saw an ice-fall confined within such plainly defined limits, or terminate so abruptly.' Nearly 150 years on the glacier is shrinking fast, but the icefall remains as dramatic as in Moore's day.

The postbus from Grimentz goes as far as the Val de Moiry roadhead at Parking du Glacier, where the hut approach begins. Take the signed track beside the *buvette* and follow it as it curves round and above a small settlement reservoir below the snout of the Moiry glacier. When the track ends a footpath continues, rising onto the north bank lateral moraine walling the glacier. It leads onto the moraine crest, where it narrows as you progress along it, then you descend left into the little ablation valley where the path continues. The way then climbs a steep slope, using fixed ropes or chains in a couple of places, before twisting in numerous zigzags up a great rocky mound on which the **Cabane de Moiry** is perched. ▶

Owned by the Montreux section of the SAC, **Cabane de Moiry** has 96 dormitory places, and is manned from the end of June until the end of September (☎ 027 475 45 34).

Cabane de Moiry, idyllically set upon rocks overlooking the Moiry glacier's icefall

ROUTE 77

Grimentz (Barrage de Moiry: 2249m) –
Haut Tour du Lac/Chemin 2500

Grade:	2
Distance:	12km
Height gain:	640m
Height loss:	640m
Time:	4–5hrs
Location:	South of Grimentz

A circuit of Lac de Moiry, on paths that keep mostly around the 2500m contour, this route is publicised locally as either the 'Haut Tour du Lac' or the 'Chemin 2500'. It's a popular and scenic walk that crosses pastures, visits small tarns, and has direct views of the cascading Glacier de Moiry and a bevy of icebound peaks. It begins at the bus stop at the eastern end of the Moiry dam.

Cross the barrage to the western side and bear left along a track which rises over grassy hillsides. Ignore the first path that cuts off to the left to return towards the lake, and instead take the second path which breaks away at about 2400m, contours along the hillside, crosses a stream and goes alongside a small lake. The path now angles uphill to the junction with another coming from the Alpage de Torrent (the Chemin 2500), and continues ahead in a southerly direction with splendid views of the head of the valley. On reaching a second small tarn there's another signed junction at 2547m, and here you bear left to descend in zigzags to the Moiry roadhead at **Parking du Glacier** (2409m), which has a small *buvette* with refreshments for sale during the high summer.

Pass to the left of the *buvette* onto a track signed to Cabane de Moiry and follow this, rising gently for a few minutes, until at about 2510m you come to a footpath on the left signed to Barrage de Moiry and Col de Sorebois. For most of the way to the dam this path maintains a fairly

even contour, with views that grow in extent down the length of the jade-green Lac de Moiry and into the valley ahead, while looking back the scene is totally different, being dominated by glaciers. Towards the end of the lake the path slopes downhill to meet a junction of tracks, and here you take the obvious route of descent to the **Barrage de Moiry** (*refreshments*) where the walk began.

From the path of the Haut Tour du Lac (the Chemin 2500), practically the whole of the Val de Moiry can be seen in a single glance

ROUTE 78

Grimentz (Barrage de Moiry: 2249m) –
Lac des Autannes (2686m)

Grade:	1–2
Distance:	4km (one way)
Height gain:	437m
Time:	1½–1¾hrs
Location:	Southwest of Grimentz

211

This short and undemanding walk leads to a beautiful mountain lake spread among pastures below the Col de Torrent, one of several crossing points in the ridge dividing Val de Moiry from Val d'Hérens. The lake and its surrounding area make an ideal site for a picnic on a bright summer's day.

The walk could be extended by continuing up to the 2916m Col de Torrent on the ridge some 230m above the lake (another 40mins), where the views are of course more extensive, and from there it is possible to scramble along the ridge to the north as far as the summit of Sasseniere (a further 45–60mins).

From the Barrage de Moiry (*refreshments*) walk across the dam and take the track that swings up the hillside and in 40mins or so brings you to the buildings of **Alpage de Torrent** (2481m) and a four-way junction. Continue ahead on an easy path that rises into the large glacial combe whose backing ridge is buttressed by the Sasseniere and Pointe du Prélet. The path brings you directly to the northern end of **Lac des Autannes**, from where exquisite views can be had looking across the lake to the turmoil of glaciers and snowpeaks that block the head of Val de Moiry. ◀

An **alternative return to Grimentz** is possible by going down-valley to the junction at Alpage de Torrent, then taking the left-hand track which crosses a col below Sex de Marinda and enters a basin within which lies

Below Col de Torrent, the Lac des Autannes glimmers among the pastures

the Lac de Lona. A footpath route continues from there
to Grimentz – detailed in Route 79.

ROUTE 79

Grimentz (Barrage de Moiry: 2249m) –
Sex de Marinda (2906m) – Grimentz (1572m)

Grade:	2
Distance:	15km
Height gain:	720m
Height loss:	1334m
Time:	5–6hrs
Location:	Southwest of Grimentz

Looming above the northwest end of Lac de Moiry, Sex de Marinda is a rocky,
round-topped peak that overlooks Grimentz and intrudes in almost every photo-
graph taken along the main street. A walk to its summit is surprisingly easy but
rewarding, while the continuing walk back to Grimentz visits Lac de Lona,
which lies in a grassy basin below the Becs de Bosson.

Take the morning postbus to the Barrage de Moiry
(*refreshments*), cross the dam to the western side of the
reservoir and walk up the farm road/track that winds into
a high pastureland. At a junction near the Alpage de
Torrent (2481m) turn right on another good track which
doubles back around the mountainside beneath the
oddly shaped rock peak of Motta Blantse and into a
combe between Sex de Marinda and the stony Diablon.
The track continues on an undemanding ascent to a col
at 2792m, known as the Basset de Lona. Here you turn
right for a final short (20mins) but steep climb to what at
first appears to be a gently rounded top, but in fact
proves to be a narrow little summit ridge with a small
cairn at the highest point of **Sex de Marinda**.

The view down to Grimentz is very fine, but the main
attraction is to the south and southeast, along Lac de

Moiry to the glacier and its icefall and up to the mighty Dent Blanche, while across the Sorebois ridge the Weisshorn and its icy neighbours can be clearly seen.

Return to the col and turn right down the track twisting into the wide basin containing Lac de Lona and several other small tarns. The track goes as far as a stream, beyond which a good path continues to the outflow from **Lac de Lona** (2640m), where it divides. Take the right branch and circle around the basin, rising slightly to a red-roofed hut then on to a shoulder below Pointe de Lona, where a sudden descent begins with a short section of metal walkway. The path edges along the rocky flanks of the mountain, losing height steadily, then turns a sharp left corner to reach the ski slopes above Grimentz. Cross a small stream to gain a ski piste/track which crosses an area with ski tows, then continue on to the top station of the Grimentz *téléphérique* at **Bendolla** (2130m). A selection of tracks and paths varying in steepness and directness lead down to the village from here.

ROUTE 80
Grimentz (1572m) – Zinal (1675m)

Grade:	1
Distance:	7.5km (one way)
Height gain:	157m
Time:	2–2½hrs
Location:	Northeast of Grimentz

This pleasant valley walk links the two upper stems of Val d'Anniviers through woodland and by way of the hamlets of Mottec, Pralong and Le Bouillet. It's the sort of walk that comes into its own when bad weather dictates that higher routes are out of the question.

From the valley station of the Bendolla *téléphérique* go onto the main road where a service road opposite slopes down to a large farm building. Continue beside the river to a road bridge, bear right and about 100m later take a footpath on the right which rises into forest. On coming to a junction of paths take the lower option ahead (sign to Ayer, Mottec and Zinal). Ignoring alternatives, this is a fine contouring path through forest virtually all the way to **Mottec** (1556m: *refreshments*), where you come onto the main road leading to Zinal.

Turn right and walk along the road beyond a settlement reservoir, then veer right through the hamlet of **Pralong** (1569m). On the south side of the hamlet rejoin the road for a short distance to **Le Bouillet** (1620m), where a footpath branches slightly left ahead and takes you to **Zinal**, which you enter near the tourist office.

Other routes from Grimentz

- A variation of Route 80 leaves the forest walk to Mottec and goes to **Mission and St-Luc** in 2hrs 15mins. Either return to Grimentz by postbus or make a circular route by descending to Vissoie and crossing the river to Mayoux, where footpaths lead to St-Jean and back to Grimentz.

- A mid-height linking of footpaths takes an interesting route along the mostly wooded hillside heading north to **Vercorin** in 3½hrs.

- From the Bendolla *téléphérique* station, the Chemin de Sotier makes a long southerly contour then a steady ascent to the **Barrage de Moiry** in a little under 2½hrs.

- Two further routes from Bendolla lead to the **Cabane des Becs de Bosson** (2985m). The first of these heads southwest round the Pointe de Lona, then approaches the hut via Pas de Lona in 2¾hrs. The alternative route is marginally shorter, and climbs roughly westward from Bendolla (sign to La Tsarva) and across a shoulder of the Becs de Bosson at 2974m to gain the hut.

ROUTE 81
Tour du Val d'Anniviers

Grade:	3
Distance:	75km
Time:	4–6 days
Start/Finish:	Sierre
Location:	A circuit of both stems of Val d'Anniviers

Making a lozenge-shaped circuit of the valley, the Tour du Val d'Anniviers leads walkers along some of the most scenic trails and visits some of the most interesting and remote lodgings in the district. With an abundance of trails, huts, dortoirs and mountain inns to choose from, many variations of the suggested tour set out below become possible. Although it would be feasible for the fit walker to complete the basic tour in a minimum of four days, the connoisseur would naturally take longer. This is a route to enjoy without the pressure of time. For more information contact: Association du Tour du Val d'Anniviers, Office du Tourisme de Sierre, Case postale 706, CH-3960 Sierre (☎ 027 455 85 35, e-mail: sierre-salgetsch@vsinfo.ch, website: www.anniviers.ch).

Day 1: The tour begins at Sierre railway station down in the Rhône valley at an altitude of only 533m, but then faces a long, steep uphill trek of nearly 1500m to mount the Gorwetschgrat, by which the route enters Val d'Anniviers high above its gorge-defended entrance. This first stage ends after about 6hrs at **Cabane de l'Illhorn** (2145m). However, if the prospect of such a demanding first day does not appeal, it's possible to take a postbus as far as Chandolin, from which Cabane de l'Illhorn is reached by a walk of just 30mins.

Day 2: Having broken the back of height gain, this second stage as far as **Hotel Weisshorn** could include a diversion to the summit of the 3025m Bella Tola (Route 64), given good conditions.

Day 3: The balcony path from Hotel Weisshorn to Zinal (Route 66) is justifiably popular on account of the magical views towards the head of the valley. These views are brought into close proximity by extending the walk from Zinal to the **Cabane du Petit Mountet** (Route 73), which is built on the lateral moraine of the Zinal glacier, with a direct view to the Weisshorn.

Day 4: This stage tackles the west wall of the Val de Zinal stem of Val d'Anniviers, and reverses Route 74 as far as the Sorebois cablecar station, then crosses Col de Sorebois (2840m) and descends to the **Barrage de Moiry** in Val de Moiry for an overnight in the *dortoir* just above the barrage.

Day 5: From the Moiry dam a pleasant hillside path leads to the Bendolla cablecar station above Grimentz, from where another path is joined which continues along the west flank of the Val d'Anniviers to the Crêt du Midi and the **Gîte de Chantovent** (2332m), with its splendid view over the Rhône valley.

Day 6: This final stage involves a descent of almost 1800m to **Sierre** by way of Vercorin and Chippis.

VAL D'HÉRENS

A great cluster of shapely peaks marks the head of Val d'Hérens: Dent Blanche, Wandfluehorn, Tête Blanche, Mont Brulé, Mont Collon and Pigne d'Arolla. Long glacial tongues project northward into a green swathe of pasture and forest – a peaceful, seemingly untroubled land where women can sometimes be seen making hay dressed in traditional costumes as their forbears have done for centuries. In the valley itself, and high on the eastern hillside terrace, several villages maintain a close link with the past, reluctant, it seems, to be drawn into the clamour for tourist favour which has led to a faceless architectural style in some regions. Traditions die hard in the Vals d'Hérens and Hérémence, where the walker can still find solitude among the high meadows and craggy passes that guard them.

ACCESS AND INFORMATION

Location:	Southeast of Sion, and west of the Val d'Anniviers.
Maps:	LS 273T *Montana* & 283T *Arolla* 1:50,000
Bases:	Evolène (1371m), Les Haudères (1436m), Arolla (2006m)
Information:	Office du Tourisme, CH-1983 Evolène (☎ 027 283 40 17, e-mail: evolene@vtx.ch, website: www.evolene-region.ch)
	Office du Tourisme, CH-1984 Les Haudères (☎ 027 283 23 04, e-mail: leshauderes@evolene-region.ch, website: www.evolene-region.ch)
	Office du Tourisme, CH-1986 Arolla (☎ 027 283 15 50, e-mail: info@arolla.com, website: www.arolla.com)
Access:	By postbus from Sion through Val d'Hérens as far as Arolla, Ferpècle and Villa, and throughout Val d'Hérémence as far south as Le Chargeur and the Grande Dixence barrage.

Val d'Hérens is a world so unlike that of the Rhône valley that it's difficult to believe it forms part of the same canton. That difference is exemplified not only by way of its landscapes and heavy-timbered villages, but by its old-time values and a local dialect barely understood by the townsfolk of Sion and Sierre. And by comparison with the Mattertal and Saastal, for example, it seems almost off the beaten track. Of course it's hardly that. But although mountaineers have known the innermost reaches of the valley, its glaciers and its summits for well over a century, tourism has had little impact, and the handful of villages hardly qualify as resorts. All these things are very much in the valley's favour.

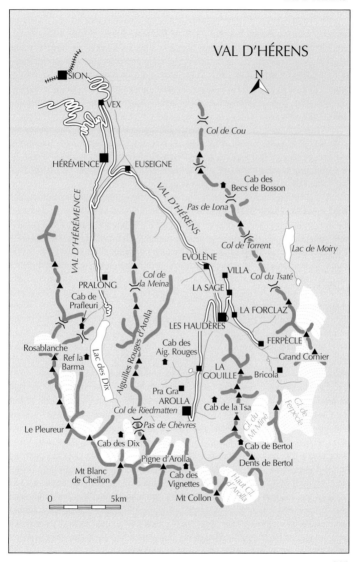

The road into Val d'Hérens climbs out of the Rhône southeast of Sion with a series of hairpin bends that ease at Vex, the first village, where it then forks. Straight ahead, the main road keeps high above the left bank of the Borgne, while the right branch climbs again to the village of Hérémence, noted for its extraordinary modern church (built 1971) that clashes with the graceful timber buildings spread around it. Beyond Hérémence the road pushes on into the southwest stem of the valley (Val d'Hérémence) as far as the huge Grande Dixence barrage, 16km from Vex.

When first built the **Grande Dixence barrage** was the largest, and one of the highest, dams in the world, while Lac des Dix which lies behind it is the largest man-made lake in Switzerland, and is fed by glaciers spilling from Mont Blanc de Cheilon and its neighbours. A summer-only cablecar rises from Le Chargeur at the foot of the dam to the upper dam wall.

Val d'Hérémence is walled to the east by the crusty ridge of the Aiguilles Rouges de Arolla, on the far side of which lies the main Val d'Hérens, accessed by the continuing road from Vex. This remains on the west bank of the Borgne and runs along a fertile hillside before making a hairpin across the Dixence tributary and tunnelling through the bizarre Pyramids d'Euseigne. The 'pyramids' give character to a remnant of old moraine that has weathered into a ragged spine, whose stalagmite-like towers have been protected from erosion by flat stone caps deposited there by the retreating glacier, who knows how many thousands of years ago.

Euseigne village nestles among walnut trees, and a little further south the road crosses to the right bank of the Borgne before entering Evolène, the main village of Val d'Hérens, about 10km from the 'pyramids'. Evolène is a delightful place, crowded above soft pastures and with a lovely view of the Dent Blanche in the southeast. On the outskirts of the village stands a huge memorial piton.

Les Haudères comes next. Just 3.5km from Evolène, and situated at the foot of the Dents de Veisivi at a confluence of glacial streams, the valley forks at this jumbled but attractive village, as does the road. The southeast stem leads among meadow and forest to Ferpècle, the Glacier du Mont Miné and Dent Blanche, with a side-road branching north along the hillside to La Sage and Villa. Meanwhile the southwest branch of the valley becomes the Val d'Arolla, growing more narrow and steep-walled until, below the impressive north face of the 3637m Mont Collon, a stupendous amphitheatre of peak, pasture, pinewood and icefield spreads in a huge arc above Arolla, the highest, smallest and simplest of the valley's three main villages. Here is a world of immense appeal to climber and walker alike, for Arolla is very much a mountaineering centre. It's not much of a village, as far as Alpine villages go, but what it has on its doorstep makes it one of great potential for all who love high mountains.

The curious Pyramids d'Euseigne in the Val d'Hérens

MAIN BASES

EVOLÈNE (1371m) is a charming village of tall, dark-timbered, stone-based houses squeezed above narrow alleyways. Hay barns stand beside shops in the single street, with flowers clustered at almost every window. Small kitchen gardens form neat squares behind some of the chalets, while meadows around the village are shorn for hay or grazed by cattle. Above rise the steep walls of the valley, but views to the south are full of promise. There are three hotels – two graded two-star and a one-star pension – several *dortoirs*, and a campsite with excellent facilities open May to end of October (☎ 027 283 11 44, e-mail: evolene@swisscamps.ch). Evolène has restaurants, PTT, tourist information, banks, a selection of food stores and a few other shops.

LES HAUDÈRES (1436m) stands at a triangle of roads – the old village of traditional Valaisian houses and *mazots* crowded on the eastern side of the valley, and more recent buildings spread along the main road. A little smaller than Evolène, it has a campsite open throughout the year, Camping Molignon (☎ 027 283 12 40, e-mail: molignon@swisscamps.ch, website: www.camping-molignon.ch). There are six hotels and a *chambre d'hôte* (b&b) – for details contact the tourist office. Les Haudères has PTT, shops, restaurants and tourist information.

AROLLA (2006m) is less obviously attractive and smaller than either Les Haudères or Evolène, but its setting is ideal, with Mont Collon in direct view,

221

Pigne d'Arolla nearby, and the abrupt wall opposite marked by the pinnacle of the Aiguille de la Tsa. Arolla is very much the mountaineering centre of Val d'Hérens, with accommodation to suit. There are five hotels and several *dortoirs* – the tourist office can supply a list – and a few houses with apartments to rent. Camping Petit Praz is located below the village, and is open from June to the end of September (☎ 027 283 22 95). There are limited shopping facilities and restaurants, but there's a PTT in the village square.

OTHER BASES

Below Arolla on the road to Les Haudères, Pension du Lac Bleu at **LA GOUILLE** has 9 rooms and 27 dortoir places (☎ 027 283 11 66, e-mail: pension lacbleu@bluewin.ch).   Above

Evolène to the southeast, and reached by road from Les Haudères, the hamlet of **LA SAGE** presides over a pastoral landscape with big mountains in view up-valley. It has Hotel de la Sage (☎ 027 283 24 20, e-mail: hoteldelasage@bluewin.ch), a *chambre d'hôte* (b&b) with three beds (☎ 027 283 11 42), while dortoir accommodation is available with 40 places at Café-Restaurant l'Ecureuil (☎ 027 283 11 38). Nearby **FERPÈCLE**, at the end of the spur road southeast of Les Haudères, has a single 20-bed hotel, the Col d'Hérens, open mid-June to mid-October (☎ 027 283 11 53).

At the head of Val d'Hérémence, Hotel Grande Dixence at **LE CHARGEUR** has modestly priced rooms and *dortoir* accommodation (☎ 027 281 13 22, e-mail: f.gessler@scopus.ch).

Mont Collon is the most prominent peak around Arolla, and is seen from the path leading from the village to Lac Bleu

MOUNTAIN HUTS

CABANE DE LA TSA (2607m) is a long, single-storey building on a rocky spur below the Pointe des Genevois northeast of Arolla. Reached in 1½hrs from Arolla, the hut is owned by the local Société des Guides, has 55 places and is manned from the end of June to late September (☎ 027 283 18 68).

CABANE DE BERTOL (3311m) is an SAC hut perched in an incredibly airy position on a narrow ridge extending northwest of the Dents de Bertol. With 80 dormitory places, the *cabane* is manned in the spring ski-touring season (mid-March to mid-May) and from late June to mid-September (☎ 027 283 19 29, e-mail: bpraz. maistre@bluewin.ch, website: www.lasage.com/ bertol). Because of its position, only those with alpine experience should attempt to reach it.

REFUGE DES BOUQUETINS (2980m) is an unmanned hut set in a splendid position in an isolated cirque dominated by Mont Brulé and Mont Collon. The 3½hr approach is via the easy Haut Glacier d'Arolla. With room for about 20, enquiries should be made on ☎ 021 845 63 21.

CABANE DES AIGUILLES ROUGES (2810m) stands amid a wild landscape of rock below the Aiguilles Rouges d'Arolla, with a fine outlook across the Val d'Arolla to the Veisivi–Bertol wall, and south to Mont Collon. Owned by the Academic Alpine Club of Geneva, it has 80 dormitory places and is manned at weekends during April, then fully from July to late September (☎ 027 283 16 49). The approach walk from Arolla takes about 2½hrs.

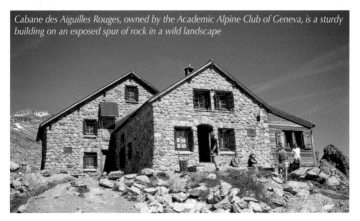

Cabane des Aiguilles Rouges, owned by the Academic Alpine Club of Geneva, is a sturdy building on an exposed spur of rock in a wild landscape

CABANE DES DIX (2928m) is a large and extremely popular hut perched on a nub of rock at the foot of the north face of Mont Blanc de Cheilon in the upper reaches of the Val d'Hérémence, known here as Val des Dix. With places for 146 in its dormitories, the hut is manned during the ski-touring season (mid-March to mid-May) and from July to mid-September (☎ 027 281 15 23, website: www.sac-cas.ch/sektionen/monte-rosa/cabane-des-dix.htm). It is owned by the Monte Rosa section of the SAC based in Martigny, and is reached in 4hrs from Arolla by way of the Pas de Chevres and the easy Glacier de Cheilon, or in 3½hrs from the Barrage de la Grande Dixence.

REFUGE DE LA GENTIANE LA BARMA (2458m) stands on the west side of Lac des Dix. A former cheese dairy, it was adapted as a mountain hut by the Gymnastic Society, La Gentiane, of Mâche, a village down-valley in Val d'Hérémence. The refuge is privately owned and often unmanned. It sleeps 30 and has self-cooking facilities. For enquiries or reservations, contact Café de Amis in Hérémence (☎ 027 281 11 97).

CABANE DE PRAFLEURI (2624m) is privately owned, and stands in the barren Prafleuri glen west of Le Chargeur in Val d'Hérémence. With 59 places, it is manned in April, and from July to the end of September (☎ 027 281 17 80).

Two other SAC huts accessible from the Val d'Hérens are the **DENT BLANCHE** and **VIGNETTES**, but both are reached by way of crevassed glaciers and require full mountaineering gear, so are not included in this guide.

Routes from Evolène
Whilst the more attractive walks of Val d'Hérens are to be had further south, Evolène has a number of recommended outings as briefly described below.

• A 6hr crossing of **Col de la Meina** (2702m) takes the walker from Evolène to Pralong in the Val d'Hérémence.

• North of Col de la Meina, the modest 2998m summit of **Pic d'Artsinol** rewards with a far-ranging panorama. A popular outing, it's usually tackled from the top of a chairlift that rises from the hamlet of Lana (30mins from Evolène) to the alp of La Meina at 2121m.

• On the east flank of the valley the small villages of **Villa** and **La Sage** are reached by footpath from Evolène, and a circular walk could be made which also links these with **Les Haudères**.

ROUTE 82
Les Haudères (1436m) – La Sage (1667m)

Grade:	1
Distance:	2.5km (one way)
Height gain:	231m
Time:	1hr
Location:	NNE of Les Haudères

This short walk makes an undemanding ascent of hill-side above Les Haudères to visit an attractive small village full of old Valaisian chalets and hay barns.

From the village square by the post office in Les Haudères walk away from the PTT along a side-street into the old part of the village, and there turn left on a signed path between buildings in the direction of La Sage and Villa. Soon rise above the village on an easily angled track, now among trees. When the track turns

La Sage, a neat little village on a shelf of hillside above Evolène

225

La Sage: Just before the tarmac road turns by Hotel La Sage, a path on the left climbs a bluff topped by a small white chapel, which provides a viewpoint from which to study the Val d'Hérens. Elsewhere, in the village itself, there are several splendid old buildings. La Sage has a café, shop, tourist information and a postbus link with Les Haudères. For an extended walk turn left along the main road in the village and follow this to the roadhead in Villa – another attractive hamlet about 15mins from La Sage.

sharply to the right, leave it for a footpath which continues straight ahead, and when this forks take the upper path between meadows and on to meet a road near La Sage.

A few paces later bear left along a narrow tarmac road winding between meadows. This eventually turns right up a slope passing Hotel La Sage, then the post office, after which you come into the heart of **La Sage** (*accommodation, refreshments*). ◀

ROUTE 83
Les Haudères
(Ferpècle: 1766m) – Bricola (2415m)

Grade:	2
Distance:	3km (one way)
Height gain:	649m
Time:	2½hrs
Location:	Southeast of Les Haudères

Bricola alp is one of those grassy belvederes from which the walker can gaze directly onto some stunning mountain scenery. Steeply below runs the Glacier de Ferpècle from a tumble of séracs. Opposite rises the dark peak of Mont Miné, with the Mont Miné icefield alongside it. Above this glacier rears the mountain wall that supports the Veisivi peaks, Pointe des Genevois and the needle-like Aiguille de la Tsa. At the head of the Ferpècle glacier sparkle Tête Blanche and Wandfluehorn, while soaring dramatically overhead is the huge cone of Dent Blanche. Bricola makes a splendid destination for a walk, with two possible extensions, as outlined below.

Either take the postbus or drive from Les Haudères to the tiny hamlet of Ferpècle, which lies about 7km to the southeast. At the hamlet entrance (Salay) there's a small parking area to the left of the road next to a large boulder. The footpath begins here, heading up the slope to the left of Hotel du Col d'Hérens (*accommodation, refreshments: open mid-June to mid-October: 20 beds,* ☎ 027 283 11 53) and rising among trees to pass behind a wall surrounding a chapel. The path then breaks away to the right along the hillside among trees and shrubs. After crossing two streams come to a junction (35mins), where you take the left-hand path signed to Cabane Rossier.

The path is clear all the way to Bricola. It climbs in steady twists up the hillside aiming southeast, with views to the glaciers ahead. There are one or two steep sections with tight zigzags, but mostly the way maintains a steady rising traverse, and about 1½hrs after setting out brings you onto the green plateau of **Bricola**, with a tall stone building standing near the edge of the alp and a number of derelict shepherds' huts lying in ruins nearby. (Allow 1hr for the return to Ferpècle from here.)

Two **extensions** of the walk may be made from Bricola that enable you to explore further and to gain even more impressive views.

* The first goes as far as **Les Manzettes** on the way to Cabane de la Dent Blanche, and is reached by taking the broad path leading southeast from the three-storey building. It crosses a sparse region of boulder-pocked pasture and, in an hour or so, gains the moraine crest between the Manzettes and Ferpècle glaciers. The view of these icefields is very fine.
* The second extension enters the high wild combe below the **west face of Dent Blanche** and is graded 3. As with the route to Les Manzettes, take the path heading southeast from the tall building at Bricola, but on reaching a fast-running stream crossed by wooden footbridge leave the main path and climb the slopes on the left, signed to the bivouac hut on the Col de la Dent Blanche. A faint path gives way to cairns and paint flashes. Climbing steeply, for much of the way following the stream, the path brings you into a shallow 'gully' walled on the left by a moraine

crest. At the head of this a very wild landscape is littered with boulders. Bear half-right towards an obvious col, then veer right to get onto a ridge overlooking the glacier-clad country to the south. Dent Blanche looks formidable, if rather foreshortened, from here (50mins from Bricola). Return to the gully and descend with care to Bricola and Ferpècle.

ROUTE 84
Les Haudères (1436m) –
Veisivi (1877m) – Roc Vieux (2213m)

Grade:	2
Distance:	6km (one way)
Height gain:	777m
Time:	2hrs 45mins
Location:	South of Les Haudères

Immediately to the south of Les Haudères, an abrupt mountain wall stands between the two upper stems of Val d'Hérens. Seen from Arolla this dividing wall has some jagged rock teeth along its crest, but there's a minor sub-peak at its northern end which is a noted viewpoint accessible to walkers. This is Roc Vieux.

Leave Les Haudères by walking along the Arolla road heading south. It crosses two glacial torrents: the first drains the Val d'Ferpècle; the second comes from Val d'Arolla. Just after crossing the Borgne d'Arolla turn left on a track by some chalets and follow this as it winds up-valley between pasture and woodland, steadily gaining height and crossing several streams along the way. The track eventually goes beneath power lines (1hr 15mins) and forks. Take the left-hand option, slope down to the main valley stream, cross to the east bank and turn north up the hillside.

The way now twists up through forest and emerges at the alp buildings of **Veisivi** (1877m: 2hrs). Continuing

across meadows the route goes through more woodland as it climbs towards the ridge and comes onto **Roc Vieux** a little under an hour from Veisivi. Enjoy the big mountain views before returning by the same path in about 1½hrs.

The alp of Remointse du Tsaté is found high above La Sage on the way to Col du Tsaté

Other routes from Les Haudères

• Four walkers' passes breach the high ridge on the east side of the valley above Les Haudères. The first and southernmost of these is **Col de la Couronne** (2987m). It's preferable to begin the approach from La Forclaz (reached by postbus or a walk of about 1hr) and climb eastward to the alp of Remointse de Bréona at 2435m. Above this you work a way through a high basin to gain the Col de la Couronne about 4–4½hrs from Les Haudères. This forms one of several routes to Cabane de Moiry, crossing the Moiry glacier on the way.

• **Col de Bréona** is next. This 2915m pass is a mere nick in a junction of ridges northwest of Couronne de Bréona, and for much of the way the route to it shares the Col de la Couronne route outlined above. The col is reached about 4hrs from La Forclaz.

229

- The third crossing point is **Col du Tsaté** (2868m), about 3hrs above and to the east of La Sage. It's a steep walk that leads past several small alp hamlets, and views are splendid for much of the way.

- The easiest of the four passes is the 2916m **Col de Torrent**. Used by trekkers tackling the Chamonix to Zermatt Walker's Haute Route, this is best started from La Sage or Villa and is gained in 3–3½hrs. Below, on the east side of the pass, lies the charming Lac des Autannes, visited on Route 78 from the Barrage de Moiry.

ROUTE 85
*Arolla (2006m) –
Lac Bleu (2090m) – La Gouille (1844m)*

Grade:	3
Distance:	5km
Height gain:	84m
Height loss:	246m
Time:	2hrs
Location:	North of Arolla

Lac Bleu is an attractive little tarn trapped in a ruck of hillside above an alp hamlet north of Arolla. It's a popular local site for picnicking families, and the route to it makes a very fine walk. After leaving the lake, the recommended route descends to La Gouille, from where it's possible to catch a postbus back to Arolla.

From the main square in Arolla by the post office, walk down the short side-street towards Hotel du Glacier, but about 40m before the hotel turn left on a narrow path climbing above chalets. Curving right it eases as you approach the red-shuttered buildings of the Centre Alpin. Pass between the buildings and come to a footpath rising into woodland. At a signed junction take the

upper branch (*Chemin difficile*) – the lower path offers an easier option to Lac Bleu.

The upper path picks a way among alpenrose and juniper, climbing steeply at times to reach the upper tree level, then going across a stream below a group of alp huts. Now cross an open slope (lovely backward views) sliced by more streams, and tackle the first of several slightly exposed sections protected by either fixed chains or cables before re-entering woodland.

The onward route follows an undulating trail across the steep wooded slope. After passing an exposed section overlooking the hamlet of Satarma, you cross a high point, then descend very steeply (caution when wet) to reach two footbridges. There follows another steeply descending section, at the foot of which the path divides. The lower branch is the easier alternative trail seen earlier. Take the upper path, cross two more streams, then twist uphill among larches, eventually coming out to a grassy bluff overlooking the aptly named **Lac Bleu** (1½hrs).

At the eastern (outflow) end of the tarn the path descends past the alp hamlet of **Louché** where cheese and milk are sometimes offered for sale. Just below the buildings veer right when the path forks, and go down a steep grass slope, then through forest to reach the roadside hamlet of **La Gouille** (*accommodation, refreshments*). Just below Pension du Lac Bleu there's a postbus halt for the ride back to Arolla. ▶

Lac Bleu is popular with visitors to Arolla, and is reached by a very pleasant walk of an hour and a half

Pension du Lac Bleu has nine rooms and a 27-place dortoir (☎ 027 283 11 66).

231

ROUTE 86

Arolla (2006m) –
Les Haudères (1436m) – Evolène (1371m)

Grade:	1
Distance:	12km (one way)
Height loss:	635m
Time:	3hrs
Location:	North of Arolla

An easy valley walk to link the three main villages of Val d'Hérens, with plenty of variety, interest and opportunities for refreshment along the way.

Begin by Arolla post office and walk down the side-road towards Hotel du Glacier. Shortly before reaching the hotel take a footpath on the right which slopes downhill and eventually brings you onto the main valley road near Hotel de la Tsa. Cross the road and walk down a track/path. Just beyond the buildings of **La Monta** cross the river and continue down-valley on the right bank. Wander through **Pramousse**, where you then briefly curve away from the river before recrossing to the road a little south of **Satarma** (1808m).

Go through the hamlet, then cross both the road and the river once more. Over the bridge the path/track arcs round meadows towards some buildings, but keeping left of these once again the way takes you back to the Borgne d'Arolla, crosses on a bridge and climbs up to the road shortly before reaching **La Gouille** (1844m: *accommodation, refreshments*). About 200m beyond the pension/restaurant, the continuing path is rejoined on the right-hand side of the road. Waymarked yellow and black, the path eases below the road and joins a track near the little white chapel of St Barthélemy (1823m). Keep ahead, and when the track forks ignore the right-hand option and walk straight ahead, with views down-valley towards Les Haudères. Eventually come onto the main road by a group of handsome old timber chalets. Turn right and walk down the road to **Les Haudères** (1436m: *accommodation, refreshments*).

The main village is set back a little on the right-hand side of the road, but the continuing route to Evolène turns left away from the road by the tourist office. After passing several old houses cross the river to the west bank, then turn right where a path leads directly to **Evolène** (1371m: *accommodation, refreshments*). An alternative waymarked path works a way above the river, goes through woodland and returns to the riverside route for the final approach to the village. Take the postbus back to Arolla.

ROUTE: 87

Arolla (2006m) – Cabane de la Tsa (2607m)

Grade:	2–3
Distance:	3.5km (one way)
Height gain:	707m
Time:	1½hrs
Location:	Northeast of Arolla

Set high above the valley on a spur of rock under the Pointe des Genevois, the Cabane de la Tsa is a single-storey hut used as a base for an assortment of climbs on the mountain wall that divides Val d'Arolla and Val d'Ferpècle. This walk to it, though steep in places, is straightforward and makes a useful training exercise, while views from just outside the hut not only unravel the extent of Val d'Arolla below, but include many fine peaks to the west and southwest – especially the Aiguilles Rouges and Pigne d'Arolla.

Walk down the road from Arolla post office as far as the left-hand hairpin bend where, just to the right of Dortoir Le Sporting (*40 dortoir places,* ☎ 027 398 39 38, e-mail: pralongsporting@bluewin.ch), a footpath descends to the river, signed to Le Tsa. Cross on a footbridge and

Cabane de la Tsa is owned by the Société des Guides du Val d'Hérens, has 55 places and is manned from the end of June to late September (☎ 027 283 18 68). The return to Arolla takes about 1hr by the same path.

continue ahead, rising gently across a meadow and passing a large boulder. The way goes through sparse woodland where the gradient is seldom demanding and height easily gained with loops and zigzags. It then steepens above the treeline, where the terrain becomes increasingly rocky. The hut flag is seen long before the building itself comes into view, for it is a long, low hut concealed by the crags on which it stands. ◀

ROUTE 88
Arolla (2006m) – Plan de Bertol (2664m)

Grade:	2–3
Distance:	5.5km (one way)
Height gain:	684m
Time:	2hrs
Location:	Southeast of Arolla

Plan de Bertol is a rough pasture with a small hut (no services) set in a rock-rimmed basin with glorious views of Mont Collon and its glaciers. The approach is almost always in view of Mont Collon, but the perspective changes on the walk in, which is quite steep and a little exposed at times.

From the post office in Arolla, walk down the road as far as the sharp left-hand hairpin, then go ahead along a minor road (sign to Cab. Bertol) towards Mont Collon and the Glacier d'Arolla. Pass an electricity works building (part of the Grande Dixence scheme) and continue ahead. About 40mins from Arolla, cross a bridge over the glacial torrent and follow waymarks that guide a path up the eastern hillside, tacking to and fro to gain height.

After about 1hr 15mins, and having gained around 350m, the path forks, with the lower option heading off to the Bouquetins refuge (which stands near the head of the Haut Glacier d'Arolla). You take the upper trail, which soon passes below some concrete struts and a statue of the Virgin. Ahead, the view of the Arolla glacier is truly impressive. The path now climbs very steeply in countless zigzags – eroded and exposed in places – before topping a lip of hillside at the **Plan de Bertol** with a small, stone-built *cabane* just ahead.

The outlook from the stone hut is wonderful, while alternative paths entice and reward with more and different views. Just to the right of the hut a path overlooks the Haut Glacier d'Arolla, with Mont Brulé at its head. Another climbs to a viewpoint on the ridge spur that extends the panorama, while the main path in the Bertol basin continues towards the SAC-owned Cabane de Bertol, seen perched on the ridge that tops the hanging valley. ▶

Note: The continuing route to Cabane de Bertol should only be attempted by equipped and competent alpinists, for it tackles a steep and shrinking little glacier, climbs its left-hand edge, then cuts across the glacier in a gently angled slant beneath the rocky cone on which the hut is built. The way then climbs by chains and ladders to gain the *cabane*.

Icefalls and glaciers form a backdrop to the path below Plan de Bertol

ROUTE 89
Arolla (2006m) – Pra Gra (2479m)

Grade:	1–2
Distance:	2.5km (one way)
Height gain:	473m
Time:	1hr
Location:	Northwest of Arolla

The alp of Pra Gra has one of the finest locations in all the Valais. Standing on a grassy terrace overlooking a wonderland of peaks, pastures and glaciers, the collection of grey stone-roofed chalets, barns and cattle byres makes an idyllic setting. Mont Collon is seen at its best from here. Pigne d'Arolla is equally impressive – the big wall supporting the Aiguille de la Tsa blocks the eastward view, but is far enough away to reveal its true stature.

From the village square by the post office walk uphill along the surfaced road. Ignore the first footpath heading towards Lac Bleu near the Centre Alpin, and continue round two more hairpin bends. At the second of these break away to the right along a broad track that winds steadily uphill across steeply sloping pastures. Keep above a small huddle of alp huts and continue to gain height – footpath sections avoid some of the long loops of the track, and the signs to follow are those that indicate the way to Cabane des Aiguilles Rouges. Eventually rise onto the hillside shelf with **Pra Gra** seen to the left.

ROUTE 90
Arolla (2006m) – Cabane des Aiguilles Rouges (2810m) – Lac Bleu (2090m) – Arolla

Grade:	3
Distance:	11km
Height gain:	804m
Height loss:	804m
Time:	4–5hrs
Location:	Northwest of Arolla

Sharing the first part of this route with the walk to Pra Gra (Route 89), the way continues over a wild patch of country marked by streams, boulders, old moraines and screes before reaching the hut, which stands on an exposed spur of rock below the peaks after which it is named. Refreshments are available at the hut, and it's a good place to relax before tackling the fairly strenuous return to Arolla by way of Lac Bleu.

Follow Route 89 as far as **Pra Gra** (1hr), and continue to the right of the alp along a clear broad path heading north across pastures to a wide plateau. Here the path swings left into a wild region of boulder slopes and gravel beds with streams running through. At the head of this minor hanging valley lie moraine ribs, snow slopes and a dying glacier, with Col des Ignes tucked below the summit of La Cassorte. The path veers to the right to cross more boulder slopes and scree, and on a short exposed section a fixed chain gives reassurance. (This stretch is neither difficult nor dangerous unless wet or icy.) The final ascent to the hut is rather steep, but not unduly arduous. **Cabane des Aiguilles Rouges** is reached in about 2½hrs. ▶

Owned by the Academic Alpine Club of Geneva, the hut has 80 dormitory places, and is manned at weekends during April and throughout July to late September (☎ 027 283 16 49). The outlook across the valley to the wall topped by the Aiguille de la Tsa, and beyond to Dent Blanche and the distant Weisshorn, then south to Mont Collon, is very fine.

To descend to Lac Bleu continue above the hut for a short distance following red waymarks (blue/white waymarks take a different route). These guide you northwest, then northeast down into a sloping valley scoured by an almost vanished glacier whose debris remains strewn throughout its bed. After crossing a stream the path becomes more clear, but descending steeply it can seem a tiring route. As you progress, you pass through different layers of vegetation, and views are shuffled and rearranged every few minutes. Though tiring, it's an

Above Pra Gra the path to the Aiguilles Rouges Hut crosses several streams draining fast-receding glaciers

interesting descent, and about an hour from the hut you arrive at the little **Lac Bleu** (2090m).

The path edges above the tarn's south shore, where there's a signed junction. Turn right here and follow the obvious path as it takes an undulating course along the hillside – sometimes among trees, sometimes across open patches with fine views to the head of the valley. Soon after leaving Lac Bleu you descend a little to cross a shallow coombe that sweeps down to Satarma and across the stream that flows through it, and then rise quite steeply on the other side. Ignoring alternative paths, the switchback trail leads directly to Arolla, with a long forest section shortly before you arrive at the village.

ROUTE 91
Arolla (2006m) – Pas de Chèvres (2855m)

Grade:	2–3
Distance:	5km (one way)
Height gain:	849m
Time:	2¾–3hrs
Location:	West of Arolla

Both Pas de Chèvres and the neighbouring Col de Riedmatten cross the high ridge separating Val d'Arolla from Val des Dix. Situated within a few metres of one another, they enjoy almost identical views, and both are used as a means of approach to the Cabane des Dix, which lies on the west side of the Cheilon glacier. However, the two passes are very different. While Col de Riedmatten is a narrow, rock-guarded cleft with a steep descent on the west side, the Pas de Chèvres is an open saddle, easy-angled on the east flank, but with an almost vertical rock wall on the other. This rock wall is surmounted by three fixed ladders, at the foot of which lies a chaos of rocks. Many walkers baulk at the idea of descending these ladders, so Route 92 offers the alternative route via Col de Riedmatten, with the suggestion that a return should be made with an **ascent** of the ladders to Pas de Chèvres – for climbing the ladders is easier for some than descending them. The route described here, then, leads to the Pas de Chèvres but not over it.

Walk up the road from Arolla's post office, and at the first hairpin bend leave the road for a track going ahead, then winding through woods of Arolla pine come to the large Grand Hotel Kurhaus. Immediately before the hotel bear right on a path waymarked with yellow flashes. The path climbs through woodland and is marked at all junctions. Signs to follow are for Cabane des Dix, Pas de Chèvres and Col de Riedmatten.

On coming to a lone building (Tsijiore Nouve) turn right and rise over open slopes, now above the treeline, and you'll reach the derelict huts of **Remointse d'Arolla** (2399m). Continue along the path which parallels the lateral moraine of the Tsijiore Nouve glacier, with splendid

An uncompromising landscape of rock, ice and snow spreads into the distance from the Pas de Chèvres

Note: Should you feel confident to descend the ladders and continue to Cabane des Dix, take care as you do so, for some of the rungs are so close to the rock-face that only the tips of your boots can be used. From the foot of the third ladder follow a faint path guided by red paint marks which stay close to the rockface heading north, then curve leftward and join the Col de Riedmatten route where it forks. One route heads down-valley to Lac des Dix, but you take the left branch and weave amongst a chaos of rocks and boulders to the edge of the glacier. The rest of the route is described below as Route 92. Allow about 45mins from Pas de Chèvres to Cabane des Dix.

views of Pigne d'Arolla and the glacier itself. After some time cross a stream on a wooden bridge and continue to gain height until reaching a rough bowl of rock-strewn pastureland where the path forks (2780m: 2½hrs). The right-hand path goes to the Col de Riedmatten, while you take the left-hand route and climb to the ridge whose lowest point is the **Pas de Chèvres**.

The ladders on the west side appear formidable, while across the Cheilon glacier can be seen the Cabane des Dix perched on a rocky knoll, with the great north face of Mont Blanc de Cheilon to its left. Looking back to the southeast there's a fabulous panorama which includes the tip of the Matterhorn poking above the horizon. Allow at least 1½hrs for the return to Arolla by the same path. ◀

ROUTE 92
Arolla (2006m) – Col de Riedmatten (2919m) – Cabane des Dix (2928m)

Grade:	3
Distance:	7km (one way)
Height gain:	963m
Height loss:	100m
Time:	4–4½hrs
Location:	West of Arolla

The alternative route for crossing the ridge dividing Val d'Arolla and Val des Dix, Col de Riedmatten, lies about 200m north of the Pas de Chèvres. Although there are no ladders to contend with, descent on the west side is very steep and gritty, and demands great care to negotiate. The onward route to Cabane des Dix involves crossing a glacier which, if the marker poles are followed, is by a crevasse-free area.

Follow the Pas de Chèvres path (Route 91) as far as the junction in the rough rock-strewn basin at about 2780m (2½hrs). The sign here gives 1hr 20mins to Cabane des Dix via Col de Riedmatten, but it could take a little longer. Leaving the Pas de Chèvres route to the left, take the right-hand path that rises to the upper basin and a vegetated moraine rib, then turns to the left towards the narrow gap of the col. On the way you gain a splendid view of the north face of Mont Blanc de Cheilon over the dip of neighbouring Pas de Chèvres. Arriving in the cleft of **Col de Riedmatten** (3hrs) views to the west are restricted, but it's worth pausing here to enjoy the immense backward view, with its sea of peaks draped with glaciers and snowfields beyond brown-grey screes and moraine banks. ▶

Note: For an even broader panorama take the narrow ledge path on the right onto the ridge for a few minutes – but take care, as it requires scrambling in places.

Col de Riedmatten is a rocky cleft at almost 3000m, from which a magnificent panorama is gained

Cabane des Dix is owned by the Monte Rosa section of the SAC. It's a large and busy hut with places for 146, and is manned from mid-March to mid-May, and from July to the end of September (☎ 027 281 15 23). Refreshments are available when open. The return to Arolla by the same path will take about 2½hrs, but you could vary the route by climbing the ladders to Pas de Chèvres and descending to Arolla from there.

The descent of the gully on the west side of the col is steep and potentially dangerous when wet or icy. Grit and small pebbles underfoot demand caution, and when the gradient eases about 10mins below the col, you should keep alert for red waymarks where the path forks. The right-hand trail continues down-valley to Lac des Dix, but for the Cabane des Dix you turn left (southwest) and weave through a chaotic mess of rocks and boulders guided by paint marks and a few cairns to reach the edge of the Glacier de Cheilon. Marker poles direct the route across the ice. Although the way should be crevasse-free, it is important to keep to the marked route and not to lose sight of the poles should visibility be poor. In reasonable conditions the hut can be seen perched like some impossible castle on its knoll on the far side.

Once off the glacier a path edges below the south side of the knoll, then cuts back to climb the final slope to reach the **Cabane des Dix**. ◀

ROUTE 93

Le Chargeur (2141m) – Cabane des Dix (2928m)

Grade:	2–3
Distance:	10km (one way)
Height gain:	787m
Time:	3–3½hrs
Location:	South of Le Chargeur (Val d'Hérémence)

This approach to the Cabane des Dix is very different to that from Arolla. There is no pass to cross, but instead there's a long lakeside walk followed by a steadily rising path along the lateral moraine that borders the Cheilon glacier before the final ascent is made up the west side of the knoll on which the hut is perched. It's an easier walk than Route 92, but every bit as interesting.

If you're staying in Val d'Hérens and have no transport, take the bus to the

Grande Dixence dam at Le Chargeur at the head of Val d'Hérémence. Note that the bus service in Val d'Hérémence is privately operated, so take the postbus from Arolla (Les Haudères or Evolène) to Vex and change there for Le Chargeur. There is a hotel at Le Chargeur and a cablecar to the top of the barrage wall which saves about 30mins of walking up a steeply twisting path.

From the western end of the Grande Dixence barrage walk along the right-hand side of the lake on a broad track which soon passes through several tunnels. The first of these is the longest and darkest, but is lit by electric lights. A switch at the tunnel entrance gives 5mins of illumination. As you progress alongside the lake fine views of the high peaks at the head of the valley draw you on.

At the southern end of the lake, about 20m before the track ends, take a signed path climbing steeply on the right. Rising at first over rough slopes of grass and rock, the way then eases onto the crest of lateral moraine that, in its higher reaches, borders the fast-receding Glacier de Cheilon. As you work your way along this moraine path, so the deep V of the Pas de Chèvres can be seen in the ridge on the western side of the valley.

Near the end of the moraine the path descends into the little ablation valley on the right; then, rising over grass slopes and scree, it gains a saddle on the north-west shoulder of the Tête Noire – on the way being rewarded by a surprise view across the western ridge to a ragged line of peaks which includes the Matterhorn, appearing like a distant stilleto point.

On gaining the saddle, the impressive north face of Mont Blanc de Cheilon is revealed, as is the hut on its abrupt knoll just below. The path slopes down into a glacial plain, crosses one or two streams, then climbs the slope leading directly to the **Cabane des Dix**. For hut details please see notes at the end of Route 92.

ROUTE 94

Le Chargeur (2141m) –
Col de Riedmatten (2919m) – Arolla (2006m)

Grade:	3
Distance:	15km
Height gain:	778m
Height loss:	913m
Time:	5½hrs
Location:	South of Le Chargeur (Val d'Hérémence)

The walk described here is one of the classic routes of the Valais. It's quite a tough walk, but it's scenically spectacular. As there are no opportunities for refreshment between Le Chargeur and Arolla, it is essential to take food and drink with you. Choose a clear day with a settled forecast and set out early.

As with Route 93, travel to Le Chargeur by bus, then ride the cablecar (or walk) to the top of the Grande Dixence barrage and head south alongside Lac des Dix, as described in the previous route. At the southern end of the lake (Pas du Chat, 2371m) take the steeply climbing path on the right. Mounting a rock and grass slope, in 10mins reach a junction marked with yellow signs fixed to a horizontal rock. Bear left (the alternative goes to Cabane des Dix) and go down to a suspension bridge spanning a narrow gorge. Across this follow the continuing path through the gorge and over a stony hillside on the east side of the valley.

Rising through the valley the waymarked path swings left and climbs steeply to gain a sloping meadow at 2550m. Turn right and angle uphill to cross a bluff, after which the path contours as far as an avalanche-scoured gully. Now climb a very steep slope of rock, grit and shale before making a delicate crossing of the gully – **caution needed!**

Once across this, contour briefly before climbing again – this time up a grass slope overlooking the Cheilon glacier, with Mont Blanc de Cheilon towering ahead. After a fairly lengthy level stretch the way crosses a slope of rust-coloured scree, then a rock tip that leads to the foot of the pass. Turn left and make the ascent through a rocky gully. ▸

Note: At the foot of the gully the path forks and red waymarks lead a faint right-hand trail to the ladders that climb to the Pas de Chèvres, about 200m to the south, for an alternative crossing.

The steep climb brings you onto the **Col de Riedmatten** (2919m), about 4hrs from Le Chargeur. This classic rocky pass presents an extraordinary window onto a world of mountains, glaciers, moraines and rough pastures. Mont Collon impresses to the southeast, as does the Dent Blanche almost due east. The Matterhorn's summit can be seen on the skyline, but everywhere you look there's something special to train the eye on. It's a tremendous panorama, and one that can be extended even further by climbing left on a narrow shelf of a path that leads up onto the ridge with a little scrambling.

Descending the eastern side of the pass a clearly defined trail leads down into a basin of grass and rock to join the route from the Pas de Chèvres. You then head down-valley through pastures and finally woodland before entering **Arolla**.

ROUTE 95
*Le Chargeur (2141m) – Cabane de Prafleuri
(2624m) – Col des Roux (2804m) – Le Chargeur*

Grade:	2
Distance:	7.5km
Height gain:	663m
Height loss:	663m
Time:	3–3½hrs
Location:	Southwest of Le Chargeur (Val d'Hérémence)

The Combe de Prafleuri is ill-named, for the 'plain of flowers' to which it refers was savagely quarried during construction work for the Grand Dixence dam, and half a century later the scars have not yet mended – although vegetation is slowly but surely taking root. The present Cabane de Prafleuri – a trekker's hut which stands in this tributary valley between Col de Prafleuri and Col des Roux – replaces the old workmen's hostel that served as a mountain hut for several decades. Although its site has a bleak outlook, the hut is an important staging post for trekkers tackling the Walker's Haute Route. From the Prafleuri cabane the circular walk described here adopts the Haute Route up to the Col des Roux, then angles down on the southern side to Lac des Dix for a return to Le Chargeur.

From the top of the Grande Dixence barrage walk along the track on the western side of the reservoir for about 2mins (see Route 93), then bear right when it forks. Twisting uphill reach a tunnel entrance at 2433m. A few paces beyond this take a signed path which tops a rocky bluff, then turns into the narrow, stony Combe de Prafleuri (watch for ibex and marmots). Keep on the south side of the valley over rock tips and landslide areas. When it narrows below the hut the way climbs along the left of a stream, then via waymarks and red-painted arrows up a rocky section to gain a desolate upper basin. At a path junction turn left and climb a short steep slope to the **Cabane de Prafleuri** (2624m, 1hr 50mins: *accommodation, refreshments*). ◀

Cabane de Prafleuri is privately owned, but is manned in April and from July to the end of September. It has 59 dormitory places (☎ 027 207 30 67).

Continue up-valley beyond the hut for about 40m, then bear left for Col des Roux – there are waymarks on rocks. Between here and the col lies a slope of rocks and boulders, but a good path has been created that winds in easy zigzags, and the 180m of ascent are achieved without difficulty. So come onto **Col des Roux** (2804m), about 20mins from the hut, to be confronted by a splendid scene where the Lac des Dix spreads through the valley below towards Mont Blanc de Cheilon.

Take the descending path on the south side of the col, dropping to more boulders before entering the pastures of a shallow valley below the Glacier des Écoulaies. Heading towards a small refuge, you then swing left to cross a stream and ease round the hillside to **Refuge de la Gentiane la Barma** (2458m). This privately owned refuge has been created in a one-time cheese dairy. Often unmanned, it can sleep 30 and has good self-catering facilities. For reservations, ☎ 027 281 11 97.

Immediately before the refuge turn left on a descending trail that brings you onto the lakeside track. Turn left and walk back along the track to the dam at the northern end of Lac des Dix.

Other routes in Val d'Hérémence

The valley offers peaceful walking in a green landscape. There are high routes with passes to cross, mountain bluffs to traverse and water courses to follow. These water courses are known in

The descent from Col des Roux leads to Lac des Dix, with Mont Blanc de Cheilon in the distance

the Valais region as *bisses*. Wooden conduits have been constructed and ditches dug to lead streams along otherwise summer-dry mountainsides in order to irrigate crops. Footpaths accompany these canals to facilitate occasional maintenance work or as an aid to farmers moving from one parcel of land to another. Two *bisse* walks are recommended.

- The **Bisse d'Ernaya** links Val d'Hérémence with Val d'Hérens. It begins by the Dixence stream at Leteygeon (1559m) and swings round the northern hillside separating the two valleys to finish at La Luette (997m) in Val d'Hérens south of Euseigne.

- The other route follows the **Ancien Bisse de Vex** from Mayens de Sion (high on the western hillside near the mouth of Val d'Hérens) south to Planchouet and Lavanthier. Bus routes serve villages at both ends of this route.

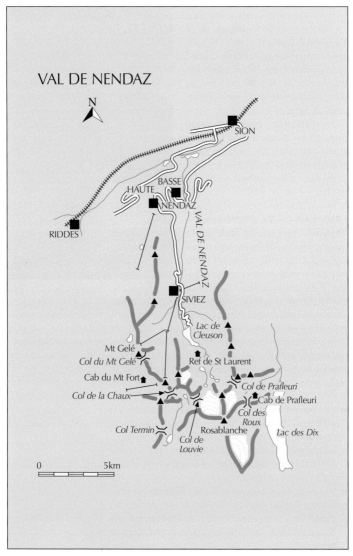

VAL DE NENDAZ

N

SION

RIDDES

BASSE

HAUTE NENDAZ

VAL DE NENDAZ

SIVIEZ

Lac de Cleuson

Mt Gelé

Col du Mt Gelé

Ref de St Laurent

Cab du Mt Fort

Col de Prafleuri

Col de la Chaux

Cab de Prafleuri

Col des Roux

Col Termin

Rosablanche

Lac des Dix

Col de Louvie

0   5km

VAL DE NENDAZ

One of the smallest of the southern glens to flow into the Rhône, the little Val de Nendaz is surprisingly pastoral despite being linked with the ski grounds of Verbier to the west, but in its upper reaches, above Lac de Cleuson, meadow and forest are traded for a wilderness of screes, moraines, bare rock slabs and shrinking glaciers. It is, nevertheless, a valley of considerable charm, with modest facilities in summer that include a privately owned mountain refuge that could be useful for walkers keen to explore the high country to the south, where the gentle strolls of the lower valley contrast with the challenge of high passes and a no-man's land traversed by the Walker's Haute Route.

ACCESS AND INFORMATION

Location:	Southwest of Sion, and west of Val d'Hérémence
Maps:	LS 273T *Montana* & 283T *Arolla* 1:50,000
Bases:	Haute Nendaz (1365m), Siviez (Super Nendaz: 1733m)
Information:	Office de Tourisme, CH-1997 Haute Nendaz (☎ 027 289 55 89, e-mail: info@nendaz.ch, website: www.nendaz.ch)
Access:	Served by postbus from Sion, a road snakes up the south flank of the Rhône valley to Haute Nendaz before easing along to Siviez.

The valley projects from an open, sunny terrace set high above the Rhône, and is gained by a scenic road that climbs among orchards of peach and apricot for 16km or so from Sion to Haute Nendaz. On the journey long views are directed through the Rhône's valley and across to the wall of Oberland peaks to the north, but then they turn to focus on the shelf of neat chalets and meadows that marks the entrance to Val de Nendaz proper. The valley slices to the south, forest-draped, pasture-trim and gentle. A few hay barns and chalets stand in the tree-shrouded meadows, then as the forest thins and the valley opens, the modern ski resort of Super Nendaz (Siviez) is reached.

More meadows stretch out to the south and the valley forks. In the southwest streams drain down from the high snows and small glaciers of Mont Gelé and Mont Fort, but the main branch leads to the barrage at Lac de Cleuson, where the road ends. Beyond the reservoir the valley, now known as Val de Cleuson, veers southeastward into a wild sanctuary headed by the snowy mass of Rosablanche (3336m) and the icefield of the Grand Désert. Up there a great knot of peaks makes a formidable wall, but in its projecting ridges this wall is breached by two or three walkers' passes that offer ways over the mountains to Lac des Dix and Val d'Hérémence in the east, and to Val de Bagnes in the west – very different worlds to that of the upper Val de Nendaz.

Nendaz has a number of mechanical aids to service a growing winter tourist trade, with Super Nendaz providing access to an extensive area of downhill terrain that spills over the western ridges into the great basin of Verbier. Happily there are still plenty of footpaths that shy away from such mechanical intrusion. Some of these follow irrigation channels (*bisses*), others wind among sloping pastures and masses of wild flowers, while yet more entice into the uncompromising landscapes of the upper regions.

Though little known and quietly unassuming, Val de Nendaz is definitely worth a visit.

MAIN BASES

HAUTE NENDAZ (1365m) gives little impression that the valley hidden behind it among pine forests holds such appeal, for the village faces away across the Rhône. There are several two- and three-star hotels and a few lower-priced auberges (lists available from the tourist office), but rather limited shopping facilities.

SIVIEZ (1733m) stands deep inside Val de Nendaz and, apart from the little alp hamlet of Les Chottes on the hillside above, is the only settlement to do so. This collection of hotels and apartment blocks has opened the valley to the downhill ski trade, and although it is very quiet in summer there are several apartments for rent.

MOUNTAIN HUTS

REFUGE DE ST LAURENT (2485m) stands on a rise at the southern end of Lac de Cleuson, some 300m above the reservoir, and is reached by a track or dirt road. Privately owned, the hut has 32 places and is manned from July to September (☎ 027 288 50 05).

At the foot of the Grand Désert glacier, a small tarn has been exposed by the receding ice

ROUTE 96

Siviez (1733m) –
Lac de Cleuson (2186m) – Siviez

Grade:	2
Distance:	11km
Height gain:	594m
Height loss:	594m
Time:	4hrs
Location:	South of Siviez

From this high path which runs along the eastern side of the valley, views are gained of mountains at the head of the Val de Cleuson and of the lush pastures that lead to the reservoir. There are woodlands and shrubs and plenty of wild flowers along the route, which also follows the course of a long-disused *bisse* – of which there are few signs remaining.

The path begins in the northeastern corner of the car park at Super Nendaz, on the right bank of the Printse – the stream which drains the valley. The way climbs for about 15mins to reach the alp hamlet of **Les Chottes** (1858m), an attractive huddle of chalets and barns that make a direct contrast to the modern buildings below. Head south (to the right) on a track which runs along the hillside – avoid that which slopes back down to the valley – and steadily gain height through woodland. About 1.5km from Les Chottes the path climbs steeply in zigzags with views opening to the south, and comes to a signed junction (2260m: 1hr 15mins). Bear right along a level path tracing the course of the Ancien Bisse de Chervé.

The footpath, which is narrow in places, makes a traverse of the hillside among shrubs and flowers, with the mountains ahead looking fine and the barrage at Lac de Cleuson coming into view below. Continue beyond the southern end of the lake until the path forks and you can descend to a narrow stretch of valley and a signpost.

Bear right and wander back along the dirt road above the reservoir to reach the barrage at its northern end.

To return from the barrage to Siviez by the direct route will take a little over an hour. Either descend directly along the road leading from the dam, or break away to the left on a footpath that leads along the crest of a wooded moraine on the western side of the valley, then down across pastures to Siviez.

ROUTE 97
Siviez (1733m) – Refuge de St Laurent (2485m)

Grade:	2
Distance:	6.5km (one way)
Height gain:	763m
Time:	3–3½hrs
Location:	South of Siviez

The approach to Refuge de St Laurent described here is an extension of Route 96. It is not the shortest nor easiest approach, but it's probably the nicest.

Follow directions given in Route 96 as far as the south-eastern end of Lac de Cleuson, where the path descends to a signed junction on the dirt road (La Gouille: about 2½hrs). Instead of turning back along the lakeside, bear left and follow the track which soon crosses the stream on a stone-built hump-backed bridge, and continues with several twists as far as the refuge.

Other routes in Val de Nendaz
To explore the high country south of the St Laurent refuge take the path which leads up to the Lac du Grand Désert (2667m) below the Bec des Etagnes and continue on the east side of its feeder stream. There's a small tarn lying at the foot of the Grand Désert glacier in exceedingly wild

At the upper reaches of Val de Nendaz, the bridge takes a track to the St Laurent refuge

country, and above this cairned routes cut across a stony landscape heading both east and west.

- Heading east you can follow cairns, waymarks and broken stretches of path to the 2965m **Col de Prafleuri** (2¼hrs from St Laurent), and from there descend into the Prafleuri glen to the **Cabane de Prafleuri** (hut details under Val d'Hérens section).

- By following waymarks on the west side of the Grand Désert glacier, you can climb to the splendid **Col de Louvie** (2921m) for views of the Grand Combin and distant Mont Blanc massif. For a longer walk continue over the col on a path that descends a narrow, rocky little valley, then forks. The right branch climbs to **Col de la Chaux** (2940m), while the continuing path leads to the easy **Col Termin** (2648m) and the delightful Sentier des Chamois. Both routes are used to access the **Cabane du Mont Fort** (see Val de Bagnes section below).

* **Cabane du Mont Fort** can also be reached by a more direct route from Siviez which rises through Val Tortin (southwest of Siviez), edges the Glacier de Tortin and crosses **Col des Gentianes** (2980m) to join a track below Col de la Chaux. However, the aesthetics of this route are sadly compromised by a plethora of mechanical lifts in and above Val Tortin.

* The 2804m **Col du Mont Gelé** and lower **Col de Chassoure** (2739m) suggest yet more ways for walkers to cross to **Cabane du Mont Fort**, but the routes to these are also fussed with the paraphernalia of the ski industry. However, a 30min scramble to the summit of Mont Gelé from the col of the same name gives a spectacular view towards the Mont Blanc massif which compensates for the pylons and tows below.

* As for easier options, the route of the **Ancien Bisse de Chervé**, partly followed on Route 96, extends for almost 11km, and may be walked in its entirety from Thyon 2000 (reached by postbus from Sion) to Lac de Cleuson. This fine hillside traverse takes about 4hrs.

* Another recommended path accompanies the **Ancien Bisse du Milieu** and the **Bisse Vieux** to link Haute Nendaz with the village of Veysonnaz on the hillside at the eastern entrance to the valley. From Haute Nendaz the way cuts into the initial stages of Val de Nendaz, then returns along the opposite hillside. Walking this path takes about 3½hrs.

VAL DE BAGNES

Val de Bagnes makes a startling contrast to the valley of the Rhône, for while the Rhône is a broad, flat-bottomed trench with vines and orchards on its slopes, the valley of the Drance de Bagnes is deep and narrow, with rugged flanks and alps perched high above. There's a string of small villages and hamlets in the bed of the valley, and big mountains liberally plastered with snowfield and glacier crowded at its head. Walks are mostly demanding, as befits the terrain, but viewpoints are spectacular, plentiful and sufficiently memorable to demand a return for more. In short, Val de Bagnes is one of the gems of the Valais region.

ACCESS AND INFORMATION

Location:	Southeast of Martigny
Maps:	LS 282T *Martigny* & 283T *Arolla* 1:50,000
Bases:	Sembrancher (717m), Verbier (1490m), Le Châble (821m), Fionnay (1491m)
Information:	Société de developpement, CH-1933 Sembrancher (☎ 027 85 12 23)
	Verbier/Bagnes Tourisme, Place centrale, CH-1936 Verbier (☎ 027 775 38 88, e-mail: info@verbier.ch, website: www.verbier.ch)
	Office du Tourisme du Châble, CH-1934 Le Châble (☎ 027 776 16 82, e-mail: bagnestourisme@verbier.ch)
Access:	By road from Martigny via Sembrancher. A local branch railway, the St-Bernard Express, travels between Martigny and Le Châble. The postbus serves the valley between Le Châble and Mauvoisin, Le Châble and Moay via Bruson, and Le Châble and Verbier. There is also cablecar link between Le Châble and Verbier.

While the great bay of hillside around Verbier is devoted to downhill skiing, with all the attendant piste-scarring and mechanical intrusion that goes with it, the vast majority of Val de Bagnes remains either green and pastoral or untamed mountain wilderness. 'The valleys here are all tremendously deep, with steeply cut walls, and lovely alps upon their higher slopes' – so wrote J. Hubert Walker, unchallenged arbiter of all that was good in Alpine scenery. And he was right.

The hugely elegant Combin massif dominates from the south, a Mont Blanc look-alike with sprawling glaciers, snowdomes and rocky protrusions. Viewed from the Sentier des Chamois or the shores of Lac de Louvie, the 4314m Grand

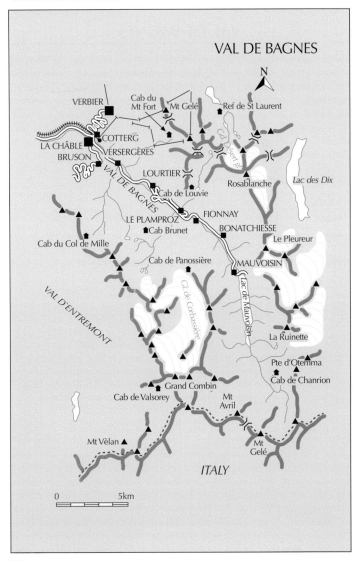

VAL DE BAGNES

N

VERBIER
Cab du Mt Fort
Mt Gelé
Ref de St Laurent
COTTERG
LA CHÂBLE
VERSERGÈRES
BRUSON
Col Dé sert Bl
LOURTIER
Rosablanche
Lac des Dix
Cab de Louvie
VAL DE BAGNES
LE PLAMPROZ
FIONNAY
Cab Brunet
BONATCHIESSE
Cab du Col de Mille
Le Pleureur
Cab de Panossière
MAUVOISIN
VAL D'ENTREMONT
Gl. de Corbassière
Lac de Mauvoisin
La Ruinette
Pte d'Otemma
Cab de Chanrion
Grand Combin
Cab de Valsorey
Mt Avril
Mt Vèlan
Mt Gelé

ITALY

0   5km

Combin presents one of the most sublime scenes in all the Alps. But it is not alone, for there are others, too, worth seeking out.

South of the monstrous Mauvoisin barrage, in the secretive, partly hidden upper reaches of the valley, a fresh horizon is revealed. This is a landscape of big mountains, glaciers and chaotic moraines, a no-compromise environment of immense appeal. From this perspective Grand Combin wears a different face, with rock walls supporting both snowbank and icefield. To the east rises that easy peak (but superb viewpoint) of La Ruinette, with Mont Blanc de Cheilon behind it. The Glacier du Giétro curls round projecting spurs, bulldozing moraine debris that is being softened by a variety of alpine plants. Other highways of ice and rock spill from more distant peaks, some of which carry the Italian border on their crests. Pools and tarns left by retreating glaciers reflect this mountain backdrop, and the Cabane de Chanrion makes a useful base from which to explore both mountain and dividing glen. Weeks of high summer could be rewardingly spent in such surroundings.

In other sections of Val de Bagnes views look west to Mont Blanc and its bristling aiguille neighbours, or northwest to the Dents du Midi. Ridge crests of grass and woodland make ideal belvederes, and there's no shortage of accommodation to exploit some of the finest views. Val de Bagnes will reward the mountain connoisseur many times over.

MAIN BASES

SEMBRANCHER (717m) is a good location from which to explore other valleys besides that of Bagnes, since it lies at the entrance to Val d'Entremont, with Val Ferret nearby. A small, unpretentious stone-walled village with limited pension accommodation but with two campsites, it has a handful of foodstores and a restaurant. Sembrancher is served by postbus and railway.

VERBIER (1490m) is perched high above the valley on the northern hillside above Le Châble, with a sprawl of hotels, apartment blocks and chalets, and numerous mechanical devices swinging up to the high ridges, lacing the peaks and pastures in giant webs of cable. There are heated indoor and outdoor swimming pools, a climbing wall, a parapente school and privately run climbing schools. Verbier has plenty of two-, three- and four-star hotels, and many more chalets and apartments offering accommodation for a week or so. At The Bunker (☎ 027 771 66 01, e-mail: sleep@thebunker.ch, website: www.thebunker.ch) low-price rooms are available for singles and groups. Although Verbier's main season is clearly the winter, the resort does not 'die' in summer, and most restaurants and shops remain in operation except for the mid-season months of April–May and October–November.

Le Châble in the Val de Bagnes

LE CHÂBLE (821m) is a modest rural community at the end of the railway line on the left bank of the river below Verbier. It's the capital of the Bagnes commune, which at around 150km² makes it the largest in Switzerland. With Villette just across the river, there are four hotels, several apartments and a caravan site, a small number of shops and restaurants, and a tourist office.

FIONNAY (1491m) is a quiet, traditional, one-time mountaineering centre and the southernmost village in Val de Bagnes. Its hotel, the two-star Grand Combin (☎ 027 778 11 22, e-mail: gdcombin @fionnay.ch, website: www.fionnay.ch), also has 48 *dortoir* places. A little further up-valley Bonatchiesse has a low-key campsite, Camping Forêt des Mélèzes (☎ 027 776 16 82).

OTHER BASES

Most villages in Val de Bagnes offer some form of accommodation for visitors. Perhaps the best is at **BRUSON**, a little resort south of Le Châble with a six-bed pension and two places with *dortoir* accommodation for groups. **LOURTIER** also has 50 *dortoir* places at La Vallée, as well as 33 conventional beds (☎ 027 778 11 75, e-mail: info@vallee.ch, website: www.vallee.ch), while at **MAU-VOISIN** below the dam, Hotel du Mauvoisin has 20 beds and 30 *dortoir* places (☎ 027 778 11 30, website: www.mauvoisin.ch). Finally, **CHAMPSEC**, some 5km southeast of Le Châble, has a campsite at 920m, La Sasse (☎ 027 778 13 23, e-mail: gabbudwilly@dransnet.ch).

MOUNTAIN HUTS

CABANE DU MONT FORT (2457m) is popular with skiers, day visitors and trekkers tackling the Walker's Haute Route. Owned by the Jaman section of the SAC, this hut stands on a grassy bluff due south of Mont Gelé, and is easily reached from Verbier. Refurbished in 2001/2002, it can sleep 66 in *dortoir*s and 4–6 bedded rooms, and is manned December to mid-May, and late June to mid-September (☎ 027 778 13 84, email: dbruchez@axiom.ch).

CABANE DE LOUVIE (2250m) enjoys a wonderful panoramic view across the Val de Bagnes to the Combin massif from its location near Lac de Louvie high above Fionnay, from which it is reached by a very steep path in a little under 2hrs. The *cabane* has 54 places in four dormitories and is open from mid-June to mid-September (☎ 027 778 17 40).

CABANE DE CHANRION (2462m) is situated among high pastures near the very head of the valley. Owned by the Genevoise section of the SAC, it has 85 *dortoir* places and is manned mid-March to mid-May, and mid-June to mid-September (☎ 027 778 12 09). It may be reached by a 4hr walk from the roadhead at the Mauvoisin barrage.

CABANE DE PANOSSIÈRE (2645m) is also known as the Cabane Françoise-Xavier Bagnoud (FXB). This popular hut stands on the right bank of the Corbassière glacier, which flows down the north flank of the Combin massif. With 103 places and a guardian in residence during the spring ski-touring season and in the summer, the hut is reached by a 4hr walk from Fionnay (☎ 027 771 33 22).

CABANE BRUNET (2104m) is located on the south side of the valley a little west of the torrent that drains the Corbassière glacier, and is reached by a path from Lourtier. The hut is open from mid-December to the end of April, and from July to the end of September, and has 65 places (☎ 027 778 18 10).

CABANE DU COL DE MILLE (2473m) has a magnificent outlook towards the Mont Blanc massif from its position on the ridge dividing Val de Bagnes from Val d'Entremont. Privately owned, and with 40 places, the hut was built in 1996 and is manned from June to October (☎ 079 221 15 16).

ROUTE 98
*Verbier (1490m) – Clambin (1730m) –
Cabane du Mont Fort (2457m)*

Grade:	2
Distance:	7km (one way)
Height gain:	967m
Time:	3hrs
Location:	Southeast of Verbier

Verbier's basin is strung about with numerous lifts that service the downhill ski trade, although a few are in operation also in summer and used by parapente enthusiasts. Despite the cluttered slopes views are splendid, and there are many kilometres of footpath that wind round pasture and forest, or that cross easy cols into Val de Nendaz, descend to the Rhône or stray along the steep hillside above Val de Bagnes. The following walk makes an easy approach to the Mont Fort hut, and if taken as a round-trip will make a good day out of about 5hrs.

From Place centrale, the main square in Verbier by the tourist information office, walk southeast along Rue de Médran towards the Médran *télécabine* station, then branch left on the Chemin de la Tinte. This winds uphill and, beneath the gondola lift, joins the Chemin de Clambin. This in turn leads eventually to **Clambin** (1730m), where a restaurant enjoys a tremendous panoramic view. Just beyond the restaurant turn left on a continuing track that twists uphill (sign to Les Ruinettes and Cabane du Mont Fort) to another junction, where you bear right. A few paces later slant left uphill to a picnic/barbecue area marked as **Le Hattey** (1860m). The path now crosses and recrosses a bulldozed piste and climbs in forest until it emerges to spectacular views of both the Combin and Mont Blanc massifs.

On coming to a track by a cableway turn right. This soon rises as a path, and at a signed junction accompanies a *bisse* (irrigation channel) to a dirt road. Across the road join another path which rises to a second *bisse*.

One of the flower-bedecked chalets at Clambin

Follow this round the hillside and you'll soon see the **Cabane du Mont Fort** standing on a bluff to the north. The path leads directly to it. ▶

ROUTE 99

Cabane du Mont Fort (2457m) –
Col Termin (2679m) – Cabane de Louvie
(2250m) – Fionnay (1491m)

Grade:	3
Distance:	9km
Height gain:	222m
Height loss:	1188m
Time:	5½hrs
Location:	Southeast of Mont Fort

Cabane du Mont Fort looks to the west and has a panoramic view that includes not only the Mont Blanc massif, but also the distant Dents du Midi. It is open throughout the year and has 80 places (☎ 027 778 13 84).

This is a tremendous walk, one of the finest and most visually spectacular in this book. But note that the path is narrow and exposed in places, and should not be

261

attempted unless conditions are favourable and the way free of ice. It's also a very tiring route – especially on the extremely steep descent from Cabane de Louvie to Fionnay, in the bed of Val de Bagnes, that will have your knees twitching for a long time afterwards! But the scenic rewards are memorable, for the Combin massif dominates almost every step of the way, a fabulous mass of snow, ice and rock that looms over the valley like a fair replica of Mont Blanc. There's a good chance of spying ibex along the path from Cabane du Mont Fort to Col Termin, while the next section to the Louvie hut is coloured by the sparkling Lac de Louvie in its deep pastoral bowl.

Descend northeast from Cabane du Mont Fort to a major path junction, where you turn right on a path signed 'Tour du Val de Bagnes et Combin'. This forks in a few metres and you bear left ahead and go down to a track, which you descend to the second hairpin bend. Leave the track here in favour of a footpath which makes a traverse of a scree slope. This is the start of the celebrated Sentier des Chamois.

Lac de Louvie and the Grand Combin

Beyond the screes the way climbs at a steady gradient and becomes a superb belvedere path, protected in places by fixed chains and cables. Keep alert for signs of ibex and chamois, and without diverting from the route you should reach Col Termin on a shoulder of the Bec Termin in about 1hr 45mins.

Bear left (ignore the alternative descent to Lac de Louvie) and cross the col on a path signed to Prafleuri and Col de Louvie. The way descends a little, then makes an undulating traverse of steep mountainside with Lac de Louvie clearly seen below to the right. About 15–20mins from Col Termin you reach a path junction and take the right-hand option, descending a rough, rocky terrain, and in a further 20mins reach a marshy area fluffed with cotton grass. This is the Plan de la Gole. After crossing a couple of streams the way divides. Bear right and soon pass a low shelter, beyond which you descend to Lac de Louvie. Pass along the right-hand side of the lake, and at the southern end come to **Cabane de Louvie** (2250m), about 3½hrs from Mont Fort. ▶

The path to Fionnay continues beyond the *cabane* and soon begins the descent, which is desperately steep in places. With hundreds of tight zigzags, and the occasional fixed chain for safety, the path eventually enters the small village of **Fionnay** about 2hrs from Cabane de Louvie.

Cabane de Louvie replaces an earlier refuge and is on a new site with a direct view of the Combin massif across the depths of Val de Bagnes. Manned from mid-June to mid-September with a full meals service, the hut can sleep 54 in four *dortoirs*. For reservations ☎ 027 778 17 40.

ROUTE 100
Fionnay (1491m) –
Cabane de Panossière (2645m)

Grade:	3
Distance:	7km (one way)
Height gain:	1154m
Time:	4hrs
Location:	South of Fionnay

One of the principal features of this route is the dramatic contrast it affords between the valley scenery at Fionnay and that which is revealed from the Panossière hut. It is an exchange of soft grassland for the arctic severity of snow-field and glacier, while the icy cataracts that hang from the north face of the Grand Combin bear witness to a world as yet resistant to vegetation. It's a raw, yet fine, sense of majesty, a heartland of big shapely peaks, lofty mountain walls and a lengthy stretch of glacier.

From Fionnay cross to the left bank of the Drance de Bagnes and take the path leading from the southern end of the tarn heading southwest and rising towards the opening of the narrow Corbassière valley. The way soon mounts more steeply in zigzags, and a little over 300m above Fionnay meets another path coming from the right. The path climbs on and swings to the right to make a traverse round the end wall of mountain. Having turned the Corbassière bluff the path angles south to pass a line of five small chalets set above a former glacier bed. Views now grow more spectacular as you gaze across the glacial trough to the Petit Combin, then to the pyramid of Combin de Corbassière on its shoulder, and finally to the Grand Combin itself at the head of the icefield.

The path now traverses roughly southward along a more-or-less level section and enters Plan Goli. At the end of this, climb steeply by way of more zigzags, then curve left along the edge of the glacier all the way to the **Cabane de Panossière** (2645m), which sits on the right bank lateral moraine. ◀

The hut is the largest in the area, with 103 places. A guardian is in residence during the spring ski-touring season and in the summer, when meals and refreshments are usually available (☎ 027 771 33 22).

Above the hut to the northeast lies the Col des Otanes (2846m), which offers an alternative way back to Fionnay. By crossing this col, whose views are spectacular, a fine circular walk is possible. The 200m climb to the col is short but steep, and about 300m below it to the northeast the path forks. One route angles across the slope to the right to Mauvoisin and the upper reaches of Val de Bagnes, but the left-hand option descends to Bonatchiesse and Fionnay.

ROUTE 101

Mauvoisin (1841m) – Lacs de Tsofeiret (2572m) – Cabane de Chanrion (2462m)

Grade:	2
Distance:	10km (one way)
Height gain:	801m
Height loss:	180m
Time:	4hrs
Location:	South of Mauvoisin

Cabane de Chanrion is popular with climbers, trekkers and with all who enjoy fine mountain scenery. It makes an obvious destination for an outing, and by linking this with a visit to the trio of tarns of Tsofeiret an extra dimension is added to the walk. In addition to the views, there's a good possibility of seeing chamois or marmots, and in early summer there will be masses of alpine flowers.

Either take the postbus to Mauvoisin or park just outside the hamlet near the massive 250m high dam. Follow the road to the head of the barrage and walk across it to the eastern side. From there a rough track heads alongside the reservoir, passing through tunnels, with the Glacier du Giètro spilling round from La Ruinette and Mont Blanc de Cheilon, its streams pouring in several cascades. After a while the track gains height by climbing the hillside in long twists, and is then replaced by a marked footpath heading south and crossing a number of streams. Across the valley the east face of the Grand Combin looks impressive, while ahead the 3403m Point d'Otemma stands above the unseen Chanrion hut.

The Combin massif appears as a great rock wall when viewed from the Lacs de Tsofeiret

In a little over 3hrs from Mauvoisin the path brings you to the **Lacs de Tsofeiret**, set among pastures from

which one gains more striking views of the Grand Combin. Continue along the path, which goes up to a low crest (Col de Tsofeiret: 2642m) and then descends over screes below the long and narrow Glacier du Brenay that comes from Pigne d'Arolla. The initial descent from the col is extremely steep and exposed, and is potentially hazardous. Fixed chains provide a degree of security, but care should still be exercised. Beyond the screes the route is straightforward and leads directly to the **Cabane de Chanrion**.

With 100 *dortoir* places and a guardian in the high weeks of summer (☎ 027 778 12 09) **Cabane de Chanrion** is owned by the Genevoise section of the Swiss Alpine Club. There are tarns nearby, an amphitheatre of mountains in the south, and a view of the Grand Combin to the west. For an alternative return to Mauvoisin an easy track leads along the west bank of Lac de Mauvoisin, while another trail runs along the slope above it. Among the recommended walks from the hut, the 2797m frontier pass of Fenêtre de Durand, noted for its alpine flowers, offers fine views into Italy and an opportunity to descend to the Valpelline. Above the Fenêtre to the northwest stands Mont Avril (3346m), whose summit is reached by an uncomplicated route along its southeast arête, where a narrow but clear path (except for a few easy rock slabs) goes all the way to the summit.

Other routes in Val de Bagnes

The Association Valaisanne de la Randonnée Pédestre promotes two multi-day circular tours that either concentrate on, or pass through, Val de Bagnes, and these are briefly outlined below.

- The **Tour du Val de Bagnes** (TVB) begins in Le Châble, makes a steep ascent of the northern hillside to Col de la Marlene below Pierre Avoi, then curves round the head of Verbier's bowl on the way to Cabane du Mont Fort. From Mont Fort the TVB traces the Sentier des Chamois to Col Termin, but instead of descending to

Lac de Louvie it remains high before cutting down to the bed of Val de Bagnes near Mauvoisin. Cabane de Chanrion is the next destination, followed by a traversing path high above the left bank of Lac de Mauvoisin which leads to Col des Otanes and Cabane de Panossière. A walk of a little under 2½hrs continues to Cabane Brunet, followed by another 2½hr walk to Cabane du Col de Mille. After that the way visits Mont Brulé before an easy descent to Le Châble completes the circuit.

- The **Tour des Combins** is somewhat longer than the TVB and strays into Italy. At present the long-promised refuge at By (2hrs from the Fenêtre de Durand) has still not materialised, so the accommodation gap is either filled by carrying a tent or by dropping to Ollomont.

The Combin massif is seen at its best from the Sentier des Chamois

The Tour des Combins takes about 6 days to complete, and usually begins in Bourg St-Pierre in the Val d'Entremont. It first heads north to Col de Mille and the refuge just below the pass, and continues to Cabane Brunet and Cabane de Panossière – thus reversing a major section of the Tour du Val de Bagnes. The next stage also reverses part of the TVB on its way to Cabane de Chanrion, but then it crosses into Italy at the Fenêtre de Durand and travels round to the meadows and hamlet of By (if the refuge has been built) or descends to Ollomont, where there's hotel accommodation. Hotel accommodation is also available at the end of the next stage of the walk, which leads to St-Rhémy below the Col du Grand St-Bernard. That col is crossed next day, with a descent into Val d'Entremont on a trail that runs parallel to the road and eventually returns to Bourg St-Pierre where the circuit began.

VAL FERRET

Val Ferret has all the neat orderliness for which Switzerland is noted. Without claiming any real resort except Champex, its string of small villages and hamlets make no pretensions, but appear as unfussed, workaday farming communities that overlook closely mown meadows and pastures grazed by bell-clattering cattle. Its chalets and hay barns exude an air of peace and well being, and there's an unhurried calm that hangs over forest and grassland alike. Yet, forming its western wall, rise the northernmost ramparts of the Mont Blanc massif: Mont Dolent, Tour Noir, the aiguilles of Argentière and Chardonnet, the Grande Fourche and Aiguilles Dorées – a lofty ridge punctuated by craggy peaks and hung about with glaciers.

ACCESS AND INFORMATION

Location:	South of Martigny
Maps:	LS 282T *Martigny* & 292 *Courmayeur* 1:50,000
Bases:	Champex (1466m), Orsières (901m), La Fouly (1592m)
Information:	Office du Tourisme, CH-1938 Champex-Lac (☎ 027 783 12 27, e-mail: info@champex.ch, website: www.champex.ch)
	Office du Tourisme, La Place, 90 Ferdinand Rausis, CH-1937 Orsières (☎ 027 783 15 31)
	Office du Tourisme, CH-1944 La Fouly (☎ 027 783 27 17)
Access:	By road from Martigny and the Rhône valley via Les Valettes and Les Grangettes (22 hairpin bends) for Champex-Lac, or via Sembrancher and Orsières for the main Val Ferret. By the St-Bernard Express branch-line railway to Orsières, and postbus throughout the valley from there.

Known to countless thousands of trekkers, thanks to the route of the classic Tour du Mont Blanc (TMB) passing through, the head of Val Ferret is border country. On the sharp little summit of Mont Dolent (3820m) the frontiers of Switzerland, France and Italy meet. From high trails on the east of the valley one looks west to French mountains, while the Grand Col Ferret makes an exciting grandstand from which to study the Italian side of the Grandes Jorasses. Yet despite this internationalism, Val Ferret itself remains undeniably Swiss.

It's a short and distinctly pastoral valley. From Orsières to the hamlet of Ferret, virtually at the roadhead, is a distance of only 15km, but in that brief stretch there's a difference in altitude of almost 600m. The valley gains that altitude in a series of

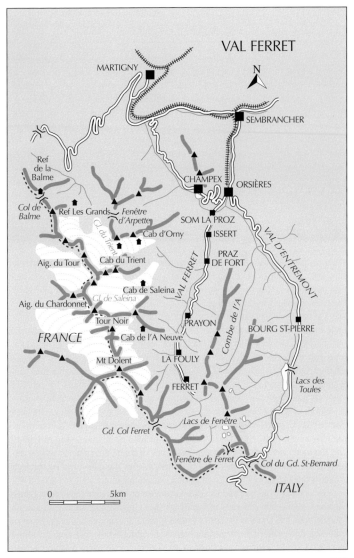

On the Swiss-Italian border, the Grand Col Ferret provides a grandstand from which to study the south side of the Mont Blanc massif

steps, with open pastures and forests hugging their margins, and when the road runs out grass slopes sweep up to hidden corners of considerable charm, where mountain lakes, streams and waterfalls add their lustre to the scene and partly concealed passes await discovery.

Val Ferret villages are modest in both size and facilities on offer to the visitor. Little more than 2km from Orsières lies the hamlet of Som la Proz, through which the road to Champex climbs in a tangle of hairpins. Overlooking a small lake, and with the wonderfully wild Val d'Arpette stretching behind it to the west, Champex (or Champex-Lac as it is also known) is the only Ferret community with ambition as a resort, and that ambition seems somewhat half-hearted, for the village has barely grown since it first came to attention in the late 19th century.

South of Som la Proz, Issert stands astride the road, clustered above the west bank of the Drance de Ferret, while Les Arlaches gathers its chalets and barns on the river's right bank, their pastures spilling away to north and south. At Praz de Fort the road crosses the river and gains a view of the Saleina glacier, whose projecting moraine, partly concealed by forest, carries the path used by the TMB along its crest.

Between Praz de Fort and La Fouly, a smattering of tiny hamlets accompanies the road, while other groups of buildings stand among the pastures. La Fouly faces across the Drance de Ferret into a glacial cirque, and acts as the main climbing and walking centre of the valley. Long-time favourite of such alpine writers as Emile Javelle and Charles Gos, La Fouly can seem overpoweringly gloomy in bad weather, although it positively sparkles when the sun shines. Just 2km beyond La Fouly stands the little hamlet of Ferret, its few chalets and attractive chapel grouped together with a view down-valley, but with pinewoods concealing the upper reaches.

Val Ferret offers a number of pleasant walks. A few are extremely strenuous, climbing as they do through the narrow shaft of a side-valley or going up to one of the huts perched high above. But some have a more fitting, more gentle quality, for they tread meadow and pasture and lead to easy passes from which to gaze off to the great peaks that raise this corner of the Alps to something rather special.

MAIN BASES

CHAMPEX (1466m) is a tranquil little resort with year-round appeal. In summer there's boating and fishing in the lake, and plenty of good walking. The village has a renowned alpine garden (Jardin botanique alpin) with an impressive collection of plants: open daily from May to September

Champex-Lac

9.00–18.00 (☎ 027 783 12 17, e-mail: fondation.aubert@bluewin.ch). Champex has restaurants, shops, PTT, tourist information, hotels ranging from one- to three-star, as well as pensions, *gîte d'étape* and camping. *Dortoir* accommodation is available at the Pension En Plein Air (☎ 027 783 23 50), Auberge de la Forêt (☎ 027 783 12 78) and Au Club Alpin (☎ 027 783 11 61). The campsite is located at the upper end of the village and is open throughout the year: Camping Les Rocailles (☎ 027 783 19 79).

ORSIÈRES (901m) lies at the junction of Vals Ferret and Entremont and the terminus of the St-Bernard Express branch railway which comes from Martigny. A small though busy little town with the best shopping facilities available for Val Ferret visitors, Orsières has a bank, post office, restaurants, tourist information and hotels in the one-, two- and three-star categories.

LA FOULY (1592m) is a good centre for walks and climbs in the area. Although small, its situation is ideal, and there's a large campsite (Camping des Glaciers)

271

on the left bank of the river at the entrance to a fine glacial cirque. For accommodation, La Fouly has hotels and pensions, two of which have *dortoir* places as well as standard bedrooms: Hotel des Glaciers (☎ 027 783 11 71) and Hotel Edelweiss (☎ 027 783 26 21). There are shopping facilities, restaurants, PTT and tourist information.

OTHER BASES

Accommodation is available elsewhere within Val Ferret. **FERRET** itself has two hotels, while between Ferret and La Fouly a *gîte d'étape* (**GÎTE DE LA LÉCHÈRE**: ☎ 027 783 30 64) is conveniently placed for TMB trekkers. Above Champex-Lac in Val d'Arpette, the **RELAIS D'ARPETTE** (☎ 027 783 12 21) offers rooms and *dortoir* accommodation, and camping places too, while at **CHAMPEX D'EN HAUT** there's a hotel and an auberge-*gîte*.

MOUNTAIN HUTS

CABANE D'ORNY (2826m) is located on the north bank of the Orny glacier, and is accessible from Champex-Lac by way of the La Breya chairlift followed by a 2hr walk. It is also reached from Champex via the Combe d'Orny, and from Praz de Fort via Plan Bagnet in about 5½hrs. Owned by the Diablerets section of the SAC, the hut has 90 places and is manned from mid-June to mid-September (☎ 027 783 18 87).

CABANE DU TRIENT (3170m) overlooks the Plateau du Trient from its position below Pointe d'Orny. Reached in about an hour from the Orny hut, Cabane du Trient is also owned by the Diablerets section of the SAC, and has *dortoir* places for 140 and a guardian in residence from mid-June to mid-September (☎ 027 783 14 38).

CABANE DE SALEINA (2691m), as its name suggests, stands within the Saleina tributary valley and overlooks the glacier which flows from the Aiguilles d'Argentière and du Chardonnet. The property of the Section Neuchâteloise of the SAC, it has 48 *dortoir* places and is manned from July to September (☎ 027 783 17 00).

CABANE DE L'A NEUVE (2735m) is the smallest of the Val Ferret refuges, for it can only sleep 28. It is found in the cirque northwest of La Fouly, where it makes a base for climbs on Mont Dolent, Tour Noir, the Aiguilles Rouges du Dolent and the Grande Lui. The hut is manned usually from early July to mid-September (☎ 027 783 24 24).

ROUTE 102
Praz de Fort (1151m) –
Plan Bagnet (1770m) – Cabane d'Orny (2826m)

Grade:	3
Distance:	7km (one way)
Height gain:	1675m
Time:	5½hrs
Location:	WNW of Praz de Fort

Although a long and strenuous route, this is the standard approach to the Orny cabane from Val Ferret. For a much shorter option from Champex via the La Breya chairlift, see Route 107.

When coming from the north the main valley road forks at the entrance to Praz de Fort. Break away from the main road and take that which skirts the western side of the village heading south. Having by-passed Praz de Fort turn right at a minor crossroads to enter the Saleina glen, a tributary valley that soon becomes very steep, with the snout of the Saleina glacier seen at its head. Keep on the road through forest until you come to a signed path which branches right. This climbs the steep mountainside

The chalets of Chanton, near Praz de Fort, stand at the entrance to the Saleina tributary glen

in a series of loops heading northwest below the crest of the Pointes de Chevrettes. As you work a way up this path, views open to include the Aiguilles d'Argentière and du Chardonnet forming the headwall of the Saleina glen. Towards the top of the slope the gradient steepens with tight zigzags. Once over the crest the path swings steadily round to the left, joins the La Breya path below the Aiguilles d'Arpettes and reaches **Cabane d'Orny**.

ROUTE 103

Ferret (1705m) – Grand Col Ferret (2537m)

Grade:	2
Distance:	6km (one way)
Height gain:	832m
Time:	2½–3hrs
Location:	Southwest of Ferret

The pass of the Grand Col Ferret is much frequented since it features on the Tour du Mont Blanc, although the vast majority of TMB trekkers tackle it in the opposite direction to that described here. From the col the whole of the Italian Vals Ferret and Veni are seen in a single glance, while the south side of the Mont Blanc range is also on display. But shortly before the col is reached, a brief diversion from the route gives an equally splendid view, this time down through the Swiss Val Ferret. For those inclined, a descent to Rifugio Elena at the head of the Italian Val Ferret will take about an hour from the col (accommodation available there), while a return to Ferret by the same path will require about 1hr 45mins.

The postbus turns around at a parking area on the south side of Ferret. From here walk up-valley along the continuing road for about 20mins to reach the roadhead below a dairy farm. Wander down a dirt road on the right, cross the Drance de Ferret and remain on the farm road/track as it winds easily up the hillside to reach another dairy farm, **Alp La Peula** (2072m: *refreshments*) about 1hr 10mins from Ferret. Pass in front of the buildings, then take the TMB path which slants left to mount the grassy hillside.

For about 150m the gradient is quite steep, but it then eases to cut round the hillside in a gentle rising traverse, with the Grandes Jorasses coming into view ahead. The way leads into a vast upland basin, with the Grand Col Ferret and its signpost seen to the west. A little over an hour from La Peula a minor path (unsigned) breaks away to the right. A 2min diversion along this brings you to a saddle with a very fine view down through the Val Ferret. Return to the original path and continue to the Grand Col Ferret, which is about 10–15mins away.

The full length of Val Ferret can be seen from a minor saddle off the path to the Grand Col Ferret

ROUTE 104

Ferret (1705m) – Lacs de Fenêtre (2495m)

Grade:	2
Distance:	7km (one way)
Height gain:	790m
Time:	2–2½hrs
Location:	Southeast of Ferret

The scant pastures that surround the Lacs de Fenêtre make a great destination for a walk and a perfect site for a picnic. From the lakeside one gains views across the upper valley to the cone of Mont Dolent, the Grandes Jorasses, Tour Noir and many other peaks. Choose a day of sunshine and calm, but stay away if there's any chance of a storm.

Just 200m above the upper lakes to the south, the Fenêtre de Ferret is an interesting walker's pass on the Swiss/Italian border. On the Italian side a path descends to the road that crosses the Col du Grand St-Bernard, and by linking the two passes a multi-day circular walk could be achieved that returns through the Val d'Entremont to Orsières.

From Ferret walk along the road heading south for about 20mins as far as the official roadhead below the dairy farm of **Les Ars dessous**. Take the track that winds past the farm, then continues up-valley to another alp farm at **Plan de la Chaux** (2041m). From here a waymarked path climbs the steep grass slope, eased with zigzags, then emerges through a rocky cleft and comes to the shore of the first of the **Lacs de Fenêtre**. Lying at 2456m this is the most attractive of the three, with beautiful views across the water from its eastern end. Two higher lakes are found a little further south, just a few minutes' walk away. Also attractive, they are somewhat more rocky round their margins than the first lake. ◀

From the shores of the Lacs de Fenêtre, outliers of the Mont Blanc massif form a ragged background

ROUTE 105

Ferret (1705m) – Champex (1466m)

Grade:	2
Distance:	18km (one way)
Height gain:	420m
Height loss:	650m
Time:	5–5½hrs
Location:	North of Ferret

Although quite a long walk, this is a relatively easy and straightforward route that forms part of the Tour du Mont Blanc. It can be broken in many places, with the possibility of catching a postbus to one of several destinations, but there are surprisingly few refreshment facilities along the way. Scenically, it's a gentle walk dominated by pasture and forest, although sudden dramatic views are also gained of rock wall or glacier.

On the south side of Ferret leave the parking area immediately before the first building on the left and descend to the river by a signed footpath. Cross on a footbridge, turn right and wander through woodland, and eventually come onto a track. Keep ahead, and after rising a little and turning a bend, leave the track on a signed path that descends on the right through a meadow, passes through a belt of trees and comes to a bridge spanning the Drance de Ferret. Cross the bridge and walk down the road to **La Fouly** (*refreshments:* 1hr).

At the village entrance bear left down a service road past the tourist information office, and cross the river once more to the left bank and enter the campsite. The route through the campsite is guided by yellow waymarks and signs for 'Chemin pedestre'. When the campsite ends continue through meadow and forest, keeping to the left of the river and alternating between footpath and dirt road.

About 40mins from La Fouly come to a junction of tracks in a clearing. Keep ahead, and soon the track slopes down to a fork near a bridge. A few minutes later leave the track at a hairpin bend where a signed footpath rises along the wooded hillside. Along this section there's an open, slightly exposed stretch safeguarded with a fixed chain, after which you continue among trees, descending once more. At a signed junction the way turns right along the wooded crest of a lateral moraine of the fast-receding Saleina glacier (unseen from here). This is known as the Crête de Saleina, a tree-crowded causeway that eventually slopes down to another dirt road near a bridge.

Bear left, and keep ahead on joining another track/dirt road which soon becomes a metalled road crossing the mouth of the Saleina glen to the chalets of **Chanton**. Along the road keep alert for a narrow footpath that cuts off to the right. This twists among trees and a few chalets and brings you to **Praz de Fort** (*refreshments*: 3¾hrs).

Turn right on the main road, cross the river and then bear left on a waymarked route through meadows leading in another 10mins to the hamlet of **Les Arlaches**. Walk ahead between attractive old chalets and barns, and 10mins later you come to **Issert** (*refreshments*: 4hrs). About 100m beyond the last buildings of the village turn left along a lane, cross a stream and go up a track which becomes a footpath and then enters forest. On the route through this forest there are several path junctions, but the way is either obvious or is marked with a yellow diamond outlined in black. As you draw near to **Champex** the path either joins or crosses the winding road that leads up to the resort and enters the village near Hotel Grand Combin at the eastern end of the lake.

ROUTE 106
Champex (1466m) – Sembrancher (717m)

Grade:	1
Distance:	8km (one way)
Height loss:	749m
Time:	2¼hrs
Location:	Northeast of Champex

On this undemanding downhill walk, the everyday life of small farming communities will be witnessed. This is a Switzerland that rarely appears in tourist brochures, but is no less interesting nor less attractive for that. As for Sembrancher, this village has a railway link with Martigny in the Rhône valley and gives easy access to the Val de Bagnes. For a return to Champex, one could ride the train to Orsières and catch a bus there for the final stage up the winding road.

At the southeastern end of Champex's lake the road forks by Hotel Grand Combin. Take the left branch and, rounding a dog-leg bend, come to the end of the road at Hotel Alpina. Take the right-hand of two footpaths (signed to Orsières) and descend into woods. On coming to a cross-track continue ahead to reach another track near the Champex–Orsières road. Cross directly ahead on a continuing path which soon joins an easy-angled track leading to the head of a dirt road.

Maintain direction to a continuing track, and on coming to a junction near the hamlet of **Chez les Rouse** keep ahead, joining yet another track coming from the right. This cuts into a cleft above a small gorge, and when the way forks you take the right branch that leads round

Gentle hillsides on the way to Sembrancher

pastureland. On coming to another fork, this time take the left-hand option and soon reach a T-junction. Bear left for just 15m, then slant right along a grass track signed to Sous la Lé, La Garde and Sembrancher. This brings you down to a gravel farm road above **Sous la Lé** (1032m).

Walk down to the village, then head left at a water trough and go through a narrow street to a junction of roads, where you keep straight ahead. Do not descend to a group of houses, but take the left-hand track signed to La Garde. Where there's a choice of tracks, keep to the upper route until reaching a second junction immediately after crossing a partly concealed stream. Ignore the left branch and continue ahead, now easing downhill between pastures to a junction of four tracks marked as **Tetou**. Go straight ahead on a path descending among trees and come to the village of **La Garde** (900m: 1¼hrs).

Passing a chapel on your right walk along a street in the direction of St-Jean and Sembrancher, then down to crosstracks where you keep straight ahead to a hairpin bend on a road. Again keep ahead on a track (to St-Jean and Sembrancher once more) following power lines. Pass to the left of the little chapel of St-Jean and descend through woodland, then beneath a railway line to finally enter the heart of **Sembrancher** (*accommodation, refreshments*). For details of facilities, please refer to the Val de Bagnes section.

ROUTE 107
Champex (La Breya: 2194m) –
Cabane d'Orny (2826m)

Grade:	2
Distance:	4.5km (one way)
Height gain:	632m
Time:	2hrs
Location:	Southwest of Champex

While Route 102 described the long ascent to Cabane d'Orny from Praz de Fort, the following walk is by far the shortest and easiest option, using the La Breya chairlift to gain 700m of height without effort. The valley station of the chairlift is found at the top end of Champex, just round the corner beyond the campsite.

From the top of the La Breya chairlift, where there's a restaurant, take the well-worn path that angles along the steep northern slope of the Combe d'Orny and provides a fine view of the rock spire of the Clochers du Portalet seen ahead. The path makes a rising traverse and joins another that comes up through the Combe from Champex (a 4hr approach). Bear right and make a steady ascent to the lateral moraine of the fast-receding Orny glacier, and so come to the **Cabane d'Orny**. ▶

Cabane d'Orny
is manned from mid-June to mid-September and has 90 places
(☎ 027 783 18 87).

ROUTE 108
Champex (1466m) –
Alp Bovine (1987m) – Col de la Forclaz (1526m)

Grade:	3
Distance:	16km (one way)
Height gain:	742m
Height loss:	682m
Time:	4½–5hrs
Location:	Northwest of Champex

The Tour du Mont Blanc has two route options for the onward journey from Champex. The easier of the two leads to Col de la Forclaz overlooking the Vallée du Trient, by way of the Bovine alp, while the more demanding alternative, via the Fenêtre d'Arpette, is described as Route 109. Although the following walk is less strenuous than the Fenêtre option, it still makes a reasonably tough day's walk, but a rewarding one at that.

From the lakeside at Champex walk up the road to pass the campsite on your right. Continue on the road beyond the La Breya chairlift to a junction with a minor road on the left. Turn along this minor road, and about 300m later come to **Champex d'en Haut**. Walk through the hamlet and down to the string of chalets of **Champex d'en Bas** about 15mins later. At the far end of meadows at the northern end of this settlement bear left on a track signed to Plan de l'Au and Bovine. After passing a few chalets a footpath leads on through woodland and out to a narrow metalled road. Turn left, and 2mins later come to the farm buildings of **Plan de l'Au**, where you can buy refreshments.

A dirt road leads on beyond the farm, and after about 20mins a footpath directs you left up a slope to the rough pastures of La Jure, where a succession of streams are crossed. After this the path enters woodland once more and climbs steeply before emerging to an open hillside, then contours to the right (north). Turn a spur and come to the simple buildings of **Alp Bovine** (*refreshments*: 3hrs 15mins) with views overlooking the Rhône valley 1500m below and to the north.

A short distance beyond the alp the path leads to a gate on the edge of larch and pinewoods. This is the so-called **Collet Portalo**, at 2049m the highest point on the walk. Through the gate the pleasant woodland path is mostly downhill all the way to Forclaz, passing another group of alp buildings on the left. Occasional views between trees show Martigny on a bend in the Rhône valley, and the road as it twists its way through the Martigny Combe. In a little over an hour from Bovine you emerge from the woodland to the **Col de la Forclaz**, where there's a hotel, shop and possibility of camping (see Vallée du Trient section for details).

ROUTE 109

Champex (1466m) – Fenêtre d'Arpette (2665m) –
Col de la Forclaz (1526m)

Grade:	3
Distance:	14km (one way)
Height gain:	1199m
Height loss:	1139m
Time:	6½hrs
Location:	West of Champex

A strenuous and demanding route, this walk crosses the high dividing ridge between the Val d'Arpette and Vallée du Trient. The Fenêtre d'Arpette is a narrow gash in the rock crest, and the contrast from one side to the other is remarkable: on the Arpette flank a great sweep of scree and rock; on the Trient slope a tremendous icefall and crevasse-riven glacier spill into the deep valley. The final approach to the pass is very steep, while the descent into the Vallée du Trient also has its steep sections. The crossing is used by laden trekkers tackling the Tour du Mont Blanc and the Chamonix to Zermatt Walker's Haute Route, so you should not expect to have the route to yourself. Please note, however, that this route should not be attempted too early in the season when snow remains on either side of the pass, nor if there's any possibility of bad weather. This is most definitely a fair-weather route.

Leaving Champex walk up the road to pass the campsite on your right. Round the corner turn left by the restaurant Le Mazot into a narrow road signed to Val d'Arpette. Very shortly come to a signpost indicating the TMB route to the right, where you pass beneath the La Breya chairlift by a small pond and enter woods. The path is joined by an irrigation channel (*bisse*), and when it forks you take the left branch. Contouring along the hillside you gain a fine view to the Dents du Midi off to the right. On coming to a diversion weir, the path climbs to a road where you turn right and come to the **Relais d'Arpette** (*refreshments*: 45mins), a hotel with *dortoir* accommodation and camping.

The road is unmade beyond the hotel, and after passing several chalets it becomes a rough track leading deeper into the lovely Val d'Arpette. About 35mins beyond the hotel look for a sign that directs a footpath to the right (direction Fenêtre d'Arpette) among trees which dodges to and fro across a stream. On coming to a more open region, the gradient becomes more severe as you climb through a vegetated gully to a path junction. Bear right, with the notch of the Fenêtre now in view on the skyline crest.

The path continues to climb along the north flank of the valley and eventually comes to a chaotic boulder tip, across which you work a way to gain a final steep, gritty slope that leads directly onto the **Fenêtre d'Arpette** (2665m: 3½–4hrs). Views are magnificent, and more than repay the effort involved in getting there.

Pass through the rocky gap, where the waymarked route swings to the right and descends across another jumble of rocks before settling to a well-made path that loops down towards the lateral moraine that borders the Trient glacier. Now and again the path descends steeply, then eases to pass the ruins of Vésevey and goes through a band of trees. About 2hrs from the Fenêtre you should reach the little *buvette* of the **Chalet du Glacier** (1583m: *refreshments*). Just beyond the building there's a path junction. Ignore the left-hand option which leads to Trient and continue ahead, now alongside another *bisse*. The path is a delight and it leads directly to the **Col de la Forclaz**. (Please refer to the Vallée du Trient section for details of facilities.)

VALLÉE DU TRIENT

The smallest of all the valleys included within this guide, the Vallée du Trient is a narrow, steep-walled glacial trough, and a product of the gouging action of several glaciers born on the fringe of the Mont Blanc massif. The most active of these, the Glacier du Trient, remains in the upper part of the valley, where it is shrinking back to the splendid high snowfield of the Plateau du Trient on the Franco-Swiss border. It's less than 8km from the tongue of this glacier to the Tête Noir gorges, where the valley empties its waters into the Eau Noire, yet there are many fine walking opportunities to exploit within this compact region.

ACCESS AND INFORMATION

Location:	Southwest of Martigny, and west of Col de la Forclaz
Map:	LS 282T *Martigny* 1:50,000
Base:	Trient (1279m)
Information:	Office du Tourisme, CH-1929 Trient (☎ 027 722 21 05, e-mail: communetrient@bluewin.ch, website: www.trient.ch)
Access:	By road from Martigny (including postbus) by way of the Col de la Forclaz.

Two of the finest multi-day treks in the Alps pass through the Vallée du Trient – the Tour du Mont Blanc and the Chamonix to Zermatt Walker's Haute Route. However, on both these treks the valley itself provides just a brief interlude between high passes, and, depending on which route option is chosen, some trekkers even avoid visiting one or other of the valley's small communities. As a result the valley is not as well known as it might be.

Trient is a combination of two hamlets, Le Peuty and Le Gilliod, although the former stands just far enough from the other to retain a degree of independence. Thanks to its being on the route of such popular long-distance treks, Trient has become an important, if understated, staging post for walkers, offering modestly priced accommodation and basic supplies at its village store, while Le Peuty has both a *gîte d'étape* and a simple campsite.

The village huddles below rough pastures, and from it the distant gleam of snowfield and glacier are sufficient to provide a constant reminder of the Alpine scale of things. Although Trient's altitude is modest enough, it's situated between passes that are 900–1300m higher, and these make lofty viewpoints

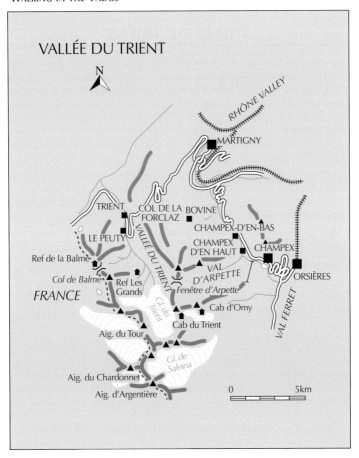

from which to enjoy uplifting mountain scenes. There are some serious walks to tackle hereabouts, as well as easier and more gentle rambles.

Though known as the smallest of Mont Blanc's seven valleys, the Vallée du Trient has more to offer the walker than its profile as a stage on a long trek might suggest. Hopefully the handful of routes described here will tempt a closer examination of what's on offer.

MAIN BASE

TRIENT (1279m) makes no pretence of being a resort. Were it not for the classic long treks that bring people here, it would be little more than an insignificant village. However, it provides all-important *dortoir* accommodation at the following: Relais du Mont Blanc – beds also (☎ 027 722 46 23), Café Moret (☎ 027 722 27 07) and Gîte La Gardienne (☎ 027 722 12 40). La Gardienne also has two apartments for rent.

OTHER BASES

The neighbouring hamlet of **LE PEUTY**, just a few minutes' stroll to the south of Trient, has 40 *dortoir* places at the *gîte*, Refuge de Peuty (☎ 027 722 09 38), and also camping with basic facilities nearby, while on the road pass of **COL DE LA FORCLAZ**, some 250m above and to the east of Trient, Hotel du Col de la Forclaz has 35 beds, 40 *dortoir* places and camping space (☎ 027 722 26 88, e-mail: forclaz@rooms.ch).

MOUNTAIN HUTS

REFUGE DU COL DE BALME (2191m) stands astride the Franco-Swiss border, from which it has a tremendous view of the Aiguille Verte, Mont Blanc and the length of the Chamonix valley. Privately owned, the hut can sleep 26 in its dormitories, and is usually manned from mid-June to late September (☎ [France] 04 50 54 02 33).

REFUGE LES GRANDS (2113m) is owned by the SAC, has 15 *dortoir* places but self-catering facilities only. This converted alp building stands on a grassy shelf below the Glacier des Grands and is infrequently manned (for reservations, ☎ 026 660 65 04).

ROUTE 110

Trient (1279m) –
Chalet du Glacier (1583m) – Trient

Grade:	1–2
Distance:	8km
Height gain:	304m
Height loss:	304m
Time:	2½hrs

This short and easy circular walk follows a bisse path which runs between the Col de la Forclaz and the Trient glacier, provides a fine view of the glacier, then returns to Trient by way of Le Peuty. Refreshments are available at the Chalet du Glacier.

Beginning by the church in Trient, walk up to the Forclaz road and turn right. A short distance along the road turn off onto a broad grass track on the left, signed to the Sentier du Bisse-Glacier. It swings easily uphill in long loops. At a junction of tracks go ahead to regain the road and cross directly ahead onto a continuing track which soon narrows to a footpath. This zigzags up to a crossing path, where you turn right alongside the irrigation channel of the Bisse du Trient. In the 19th century rails were laid alongside the *bisse* on which blocks of ice were transported from the Glacier du Trient to the hotel on the Col de la Forclaz.

This delightful level footpath is mostly along a wooded hillside, but from it you can see the Col de Balme at the head of a tributary glen across the valley. About 1hr 20mins after leaving Trient you come to the **Chalet du Glacier** (1583m: *refreshments*), a small *buvette* on the edge of woods with a view of the Trient glacier.

After you've had enough of the view, backtrack a few paces to a path junction where you turn left, cross a footbridge over the glacial torrent, then turn right on a crossing path. This soon brings you onto a narrow tarmac road where you bear left, but there are footpath shortcuts

that avoid too much road walking, so you descend among shrubs and trees until you come onto the road once more on the way to **Le Peuty**. From here to **Trient** will take an easy 10mins.

The Glacier du Trient

ROUTE 111

Trient (1279m) –
Col de Balme (2191m) – Croix de Fer (2343m)

Grade:	2–3
Distance:	6km (one way)
Height gain:	1064m
Time:	3¼–3½hrs
Location:	Southwest of Trient

The Croix de Fer viewpoint, northeast of Col de Balme, is the culmination of a narrow grassy ridge that forms part of the left-hand boundary wall of the Nant Noir glen. From it a very fine 360° panorama includes, among others, Mont Blanc, the Aiguilles Rouges, the Emosson lakes and the Trient glacier. There's nothing difficult about the walk, although the final approach to the Croix de Fer

289

might bother walkers who suffer vertigo. If so, they should return to Col de Balme and enjoy the views from there.

Walk up the road from Trient to Le Peuty where a signed path (to Col de Balme) strikes south across meadows fanning out at the mouth of the Vallon de Nant Noir. The way crosses the Nant Noir stream, and on entering woods begins to climb in numerous steep zigzags up the south flank of the valley. The gradient eventually eases above the trees, where you angle across a more open hillside to the hutments of Les Herbagères (2036m). From here the path steepens again with more zigzags to gain the **Col de Balme** about 2½hrs from Trient.

Do not go as far as the refuge, but take the right branch where the path forks at a signpost in the direction of Vallorcine and Col des Montets. In a little under 2mins from this junction, take another path on the right which is seen heading towards a minor saddle between the Tête de Balme and the Croix de Fer (there could well be snow here even in mid-summer). Come onto the saddle (2330m) about 30mins from Col de Balme, then turn right along a narrow crest path which leads in another 15mins to the rocky eminence of the **Croix de Fer**. The cross itself stands just beyond the summit. (Return to Trient by the same path in about 2½hrs.)

ROUTE 112
Trient (1279m) – Refuge Les Grands (2113m) – Col de Balme (2191m) – Trient

Grade:	3
Distance:	15km
Height gain:	912m
Height loss:	912m
Time:	6–6½hrs
Location:	South and southwest of Trient

Adopting a TMB variante via Refuge Les Grands, this rather strenuous circular walk is both challenging and rewarding. Full of variety, in terms of scenery, vegetation and demands, it has as its high point the grandstand of Col de Balme that enjoys one of the great views of the Alps.

Follow directions given under Route 110 alongside the Bisse du Trient as far as the path junction a few paces before the **Chalet du Glacier** (1hr 20mins: *refreshments*). Turn right to cross the glacial torrent on a footbridge, then bear left at a crossing path. This angles up a wooded hillside, gaining height steadily, then forks. Take the upper path, soon emerging from the pinewoods in a scoop of a valley, above which can be seen the Glacier des Grands. After passing a few ruins the gradient steepens, with the path climbing in zigzags before slanting to the right along a narrow shelf against a rock slab, where it's safeguarded with a fixed cable. Twisting uphill again you come to the converted alp buildings of the **Refuge Les Grands** (2113m: 2¾–3hrs).

Below the Chalet du Glacier a bridge spans the torrent coming from the Trient glacier

291

Pass to the right of the buildings and continue to climb a little further to gain a high point of about 2150m. The way now twists among rocks, then eases among shrubbery as a pleasant balcony path with a distant view of the Dents du Midi out to the north-north-west. Several minor spurs are turned as the path takes an undulating course above the Vallon de Nant Noir. Then, angling towards the southwest, the hillside becomes more stony, with old slips of snow often remaining through the summer. But then the way rises a little and comes to a path junction on the saddle of **Col de Balme** a few paces south of the refuge (2191m: 4½hrs: *refreshments*). Given good conditions, the views from here are outstanding.

Bear right, and just beyond the refuge come to a second signed path junction, where you take the right-hand option to descend through the Nant Noir glen. This is the standard route of the Tour du Mont Blanc, although most TMB trekkers tackle it in the opposite direction. The path is clear, and after passing the old hutments of Les Herbagères in a hollow, it cuts down the right flank of the valley, then descends a steep wooded spur with tight zigzags. At the bottom of the slope you then cross the mouth of the Nant Noir valley to Le Peuty, and continue for another 10mins to reach **Trient**.

Other routes in the Vallée du Trient

• By adopting another *variante* of the Tour du Mont Blanc, an interesting 4–4½hr walk can be taken to **Vallorcine**, a French village on the north side of the Col des Montets. On leaving Trient, the path, which is clearly marked on the LS map, tacks up the wooded hillside west of the village to the alp of Les Tseppes (1932m) in about 2hrs. The way then turns a spur (the north ridge of Croix de Fer) and contours round the hillside to Catogne (2011m), where there's a junction of paths. Take the right fork, where the Vallorcine route begins to descend by heading northwest, with much of the final approach to the village being through the Forêt Verte. Vallorcine is on the

Chamonix–Martigny railway line, and is also linked with Trient by road.

- A variation of the Vallorcine route outlined above gives an opportunity to make a **circuit via Catogne, Tête de Balme and Col de Balme**. For this, take the TMB variante from Trient to Catogne (2hrs 45mins), then choose the left-hand path at the junction to climb southwest to the Franco-Swiss border below the Tête de Balme. The way then curves round the French slopes of the Tête on a contouring path that returns to Swiss territory at the Col de Balme. To return to Trient descend through the Vallon de Nant Noir as described at the end of Route 112.

- A **two-day circular walk** can be achieved by crossing the Fenêtre d'Arpette and descending to Champex via the Val d'Arpette (Route 109 in reverse), and next day returning to Trient by way of Alp Bovine described as Route 108.

MULTI-DAY TOURS

By far the majority of routes contained in this guide are day walks beginning and ending at a valley base, but it will be evident that numerous possibilities exist for linking routes together into multi-day journeys, circuits of mountains, and the traverse of individual valleys or a number of valleys by crossing accessible passes. Some such possibilities have already been described in detail elsewhere in this guide, and a few others have been given in basic outline. But there are yet more that are worth considering, and for those mountain trekkers for whom this type of travel is the most rewarding of all, the following suggestions are offered. Please note that some of these routes are included in a useful booklet published by the Association Valaisanne de la Randonnée Pédestre: *Les Tours – Sentiers Valaisans*, available from the Valais tourist office in Sion.

ROUTE 113
Tour of the Weissmies

Grade:	3
Location:	The Saastal and Simplon pass region
Maps:	LS 274T *Visp*, 284T *Mischabel* & 285T *Domodossola* 1:50,000
Length:	7–8 days (46hrs walking time)
Accommodation:	Mountain huts, inns and village hotels
Start:	Gspon, Saastal
Finish:	Gspon

With the single exception of Monte Leone above the Simplon pass, the Weissmies–Fletschhorn group overlooking the Saastal marks the eastern limit of the big snow massifs of the Valais region. On both sides of this massif there are some fine valleys and an assortment of trails, and by linking a number of existing paths a tour may be created that would suit experienced wild-country trekkers. The anti-clockwise circuit outlined below is a demanding one, for it journeys across some remote and rugged country and crosses several high passes. Some stages are necessarily long in order to reach accommodation. Trekkers attempting this route need to possess good map-reading skills.

Gspon (1895m) – Gspon Höhenweg – Kreuzboden (2400m) – Almagelleralp (2194m) – Furgtälli – Antrona pass (2838m) – Valle d'Antrona – Antronapiana (908m) – Rifugio Andolla (2052m) – Passo Andolla (2448m) – Passo Busin (2487m) – Passo della Preja (2321m) – Rifugio Gattascosa (1980m) – Passo di Monscera (2103m) – Zwischbergen (1359m) – Gstein (1240m) – Simplon Dorf (1460m) – Simplon pass (2006m) – Bistinepass (2417m) – Nanztal – Gebidumpass (2201m) – Gspon

ROUTE 114
Tour of Monte Rosa

Grade:	3 – glacier crossing involved
Location:	Saastal, Mattertal and the Italian side of Monte Rosa
Maps:	LS 274T *Visp* & 284T *Mischabel* and IGC Sheets 5 *Cervino-Matterhorn* & *Monte Rosa* & *10 Monte Rosa, Alagna & Macugnaga* 1:50,000 Kümmerly + Frey has a special 1:50,000 map for this route: *Tour Monte Rosa*
Length:	9–10 days (64hrs walking time)
Accommodation:	Mountain huts, inns and village hotels
Start:	Saas Fee, Saastal
Finish:	Saas Fee

Making a circuit of the Monte Rosa massif, this splendid 9–10 day tour has several variations, and a longer version is suggested as Route 115. However, the basic tour outlined here is a classic circumnavigation that follows a number of traditional trade routes as well as more recently created paths. Since it visits two of the most popular centres in Switzerland (Saas Fee and Zermatt), and passes above one of the busiest on the Italian side (Breuil-Cervinia), there will be sections of the walk lacking in solitude. But the scenery is spectacular throughout, accommodation good and waymarking, for the most part, more than adequate. Note that a crevassed glacier has to be crossed on the descent from the Théodule pass, and this should be treated with respect and by taking normal precautions. Being a circular trek the tour could be tackled either clockwise or counter-clockwise and begun at one of several different places. The suggestion here is to begin in Saas Fee and walk in a clockwise direction. See *The Tour of Monte Rosa* by Hilary Sharp (Cicerone Press).

Saas Fee (1809m) – Monte Moro pass (2868m) – Rifugio Città di Malnate (2810m) – Macugnaga (1320m) – Rifugio Pastore (1575m) – Colle d'Olen (2881m) – Rifugio Guglielmina (2880m) – Stafal (1820m) – Colle di Bettaforca (2672m) – Resy (2072m) – Colle Sup. Delle Cime Blanche (2982m) – Plan Maison (2555m) – Théodule pass (3301m) – Zermatt (1620m) – Europaweg – Täschalp (2214m) – Europa Hut (2220m) – Grächen (1618m) – Hannigalp (2121m) – Balfrin Höhenweg – Saas Fee

ROUTE 115
Grand Tour of Monte Rosa

Grade:	3
Location:	Both sides of the Pennine Alps between the Fenêtre de Durand at the head of Val de Bagnes and the Monte Moro pass at the head of the Saastal
Maps:	LS 273T *Montana*, 274T *Visp*, 282T *Martigny*, 283T *Arolla*, 284T *Mischabel*, 293T *Valpelline* & 294T *Gressoney* and IGC Sheets 5 *Cervinia-Matterhorn* & *Monte Rosa* and 10 *Monte Rosa, Alagna & Macugnaga* at 1:50,000
Length:	14–18 days (depending which options are used)
Accommodation:	Mountain huts, inns and village hotels
Start:	Le Châble, Val de Bagnes
Finish:	Le Châble

Making a traverse of several valleys that drain both the Swiss and Italian flanks of the Pennine Alps, this epic trek has no official recognition, but is nonetheless treated to a two-volume guide, *The Grand Tour of Monte Rosa* (C.J. Wright, published by Cicerone Press). The route has numerous variations, for most of the transverse ridges are broken by two or more walkers' passes, and since the guide describes all the options, the trekker is able to choose the most suitable route to match prevailing conditions and his own fitness or ability. A basic outline only is given here, following Wright's preferred direction of travel, which is anti-clockwise.

Le Châble (821m) – Mauvoisin (1841m) – Cabane de Chanrion (2462m) – Fenêtre de Durand (2797m) – Ollomont (1356m) – Col de Breuson (2492m) – Close (1457m) – Bionaz (1606m) – Col de Montagnaya (2899m) – Lignan (1633m) – Fenêtre di Tzan (2734m) – Paquier (1528m) – Colletto Roisetta (2826m) – St Jacques (1689m) – Colle di Bettaforca (2672m) – Gressoney-la-Trinité (1624m) – Colle d'Olen (2881m) – Alagna (1190m) – Colle Piglimo (2485m) – Rima (1411m) – Colle di P. Altare (2630m) – Macugnaga (1320m) – Rifugio Città di Malnate (2810m) – Monte Moro pass (2868m) – Saas Fee (1809m) – Balfrin Höhenweg – Hannigalp (2121m) – Grächen (1618m) – St Niklaus (1127m) – Augstbordpass (2894m) – Gruben (1822m) – Meidpass (2790m) – Hotel Weisshorn (2337m) – Zinal (1675m) – Col de Sorebois (2840m) – Barrage de Moiry (2249m) – Col du Tsaté (2868m) – Les Haudères (1436m) – Arolla (2006m) – Pas de Chèvres (2855m) – Cabane des Dix (2928m) – Col des Roux (2804m) Cabane de Prafleuri (2624m) – Col de Prafleuri (2965m) – Col de Louvie (2921m) – Col de la Chaux (2940m) – Cabane du Mont Fort (2457m) – Le Châble

ROUTE 116

Tour of the Matterhorn

Grade:	3 – with glacier crossings
Location:	Swiss and Italian valleys of the Pennine Alps, between Col Collon above Arolla and the Théodule pass above Zermatt
Maps:	LS 273T *Montana*, 274T *Visp*, 283T *Arolla* & 284T *Mischabel*, and IGC Sheet 5 *Cervino-Matterhorn & Monte Rosa* at 1:50,000
Length:	8–10 days
Accommodation:	Mountain huts, inns and village hotels
Start:	Gruben, Turtmanntal
Finish:	Gruben

The Tour of the Matterhorn (Tour du Cervin in French) is a relatively new route which makes a circumnavigation of the most famous of Swiss mountains, but unlike the long-established Tour du Mont Blanc (Route 120), it has to negotiate crevassed glaciers where it crosses the international frontier in both directions. Because of this, the route is only suitable for trekkers equipped for, and experienced in, glacier travel. The tour is a demanding one, and is outlined as an anti-clockwise route. See *Tour of the Matterhorn* by Hilary Sharp (Cicerone Press).

Gruben (1822m) – Meidpass (2790m) – Zinal (1675m) – Col de Sorebois (2840m) – Barrage de Moiry (2249m) – Col de Torrent (2916m) – Evolène (1371m) – Arolla (2006m) – Col Collon (3082m) – Rifugio Nacamuli (2818m) – Prarayer (2005m) – Col de Valcournera (3066m) – Paquier (1528m) – Breuil-Cervinia (2006m) – Plan Maison (2555m) – Théodule pass (3301m) – Zermatt (1620m) – Europaweg – Täschalp (2214m) – Europa Hut (2220m) – Gasenried (1659m) – St Niklaus (1127m) – Augstbordpass (2894m) – Gruben

ROUTE 117
Tour of the Val d'Hérens

Grade:	2–3
Location:	The Vals d'Hérens and Hérémence, southeast of Sion
Maps:	LS 273T *Montana* & 283T *Arolla* 1:50,000
Length:	5–6 days (32hrs walking time)
Accommodation:	Hotels and mountain huts
Start:	Sion, Rhône valley
Finish:	Sion

One of the shortest in this collection of multi-day tours, the Tour of the Val d'Hérens would make a splendid introduction to trekking in the Alps. However, despite an overall grading of 2–3, the crossing of either Col de Riedmatten or the neighbouring Pas de Chèvres makes this particular stretch a demanding stage and a worthy grade 3. On the northward trend along the right flank of Val d'Hérens, there are several options to consider, but the prescribed route makes an interesting diversion to briefly sample the upper reaches of the neighbouring Val de Réchy. The tour is described in an anti-clockwise direction.

Sion (491m) – Les Agettes (1164m) – Thyon 2000 (2095m) – Le Chargeur (2141m) – Col de Riedmatten (2919m: or Pas de Chèvres: 2855m) – Arolla (2006m) – Les Haudères (1436m) – La Sage (1667m) – L' A Vieille (2368m) – Pas de Lovégno (2169m) – Col de Cou (2528m) – Nax (1265m) – Sion

ROUTE 118
Tour of the Dents du Midi

Grade:	3
Location:	Northwest of Martigny
Map:	LS 272T *St Maurice* 1:50,000
Length:	3 days
Accommodation:	Mountain huts
Start:	Mex, reached from St Maurice
Finish:	Mex

Apart from the last few summits of the Jura crest to the north of Lac Léman, the Dents du Midi form the most westerly group in Switzerland. Surrounded by charming alpine meadows, these are attractive limestone mountains whose highest summit is the relatively easy 3257m Haute Cime. The Tour of the Dents du Midi provides a short but rewarding anti-clockwise trek, using manned mountain huts for overnight accommodation.

Mex (1112m) – Les Jeurs (1555m) – Valerette (1702m) – Signal de Soi (2054m) – Refuge d'Antème (2037m) – Cabane de Susanfe (2102m) – Col de Susanfe (2494m) – Lac and Cabane de Salanfe (1935m) – Col du Jorat (2210m) – Mex

ROUTE 119
Chamonix to Zermatt, the Walker's Haute Route

Grade:	3
Location:	Travelling west to east across the Swiss flank of the Pennine Alps
Maps:	LS 5003 *Mont Blanc-Grand Combin* & 5006 *Matterhorn-Mischabel* 1:50,000
Length:	14 days
Accommodation:	Mountain huts, inns and village hotels
Start:	Chamonix
Finish:	Zermatt

Today, mention of the Haute Route usually means the classic ski-mountaineering expedition between Chamonix (or Argentière) and Zermatt (or Saas Fee). This traverse of some of Europe's finest mountains originated in the 19th century as a summer tour for mountaineers, for it involved the crossing of a whole series of glacier passes, travelling from hut to hut – or from one bivouac to another where no huts existed. It was (and still is) a magnificent challenge, but one that demanded a high degree of mountaineering expertise. With increased glacial shrinkage, a number of those former glacier passes are now endangered by rockfall.

There is, however, an alternative high route for fit mountain walkers that avoids glaciers (except for one, where there are normally no crevasses to worry about), but which makes a traverse of the most spectacular valleys and ridges in the Valais region, with marvellous scenic rewards on every stage. Several of these stages have been described in detail elsewhere in this guide. The route is a delight. It's long and reasonably demanding, for it crosses the grain of the country – the ridges run south to north, while the Haute Route heads east – so practically every stage is marked by a steep ascent or descent, but the rewards are plentiful. The Walker's Haute Route is a strong contender for the title of Europe's Most Beautiful Walk. The full route, with variations, is described in detail in the guidebook: *Chamonix to Zermatt: The Walker's Haute Route*, published by Cicerone Press.

Chamonix (1062m) – Col de Balme (2204m) – Trient (1279m) – Col de la Forclaz (1526m: or Fenêtre d'Arpette: 2665m) – Champex (1466m) – Sembrancher (717m) – Le

Châble (821m) – Cabane du Mont Fort (2457m) – Col de Louvie (2921m) – Col de Prafleuri (2965m) – Cabane de Prafleuri (2624m) – Col des Roux (2804m) – Col de Riedmatten (2919m: or Pas de Chèvres: 2855m) – Arolla (2006m) – Les Haudères (1436m) – La Sage (1667m) – Col de Torrent (2916m: or Col du Tsaté: 2868m) – Barrage de Moiry (2249m: or Cabane de Moiry: 2825m) – Col de Sorebois (2840m) – Zinal (1675m) – Forcletta (2874m: or Meidpass: 2790m) – Gruben (1822m) – Augstbordpass (2894m) – St Niklaus (1127m) – Gasenried (1659m) – Europaweg – Europa Hut (2220m) – Täschalp (2214m) – Zermatt (1620m)

ROUTE 120
Tour of Mont Blanc

Grade:	3
Location:	The Mont Blanc massif. The circuit travels through valleys in Switzerland (Val Ferret), Italy and France
Maps:	IGN 3530 ET *Samoens, Haut-Giffre*, 3531 ET *Ste-Gervais-Les-Bains, Massif du Mont Blanc* & 3630 OT *Chamonix, Massif du Mont Blanc* 1:25,000
Length:	10–12 days
Accommodation:	Mountain huts, inns and village hotels
Start:	By tradition, Les Houches (Chamonix valley), but Champex, Val Ferret, is a good alternative
Finish:	Les Houches or Champex

The Tour of Mont Blanc warrants inclusion in this book as it passes through the region via Val Ferret and Vallée du Trient. Without question the most popular mountain trek in Europe, the TMB circles the Mont Blanc massif to provide ever-changing – but always memorable – views, not only of a whole range of dramatic peaks and glaciers, but of their valleys too. Those of the Valais region have already been treated to full description in this guide, but when included in a long trek such as the TMB, a fresh perspective is gained. The traditional route is walked in an anti-clockwise direction beginning and ending in Les Houches, down-valley from Chamonix, but when tackled as a clockwise trek it is preferable to begin in Champex, above the Val Ferret, and this is how the route is outlined here. The Cicerone guide to the TMB, *Tour of Mont Blanc*, describes the route in both directions and gives details of accommodation throughout.

Champex (1466m) – La Fouly (1610m) – Ferret (1705m) – Grand Col Ferret (2537m) – Rifugio Elena (2062m) – Rifugio Bonatti (2150m) – Pas Entre-Deux-Sauts (2524m) – Col Sapin (2436m) – Rifugio Bertone (1970m) – Courmayeur (1226m) – Col Chécroui (1956m) – Rifugio Elisabetta (2300m) – Col de la Seigne (2516m) – Refuge des Mottets (1870m) – Les Chapieux (1554m) – Refuge de la Croix du Bonhomme (2443m) – Col de la Croix du Bonhomme (2483m) – Les Contamines-Montjoie (1167m) – Bionnassay (1314m) – Col de Voza (1653m) – Les Houches (1007m) – Refuge de Bellachat (2152m) – Le Brévent (2526m) – Col du Brévent (2368m) – Refuge la Flégère (1875m) – Tré-le-Champ (1417m) – Col de Balme (2191m) – Trient (1279m) – Fenêtre d'Arpette (2665m) – Champex

APPENDIX A: USEFUL ADDRESSES

Tourist Information
NB Details of offices in specific resorts are given at the head of each valley section.

Switzerland Travel Centre Ltd
Swiss Centre
30 Bedford Street
London WC2E 9ED
☎ (Freephone) 00800 100 200 30
e-mail: info.uk@myswitzerland.com
website: www.MySwitzerland.com

Switzerland Travel Centre
Swiss Center
608 Fifth Avenue
Suite 202
New York
NY 10020
☎ 1877 794 8037
e-mail: info.usa@myswitzerland.com

Valais Tourism
Rue Pré-Fleuri 6
CH-1951 Sion
Switzerland
☎ (0041) [0]27 327 35 70
e-mail: info@valaistourism.ch
website: www.valaistourism.ch

Fédération Suisse de Tourism Pédestre
(Swiss Hiking Federation)
Im Hirshalm 49
CH-4125 Riehen
Switzerland
☎ (0041) [0]61 606 93 40
e-mail: info@swisshiking.ch
website: www.swisshiking.ch

Club Alpin Suisse (Swiss Alpine Club)
Monbijoustrasse 61
Postfach
CH-3000 Bern 23
Switzerland
☎ (0041) [0]31 370 18 18
website: www.sac-cas.ch

Map Suppliers
Cordee
3a De Montfort Street
Leicester LE1 7HD
☎ 0116 254 3579
e-mail: sales@cordee.co.uk
website: www.cordee.co.uk

Edward Stanford Ltd
12–14 Long Acre
London WC2E 9LP
☎ 020 7836 1321
e-mail: sales@stanfords.co.uk
website: www.stanfords.co.uk

Maps by Mail
☎ 020 8399 4970
website: www.mapsbymail.co.uk

The Map Shop
15 High Street
Upton-upon-Severn
Worcs WR8 0HJ
☎ 0800 085 4080
website: www.themapshop.co.uk

Rand McNally Map Store
10 East 53rd Street
New York
NY

Omni Resources
PO Box 2096
1004 South Mebane Street
Burlington
NC 27216020096
e-mail: custserv@omnimap.com
website:
www.omnimap,com/maps.htm

Map Link Inc
30 South La Patera Lane
Unit #5
Santa Barbara
California 93117

APPENDIX B: BIBLIOGRAPHY

General Tourist Guides

- *The Alps* by R.L.G. Irving (Batsford, London 1939) – Long out of print, but available on special order from public libraries or via internet book-search sites, this volume by a noted Alpine connoisseur contains lengthy passages of interest to visitors to the Valais.

- *Blue Guide: Switzerland* by Ian Robertson (A. & C. Black, London/W.W. Norton, New York) – regularly updated, and with near-comprehensive coverage.

- *The Rough Guide to Switzerland* by Matthew Teller (Rough Guides Ltd) – Perhaps the best general guide to the country available at present.

- *The Green Guide: Switzerland* (Michelin) – Presented in gazetteer form with a wide range of illustrations, but inaccuracies abound.

Mountains and Mountaineering

Countless volumes devoted to mountaineering pack the bookshelves. Those containing references of particular interest to visitors to the Valais are listed below. It's a small selection, but there should be sufficient to provide a good background introduction and to whet the appetite for a forthcoming visit.

- *Alps 4000* by Martin Moran (David & Charles, Devon 1994) – The account of Moran's and Simon Jenkins's epic journey across all the 4000m summits of the Alps in one summer of activity.

- *Scrambles Amongst the Alps* by Edward Whymper (John Murray, London – many editions) – 'Scrambles' is the classic volume of mountaineering literature, covering Whymper's Alpine campaigns between 1860 and 1865 including, of course, the account of his fateful first ascent of the Matterhorn, but much else besides related to the Valais.

- *The Alps in 1864* by A.W. Moore (latest edition in 2 vols, Blackwell, London 1939) – Moore was with Whymper and Horace Walker during the summer of 1864, during which they were active on mountains that feature throughout this guide.

- *Wanderings Among the High Alps* by Alfred Wills (Blackwell, London – latest edition 1939) – Another record of Victorian adventures with guides on peaks and passes above Zermatt, Saas Fee, etc.

- *The High Mountains of the Alps* by Helmut Dumler & Willi Burkhardt (Diadem, London/The Mountaineers, Seattle 1993) – A beautifully produced volume, packed with excellent colour photographs and with an intelligent text, depicting all the Alpine 4000m peaks, many of which are in the Valais. Highly recommended.

- *Men and the Matterhorn* by Gaston Rebuffet (Kaye & Ward, London 1973/OUP, New York 1967) – A well-illustrated volume dedicated to the most famous mountain in Europe.

- *The Mountains of Switzerland* by Herbert Maeder (George Allen & Unwin, London 1968) – Large-format book with splendid monochrome illustrations.

- *The Outdoor Traveler's Guide: The Alps* by Marcia R. Lieberman (Stewart, Tabori & Chang, New York 1991) – With numerous fine colour illustrations by Tim Thompson, this book has a section devoted to the Valaisian Alps.

- *The Mountains of Europe* by Kev Reynolds (Oxford Illustrated Press, Sparkford 1990) – All the major mountain areas of continental Europe described, including the Pennine Alps of the Valais.

- *Valais West* by Lindsay Griffin and Valais East by Les Swindin and Peter Fleming (Alpine Club, London) – Guidebooks for climbers; authoritative as one would expect of AC publications.

Walking

- *Walking in the Alps* by J. Hubert Walker (Oliver & Boyd, Edinburgh and London 1951) – Long out of print, but available on special order from some libraries, this is probably the best and most readable volume of inspiration to mountain walkers. A large section is dedicated to the Pennine Alps of canton Valais, although some of the information is no longer applicable, as a number of valleys have been irrevocably changed by hydro-schemes and downhill ski development.

- *Walking in the Alps* by Kev Reynolds (Cicerone Press, Milnthorpe 2nd ed 2005) – Based on Walker's classic volume (see above), this all-colour 495-page tome describes 19 regions of the Alps, from the Alpes Maritimes to the Julians of Slovenia, and includes, of course, the Valais from a walker's perspective.

- *Backpacking in the Alps and Pyrenees* by Showell Styles (Gollancz, London 1976) – Contains an account of a backpacking journey across part of the Walker's Haute Route.

- *Classic Walks in the Alps* by Kev Reynolds (Oxford Illustrated Press, Sparkford 1991) – A large-format book with several routes from the Valais selected.

- *Trekking and Climbing in the Western Alps* by Hilary Sharp (New Holland, London 2002) – One of a series of well-illustrated books dedicated to activity in the major ranges, Hilary Sharp's authoritative text makes this both useful and readable. Among others, it includes an account of both the Walker's Haute Route and the glacier route between Chamonix and Zermatt.

- *Walking in Switzerland* by Clem Lindenmayer (Lonely Planet, London, Melbourne etc, 2nd edition 2001) – A typically fat Lonely Planet book, strong on background but less useful when it comes to walks, for by trying to cover most of the country the routes are rather thinly spread. Useful for pre-holiday research.

- *Walking Switzerland the Swiss Way* by Marcia and Philip Lieberman (Cordee, Leicester/The Mountaineers, Seattle 1987) – A selection of walks in various regions of Switzerland, including the Valais.

- *Chamonix to Zermatt: the Walker's Haute Route* by Kev Reynolds (Cicerone Press, Milnthorpe, 4th edition 2007) – Stage-by-stage route guide to this classic long trek, with variations and accommodation details.

- *Tour of Mont Blanc* by Kev Reynolds (Cicerone Press, Milnthorpe 2nd ed 2007) – Included here as the TMB passes through two valleys of the Valais. Route descriptions are given for both the clockwise and anti-clockwise routes; accommodation details and full colour photographs throughout.

- *The Grand Tour of Monte Rosa* by C.J. Wright (Cicerone Press, Milnthorpe 1995) – A two-volume guide to this epic circuit. Volume 1 details the route from Martigny to Valle delle Sesia via the Italian valleys. Volume 2 describes the GTMR from Alagna Valsesia to Martigny across the Valais.

- *100 Hut Walks in the Alps* by Kev Reynolds (Cicerone Press, Milnthorpe 2nd ed 2005) – As the title suggests, a large selection of mountain huts across the Alpine ranges, several of which are located within the Valais.

- *Valais* (Rother, Munich) – Walking guides in two volumes (East and West). Some of the accuracy seems to have been lost (in translation from the German?), but the books are useful in providing route ideas for readers to work out for themselves.

- *Tour of the Matterhorn* by Hilary Sharp (Cicerone Press, Milnthorpe 2006) – Destined to become one of the great walks of the Alps, this multi-day tour is described as an anti-clockwise circuit.

- *The Tour of Monte Rosa* by Hilary Sharp (Cicerone Press, Milnthorpe 2007) – Similar to the Matterhorn tour, with which it shares some trails, this trek also promises to become very popular.

APPENDIX C: GLOSSARY

GERMAN	FRENCH	ENGLISH
Abhang	pente	slope
Alp	alpage	alp
Alpenblume	florealpe	alpine flower
Alpenverein	club alpin	alpine club
Alphütte	chalet de alpage	alp hut
Arzt	docteur	doctor
Auskunft	renseignements	information
Aussischstpunkt	belle vue	viewpoint
Bach	ruisseau	stream, river
Bäckerei	boulangerie	bakery
Bahnhof	la gare	railway station
Berg	montagne	mountain
Bergführer	guide de montagne	mountain guide
Berggasthaus	hotel en haut	mountain inn
Bergpass	col	pass
Bergschrund	rimaye	crevasse between glacier and rock wall
Bergsteiger	alpiniste	mountaineer
Bergweg	chemin de montagne	mountain path
Blatt	feuille	map sheet
Brücke	pont	bridge
Dorf	village	village
Drahtseilbahn	télépherique	cable car
Ebene	plaine or plan	plain
Feldweg		meadowland path
Fels	rocher	rock wall or slope
Fereinwohnung	appartment de vacances	holiday apartment
Firn	névé	snowfield
Fluss	rive	river
Fussweg	sentier or chemin	footpath

GERMAN	FRENCH	ENGLISH
Garni	garni	hotel with breakfast only
Gästezimmer	chambres d'hôte	bed & breakfast
Gasthaus or gasthof	auberge	inn or guesthouse
Gaststube	salon	common room
Gefährlich	dangereux	dangerous
Gemse	chamois	chamois
Geröllhalde	éboulis	scree
Gewitter	orage	thunderstorm
Gipfel	sommet, cime	summit, peak
Gletscher	glacier	glacier
Gletscherspalte	crevasse	crevasse
Gondelbahn	télécabin	gondola lift
Grat	arête	ridge
Grüetzi	bonjour	greetings
Haltestelle	halte de l'autobus	bus stop
Heilbad	bains chaud	spa, hot springs
Hilfe	au secours	help
Hirsch	cervides	red deer
Hoch	haut	high
Höhe	altitude	height
Höhenweg	haute route	high route or path
Horn	pic	horn, peak
Hügel	colline	hill
Hütte	cabane, refuge	mountain hut
Joch	col	col, pass or saddle
Jugendherberge	auberge de jeunesse	youth hostel
Kamm	crête	crest or ridge
Kapelle	chapelle	chapel
Karte	carte	map
Kirche	église	church
Klamm	gorge, ravin	gorge
Kumme	combe	combe or small valley

GERMAN	FRENCH	ENGLISH
Landschaft	paysage	landscape
Lawine	avalanche	avalanche
Lebensmittel	épicerie	grocery
Leicht	facile	easy
Links	á gauche	left (direction)
Massenlager	dortoir	dormitory
Matratzenlager	dortoir	dormitory
Moräne	moraine	moraine
Murmeltier	marmot	marmot
Nebel	brouillard	fog, low cloud, mist
Nord	nord	north
Ober	dessus	upper
Ost	est	east
Pass	col	pass
Pension	pension	simple hotel
Pfad	sentier, chemin	path
Pickel	piolet	ice axe
Quelle	source, fontaine	spring
Rechts	á droite	right (direction)
Reh		roe deer
Rucksack	sac à dos	rucksack
Sattel	selle	saddle, pass
Schlafraum	dortoir	bedroom
Schloss	château	castle
Schlucht	ravin, gorge	gorge
Schnee	neige	snow
Schnell	vite	quick
See	lac	lake
Seil	corde	rope
Seilbahn	télépherique	cable car

GERMAN	FRENCH	ENGLISH
Sesselbahn	télésiège	chairlift
Stausee	réservoir	reservoir
Steigeisen	crampons	crampons
Steinmann	cairn	cairn
Steinschlag	chute de pierres	rockfall
Stop	halte	stop
Stunde(n)	heure(s)	hour(s)
Sud	sud	south
Tal	vallée	valley
Tobel	ravin boisé	wooded ravine
Touristenlager	dortoir	dormitory
Über	via, par-dessus	via or over
Unfall	accident	accident
Unterkunft	logement	accommodation
Verkehrsverein	office du tourisme	tourist office
Wächte	corniche	cornice
Wald	forêt, bois	forest
Wanderweg	sentier, chemin	footpath
Wasser	l'eau	water
Weide	pâturage	pasture
West	ouest	west
Wildbach	torrent	torrent
Zeltplatz	terrain de camping	campsite
Zimmer - frei	chambres	bedroom vacancies

APPENDIX D: ROUTE INDEX

LISTING OF CICERONE GUIDES

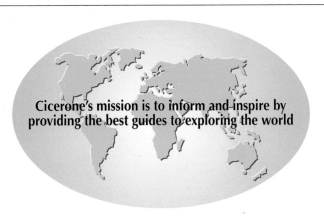

Cicerone's mission is to inform and inspire by providing the best guides to exploring the world

Since its foundation over 30 years ago, Cicerone has specialised in publishing guidebooks and has built a reputation for quality and reliability. It now publishes nearly 300 guides to the major destinations for outdoor enthusiasts, including Europe, UK and the rest of the world.

Written by leading and committed specialists, Cicerone guides are recognised as the most authoritative. They are full of information, maps and illustrations so that the user can plan and complete a successful and safe trip or expedition – be it a long face climb, a walk over Lakeland fells, an alpine traverse, a Himalayan trek or a ramble in the countryside.

With a thorough introduction to assist planning, clear diagrams, maps and colour photographs to illustrate the terrain and route, and accurate and detailed text, Cicerone guides are designed for ease of use and access to the information.

If the facts on the ground change, or there is any aspect of a guide that you think we can improve, we are always delighted to hear from you.

Cicerone Press
2 Police Square Milnthorpe Cumbria LA7 7PY
Tel:01539 562 069   Fax:01539 563 417
e-mail:info@cicerone.co.uk   web:www.cicerone.co.uk